Ginny + Jim,

It was great seeing you all last week.

Hope you enjoy this!

Michael Lewis

THE COMING OF SOUTHERN PROHIBITION

SOUTHERN PROHIBITION

THE DISPENSARY SYSTEM *AND* THE BATTLE OVER
LIQUOR IN SOUTH CAROLINA, 1907–1915

Louisiana State University Press

Baton Rouge

Published by Louisiana State University Press
Copyright © 2016 by Louisiana State University Press
All rights reserved
Manufactured in the United States of America
First printing

Designer: Michelle April Neustrom
Typefaces: Sentinel, text; Brothers, display
Printer and binder: Maple Press (Digital)

Frontispiece: North Augusta Dispensary, ca. 1908. Arts and Heritage Center
of North Augusta. Photo by Charles Petty. Used by permission.

Library of Congress Cataloging-in-Publication Data
Names: Lewis, Michael, 1965–
Title: The coming of Southern prohibition : the dispensary system and the
    battle over liquor in South Carolina, 1907–1915 / Michael Lewis.
Description: Baton Rouge : Louisiana State University Press, [2016] |
    Includes bibliographical references and index.
Identifiers: LCCN 2015043015| ISBN 978-0-8071-6298-9 (cloth : alk. pa-
    per) | ISBN 978-0-8071-6299-6 (pdf) | ISBN 978-0-8071-6300-9 (epub) |
    ISBN 978-0-8071-6301-6 (mobi)
Subjects: LCSH: Prohibition—South Carolina—History—20th century. | Li-
    quor Industry—South Carolina—History—20th century. | Dispensaries—
    South Carolina—History—20th century. | Liquor laws—South Carolina—
    History—20th century.
Classification: LCC HV5090.S6 L49 2016 | DDC 363.4/10975709041—dc23
    LC record available at http://lccn.loc.gov/2015043015

To Regina, with all my love

CONTENTS

PREFACE

"**E**verybody knows a place like that," a friend remarked when I first told him about the North Augusta liquor dispensary, a shop that, because of its location fifty feet from the state line separating South Carolina and Georgia, sold close to four million dollars of liquor in the year after Georgia adopted prohibition. Sure enough, every time I shared my research listeners would nod their heads knowingly and launch into their own stories about the liquor store located just beyond the county line from where they grew up or went to college or near their grandmother's house. Southerners in particular were fond of such tales. It seemed that everyone who had spent any kind of time below the Mason-Dixon Line had their own favorite oasis. Looking back now, I realize I should not have been surprised by the plethora of similar stories. For decades following the repeal of national prohibition, the South was honeycombed with dry counties and towns; my very unscientific count revealed over one hundred of them still scattered across the region. It only makes sense that folks would create and frequent nearby establishments to shorten the distance to legal liquor.

Perhaps the reason I was surprised by the prevalence of these alcohol oases lying just beyond dry county borders is that this aspect of the region's alcohol policy is largely absent in scholarly discussions. We know a great deal about Southern Baptists, Methodists, and the like and their historical and contemporary antipathy to alcohol. We know, too, of the contribution the region's tortured race relations made to its drive toward prohibition in the early twentieth century. Finally, we know quite a bit about how class and gender played into the onset of prohibition, not only in the South but nationwide. Yet in all that scholarship scant attention is paid to the shops that continued to dispense liquor. Nor have we reckoned with the motives of county and municipal governments that, starved for extra dollars, sought to take advantage of their neighbors' moral zealousness. This book seeks in part to remedy that oversight.

The story I will tell is about how one town, little more than a dot on the map, first resisted the introduction of liquor sales into its community and then, upon seeing how much money could be made from liquor, quickly reversed course and used these funds to support all sorts of civic improvements while at the same time completely canceling its local taxes. The importance of the liquor dispensary to North Augusta's history was indeed so great that it is still considered one of the town's most important historic institutions, even though it has been gone for almost a century. The little shop in the hollow, as my friend pointed out, was not the only shop of its kind, but few had as big an impact or are as fondly remembered.

ACKNOWLEDGMENTS

Throughout my work on this project I have been fortunate to receive the support of many people. Taken together, their consistent willingness to give their best on my behalf has left me humbled and truly grateful.

This project began with a memo by Richard Hamm entitled "Five Easy Pieces on the South Carolina Dispensary," in which he pointed to vast resources that had gone largely untapped and promised to share what he knew with any willing researcher. Staying true to his word, Dr. Hamm greeted my inquiry with abundant generosity, sending along advice and a rather large box of research materials he had already gathered.

Armed with little more than that boxful of materials and a vague sense of where they would lead, I asked for and received a research sabbatical. I thank my colleagues and the administration at Christopher Newport University for their willingness to take a leap of faith in support of this project; the time I subsequently spent in the South Carolina Department of Archives and History gave me the jump-start I desperately needed. I would especially like to thank Bob Colvin, Marion Manton, Linda Waldron, and Mai Lan Gustafsson, whose kindness throughout this time consistently reminds me of the true meaning of that word.

The staff at the South Carolina state archives, despite working under increasingly dire budgetary constraints, gave generously of their time and vast knowledge. In Augusta I benefited from several visits to the Reese Library Special Collections at Augusta State University. I owe a special thanks to the local museum directors and historians. In North Augusta, Andree Wallgren and Milledge Murray have given both their time and expertise in securing pictures of the dispensary and sharing local lore about its infamous past. At the Aiken County Historical Museum, Brenda Baratto has become a fellow sleuth, searching for local dispensary items, as well as a constant cheerleader and a friend.

As I began to put form to my ideas, I received an invitation to share them at the 2013 Southern Historical Association meetings. My thanks go to Joseph Locke for reaching out and inviting me to join the panel and to Lee Willis and Paul Harvey for giving thoughtful feedback. At the University of North Carolina–Chapel Hill, Andy Andrews and Charles Seguin have offered consistent encouragement and many enjoyable hours debating the real causes for the success and failure of the prohibition movement, in South Carolina and beyond. These discussions have sharpened my thinking and made this book far better than it otherwise might have been.

At Louisiana State University Press my editor, Rand Dotson, has shown great patience with the slow evolution of this project. I would also like to thank the press's anonymous reviewers for their comments, which helped push the manuscript forward in several key ways, as well as the many others at the press who helped guide it through to publication.

Special thanks are due my in-laws, Heidi and Steve MacAlpine, for their gifts of time, encouragement, and interest in a project that no doubt seemed arcane. My father, David Pinto, and my uncles Allen Pinto and Michael Greenberg have collectively nurtured my love of history, instilled an appreciation for finely honed arguments, and encouraged my intellectual development in ways too numerous to count. To each of them I owe more than can ever be repaid.

My wife, Regina A. Root, and my stepdaughter, Audrey Root, have had to live with my obsession with liquor dispensaries for far too long. They have endured more tales of Pitchfork Ben Tillman, women's temperance campaigns, and corrupt liquor officials than anyone should have to bear. They have spent far too many hours without me, giving me space while I tapped away at the computer trying to get my thoughts clear. Yet in the midst of everything they always knew to check in, whether it be Audrey taking a seat in the chair across from me and sharing an arcane detail about Taylor Swift or Regina dropping in with news from a friend or just a quick smile. I love you ladies and am grateful for every day we have together.

THE COMING OF SOUTHERN PROHIBITION

INTRODUCTION

O n August 9, 1907, the citizens of North Augusta, South Carolina, awoke
to a notice on the front page of their county newspaper: "The action of
the legislature of Georgia, establishing prohibition in that state on January 1,
1908, has resulted in a movement to place a [liquor] dispensary at North Augusta in Aiken County, just a few miles from Augusta. . . . It was rumored last
night at police headquarters that arrangements had been made to open up a
dispensary at an early date."[1]

As residents of "the newest suburb of Augusta, and beyond question one
of the prettiest residence localities in the whole South," North Augustans had
grown accustomed to a fair bit of isolation from Augusta and its social ills.
Their lone connection to the city proper was "a magnificent steel bridge" that
took suburban pedestrians and trolley passengers from their homes to Augusta's business and shopping district.[2] Now it appeared that the same bridge
would serve swarms of desperate Georgians in search of legal liquor.

Over the next eight months North Augustans fought a concerted campaign
against the proposed dispensary. Led by local physician Dr. William E. Mealing, they protested "placing a dispensary in a residential town with no adequate police force to handle the 30,000 negroes and low class of whites from
Augusta." Concerned for the welfare of "wives and daughters who have to pass
this mob on their way to and from the city," Mealing pledged that "the citizens
of North Augusta are going to ask the South Carolina state legislature to give
us our God-given right to say what we want."[3]

Arrayed against North Augusta's petitioners were those who argued for
the dispensary and the potentially vast profits that could be raised by sell-

ing liquor to Augusta's citizenry. "If a dispensary is placed in North Augusta," opined the editor of the *Aiken Journal and Review,* "it would clear twice as much as the present dispensaries do, or $60,000. . . . The expenses of the county should not be more than $40,000 so there would be a surplus."[4] Sensing an opportunity to use this surplus to reduce taxes and fund civic projects, Aiken county voters supported the dispensary.

Over the course of the next few years North Augustans' resistance gradually turned to acceptance as the expected dispensary profits began to materialize and the anticipated social chaos did not. Fortified with dispensary funds, North Augusta and Aiken County built new schools, paved more miles of road than all but one other South Carolina county, and still had the largest budget surplus in the state, which allowed Aiken to lower its residents' tax rate, making it the only county in the state to do so.

Seeking to emulate North Augusta's success, other South Carolina counties began reinstating their dispensaries. As they did so, they created greater competition among counties dealing liquor, thereby cutting drastically into their own hoped-for profits and Aiken County's existing liquor fueled expansion. Faced with increasingly limited liquor money in their county treasuries, Aiken and the other dispensary counties reasoned it was no longer worth the trouble of policing drunken people in their towns and in September 1915 voted for statewide prohibition by huge margins.

THE SOUTHERN ANTI-LIQUOR MOVEMENT

North Augusta's failed campaign and its accommodation to the local dispensary offers a challenge of sorts to understandings of the southern anti-liquor movement. Most of what we know about southern dry counties comes from various state and local monographs, investigations of southern progressivism, and studies of southern religious groups, especially evangelical Christians. These accounts make clear that southern anti-liquor campaigners' concerns fell broadly into three areas.[5]

The first such concern had to do with the safety and welfare of their children.[6] Across the country the positioning of saloons and the liquor trade as antifamily and a danger to youth spawned campaigns to "kill the beast and save the boys."[7] For southerners in particular, roughly 90 percent of whom were Baptist or Methodist, the tenets of evangelical Protestantism added extra urgency, as the fate of young people, not only in this life but for all eternity, seemed to hang in the balance. "If we are to win and keep children for Christ," wrote a Woman's Christian Temperance Union member from North Carolina, "the Church must train children in the ways of temperance and the Church must get into close grip with the wolf in the shape of the liquor traffic."[8]

The second concern of anti-liquor advocates related to the protection of home, family, and the sanctity of domestic womanhood—all of which were said to be threatened by degradation by husbands if they were under the influence of alcohol. Male drunkenness, Ted Ownby notes, "squandered money that could be used to support the family, wasted time that could be spent more profitably, and rendered the drunkard unfit for either work or family life."[9] In addition to poverty, neglect, and destitution at the hands of their husbands, alcohol consumption put white women at risk from the supposed ravages of black men. Drawing on the increasingly negative and animalistic portrayal of black men that accompanied the campaign for disfranchisement, anti-liquor campaigners wove tales of liquor-crazed black men ravaging and killing innocent white women. "White hysteria about black brutes assaulting white women that swept the South in the early 1900s put the prohibition cause back in the public spotlight. Evangelical prohibitionists capitalized on this public concern over alcohol and successfully pushed prohibition as the solution to black savagery."[10]

The third broad area of concern driving southern anti-liquor activism stemmed from industrialization and its resulting social disorder. As a "New South" increasingly made up of factories and mill villages began to take shape in southern cities and towns, reformers worried about the effects this new working class would have on southern society and in turn the impact of alcohol on the new working class. For individual workers alcohol was thought to reduce self-control, frugality, and sobriety, the very habits necessary for a successful transition from farm to factory life.[11] Collectively, the presence of saloons near heavily populated mill villages threatened the public order of the towns surrounding them. Attempts to combat such disorder "united ministers, journalists, teachers, club women and businessmen in . . . a common perception that one of the major barriers to its realization was a 'shiftless' undisciplined operative class."[12]

SOUTHERN ANTI-LIQUOR AND
THE NORTH AUGUSTA DISPENSARY

North Augustans' initial animas toward their local dispensary and its clientele shared themes with the southern anti-liquor movement. Given this stance, the belated adoption of prohibition by Aiken County's citizens and North Augustans' accommodation to their local liquor shop during the eight years of its existence only to then change their minds and go dry is puzzling. The previous literature identifies few examples of southern localities that waffled on the liquor question or openly elected to retain their liquor shops, and these exceptions (e.g., Charleston) are usually distinguished from the rest of the region by their more urbane populations.

Aiken County was not such an exception. At the time of the dispensary campaign Aiken County boasted a population of 41,849 people, only 14 percent of whom lived in incorporated towns: Aiken, the county seat (pop. 3,911), followed by North Augusta (1,136), Wagener (362), Salley (311), and Perry (179). Roughly 85 percent of Aiken County residents were Southern Baptist, and only eighty-three hailed from outside the United States. Alongside this largely rural, pietist population were a fair number of African Americans (who made up 50.5 percent of the county) and several mill villages in the Horse Creek Valley—populations that across the South often sparked anxiety among those in power, leading to anti-liquor legislation.[13]

One response to Aiken County's pietists' seemingly odd decision to retain liquor sales is to treat this case as an anomaly in the broad sweep of southern prohibition adoption and dismiss it as not worthy of investigation. But if we pull the lens back to examine the whole South, we see a pattern that makes Aiken County seem not all that unusual.

Local option laws let the voting unit in question, in the South typically the county, determine for itself the status of liquor sales. Within this broad category laws varied by state, with some adopting mile laws (which stipulated how far from a given location liquor could be sold), others adopting dispensaries, and others requiring rural prohibition and permitting only incorporated towns to vote on the liquor question.[14] Table I.1 shows the percentage of counties by liquor status for eleven southern states during the period of local option. Of the roughly nine hundred southern counties that held local option contests, better than one in ten retained liquor sales until the onset of statewide prohibition. Granted, forty of them housed a considerable num-

Table I.1. Dry counties across the South during the local option era

State (local option era)	No. of counties	No. of counties with legal liquor sales	No. of legal liquor counties with at least 10% non-pietist population	No. of legal liquor counties with less than 10% non-pietist population
Alabama (1907–9)	67	7 (10.4%)	1 (1.4%)	6 (9.0%)
Arkansas (1881–1914)	75	8 (10.6%)	0	8 (10.6%)
Florida (1886–1918)	49	4 (8.1%)	2 (4.0%)	2 (4.0%)
Georgia (1885–1907)	137	18 (13.1%)	1 (0.7%)	17 (12.4%)
Kentucky (1912–19)	120	9 (7.5%)	3 (2.5%)	6 (5.0%)
Louisiana (1884–1919)	59	28 (47.4%)	24 (40.6%)	4 (6.7%)
Mississippi (1886–1908)	75	6 (8.0%)	4 (5.3%)	2 (2.7%)
North Carolina (1903–8)	97	19 (19.5%)	0	19 (19.5%)
South Carolina (1904–15)	42	6 (14.2%)	1 (2.3%)	5 (11.9%)
Tennessee (1887–1909)	95	4 (4.2%)	0	4 (4.2%)
Virginia (1909–14)	95	8 (8.4%)	4 (4.2%)	4 (4.2%)
Total	913	117 (12.8%)	40 (4.3%)	77 (8.4%)

Source: County status derived from Sechrist, *Prohibition Movement in the United States* (data source). To check this data I consulted state auditor reports, which list taxes on liquor sellers by county for each year, as well as local option voting results found in state blue books and secondary histories of prohibition movements in each state.

ber of non-pietist Christians, but far more common were counties that demographically looked like Aiken County: overwhelmingly pietist populations that seemed to go against the prevailing sentiment by clinging to their liquor sales. Previous literature overlooks these cases because scholars have been more focused on accounting for prohibition's adoption, and at least at first glance, counties such as Aiken do not serve that task. Examining such cases, however, can throw light on the limits of prohibition's appeal to southerners and perhaps provide a more nuanced understanding of the factors that were most essential to the anti-liquor movement's success.

UNDERSTANDING AIKEN COUNTY

The key to a more refined understanding of southern attitudes toward liquor is to separate dry campaigners' diagnosis of the liquor problem and their prognosis of prohibition as the best solution to address it. Previous research makes clear that southerners in the main believed the diagnosis that liquor was a source of multiple social problems. What is less well understood is how southerners evaluated prohibition as a solution to their liquor problem. Although prohibitionists claimed their solution would end the liquor traffic, many southerners were dubious that it would in fact accomplish that goal, and their doubts led them to consider alternatives—high license fees, mile laws, and dispensaries—that would remove the traffic's worst excesses.

In Aiken County these assessments were intimately intertwined with two confounding factors: the lack of "dangerous drinkers" in close proximity to the county's dispensaries; and the promise of profits from future liquor sales. In considering these factors, Aiken County residents were like most southerners. They, too, granted the dry arguments about the necessity of limiting alcohol sales in the interest of public safety—for women, for children, for politics free from corruption, for public spaces free from disorder. What differed in Aiken County was the assessment of risk to the public of permitting alcohol sales. Within the county only North Augusta had a dispensary located near a large working-class population. Its other dispensary towns—Aiken, Salley, and Wagener—were each at least twenty miles from Augusta and ten miles from the county's other mill villages.

Aiken County's citizens were also like many other southerners (then as well as now) in their aversion to taxation. Business and community leaders across Aiken County and within North Augusta who sought development (e.g., roads, electric lighting, better schools) faced an uphill battle in convincing their fellow citizens to pay for these improvements; rather than fight that battle, they sought out dispensary profits as a way forward. Of course, many southern county governments likely considered using funds from liquor sales to pay for civic progress; most innovations intended to control the liquor traffic, short of prohibition, can be understood as attempts to do just that. No other county had the advantages Aiken did.

Aside from a small pocket of counties in eastern North Carolina and a pair along Georgia's coast that had few pietist adherents and thus few folks to push for prohibition, the primary motivator behind retaining liquor sales was the likelihood of profit (table I.2). This profit came from one of three sources: urban areas whose large populations led to greater liquor sales; counties located on the border of dry states that could sell liquor to those otherwise unable to purchase it; and the dispensary system, which licensed counties as liquor sellers, thus entitling them to all profits from liquor sales, rather than just taxing liquor dealers who then kept those profits. Within the Carolinas, where use of the dispensary was most common, counties housing larger cities and those nearby dry areas were in especially advantageous positions. Among them Aiken County stood out: the North Augusta dispensary was located just across the river from one of the South's largest dry populations—an ideal situation promising untold riches.

Over time, however, Aiken County's perceived source of riches diminished, and its residents' attitudes toward liquor changed as well. No longer able to rely on liquor profits to fund civic improvements, line the pockets of the county treasury, or lower citizens' taxes, Aiken County's leaders began to advocate for getting rid of the dispensary in the hopes of diminishing the lawlessness and corruption associated with it. Aiken County voters followed their lead, supporting statewide prohibition by an almost four-to-one margin less than a decade after they had openly welcomed liquor sales as their county's savior.

Table I.2. Sources of continuous liquor sales in pietist counties across the South

State	Low pietist church membership	City	Border	Dispensary	Two or more revenue sources	Total
Alabama	—	2	3	1	—	6
Arkansas	—	4	4	—	—	8
Florida	—	2	—	—	—	2
Georgia	2	4	—	11	—	17
Kentucky	—	2	4	—	—	6
Louisiana	—	—	4	—	—	4
Mississippi	—	2	—	—	—	2
North Carolina	6	3	2	5	3	19
South Carolina	—	—	—	—	5	5
Tennessee	—	4	—	—	—	4
Virginia	—	3	1	—	—	4
Total	8	26	18	17	8	77

Sources: U.S. Bureau of the Census, *Religious Bodies, 1906;* state auditor reports for each state.

Note: This table includes only the seventy-seven counties that did not have significant percentages of non-pietists (see table I.1).

So, the story of the North Augusta dispensary is about what happened when the prohibitionist desire for morality, sobriety, and public order runs headlong into the economic imperative to improve other aspects of southern civic life without raising taxes. Such a story improves our understanding of southern prohibition by locating the choice to go dry within a localized economic context alongside more traditional discussions of the political and cultural settings. Although class, religious, and racial worldviews about liquor and drunkenness were no doubt necessary preconditions for Aiken County's adoption of prohibition, North Augusta's dispensary story demonstrates that anti-liquor activism aiming to unite citizens in common cause against the saloon could only succeed if those citizens reasoned that their daily existence would be materially better without the saloon.

PART I

THE SOUTH CAROLINA DISPENSARY

Considered a unique innovation in liquor control when it was adopted in 1893, the South Carolina dispensary system concentrated all alcohol sales in state-run liquor stores. In its role as intermediary between liquor dealers and its own citizens, South Carolina's government set all the terms for these transactions and in the process reaped enormous profits for the state. As might be expected with so much money at stake, corruption soon became rife within the system. Revelations of graft surfaced at the highest levels of government, prompting South Carolina's citizenry to abolish the state dispensary and permit counties to adopt their own liquor stores.

The crucial factors determining which counties retained their dispensaries and which adopted prohibition go beyond religion, race, gender, and social class—factors that were largely constant across all of South Carolina's counties. What was less constant was the amount of money a county could make from the sale of liquor and how much social disorder might result if dispensaries were allowed to continue operating. The counties that most quickly adopted prohibition were those that had either little or no liquor profits or had a significant number of dangerous drinkers in their dispensary towns. Counties that could make higher profits with less risk of social disorder kept their liquor shops.

1

THE POLITICS OF THE SOUTH CAROLINA DISPENSARY

O ver the course of the late nineteenth and early twentieth centuries South Carolinians' discussions about the "liquor problem" were at once similar to and considerably different from those of their southern neighbors. As was the case across the South, South Carolinians worried that the uncontrolled use of liquor would contribute to racial unrest, put women and children at risk, and promote greater social disorder. Although some Palmetto State citizens advocated statewide prohibition as the best anti-liquor policy, others worried that prohibiting the sale of liquor could not effectively prevent alcohol consumption and instead sought out less drastic measures to combat the liquor trade.

It was the institution of one such alternative, the state dispensary system, that distinguished South Carolina's anti-liquor campaigns from those of other southern states.[1] Although Alabama, Georgia, North Carolina, and Virginia permitted county dispensaries, nowhere was the dispensary idea embraced as wholeheartedly as in South Carolina. The dispensary system's mandate that all liquor purchases be made through state-run outlets meant that all profits went directly to state and local governments. Thus, monetary considerations played a more central role in South Carolina anti-liquor policy than in states adopting restrictions with less direct government involvement.

BACKGROUND AND FORMATION OF THE DISPENSARY

South Carolina anti-liquor agitation saw its first spate of activity in the years following the Civil War and bore its first fruit in local option contests that by the 1880s resulted in successful prohibition campaigns in seventy-six South

Carolina towns. Sadly, the majority of these towns saw only their profits from liquor sales dry up but not their citizens; the transportation of liquor from license to prohibition counties continued undisrupted. Frustrated, many towns returned to the license system; as of 1892, the state licensed 613 saloons, and only two counties (Marlboro and Williamsburg) were completely dry.

Confronted with the limits of municipal option, South Carolina liquor opponents began agitating for statewide prohibition legislation. In 1890 they successfully maneuvered a prohibitory measure through the state house, only to see it defeated in the Senate. Encouraged by this near miss, prohibitionists redoubled their efforts and secured from the Democratic executive committee approval for a prohibition poll to be run conjointly with the 1892 Democratic primary. Under this plan voters at each precinct were shown two boxes, one supporting prohibition, the other against it, and voters could choose to place a ballot in one or the other box or in neither if they wished to abstain. The result of the referendum was 38,988 for prohibition and 29,527 against it. Tempering this apparent dry victory were the roughly 20,000 South Carolinians who registered no opinion, thereby preventing drys from claiming an absolute majority.

Just when it seemed that dry forces might achieve their goal, the state's governor, Benjamin Tillman, opted for a different course.[2] His 1892 message to the state senate, in which he laid out the case for a statewide dispensary system, presaged the broad outlines of the liquor debate that would consume South Carolinians for the next generation. Tillman began by acknowledging that "liquor drinking is the cause directly or indirectly of most of the crimes committed in our country" and that it also "produced much of the poverty and misery among certain classes,"[3] thereby joining his fellow citizens in seeking out the best method to curb this insidious evil.

Despite the harm caused by liquor, Tillman argued that prohibition was not a viable solution, as both human nature and previous experience demonstrated that the measure did not achieve its intended goal. "The human family," he asserted, "cannot be legislated into morality. All classes of men and women alike, feel, at times the need for stimulants and many who are never guilty of excess in their use resent any law infringing upon personal liberty."[4] As evidence to support his contention, Tillman noted that "town after town in this state has tried it, and, finding the adverse sentiment so strong and the evasion of the law so common, they returned in disgust to the license system."[5]

In addition to testing the limits of human frailty and law enforcement, prohibition also made likely the need for higher taxes to make up for the loss of liquor revenue and strained already deep divisions between town and country. "The liquor men live in the towns, they make money selling the liquor; the towns make money; the country suffers; the country pays for it; the country pays increased taxes for it."[6] Allowing that the prohibition referendum had "indicate[d] a wish on the large part of our people that there be some restrictive legislation in regard to the liquor traffic," Tillman nevertheless suggested that the referendum results be set aside because "this question did not enter into the issues of the campaign [and therefore] cannot be considered a conclusive test of the popular will."[7]

Instead of supporting a prohibition law, Tillman proposed eliminating the state's barrooms through the creation of a statewide dispensary system. The governor called for a prohibition on all sales of intoxicants in South Carolina except for those sold through state-run liquor stores. The manufacture of spirits was to be outlawed entirely. The state government would run the dispensary system through the activities of a commissioner (who was responsible for purchasing liquors and reselling them to local dispensaries at up to 50 percent over net cost) and a state board of control consisting of three members. The board in turn appointed county boards of control that were tasked with identifying sites for their dispensaries and appointing dispensers who would be responsible for the day-to-day operations of each liquor store. Profits from each dispensary were divided into three parts, with 50 percent going to the state, 25 percent to the county, and 25 percent to the municipality in which the dispensary was located.

A person wishing to purchase liquor was required to file an application with the dispenser stating the kind and quantity of the liquor desired. If the applicant was intoxicated or known to be an alcoholic, he was to be denied the right to purchase liquor.[8] Liquor was to be sold only between sunrise and sunset and could only be handled in sealed packages, which were not to be opened on the premises. To control illegal private sales, a state constabulary system was also created, and the governor was given the further authority to withdraw a municipality's share of dispensary revenue if he determined that municipality had been negligent in terms of enforcement.

Because Tillman came to the dispensary idea late in the state legislature's debate on the liquor question, prohibitionists initially thought it would gain little traction, especially given the prevailing dry sentiment throughout the state, a belief that seemed to be reaffirmed after the House passed a bill providing for statewide prohibition. Shortly thereafter, Senator John Gary Evans, a close confidant of Tillman, offered an alternative based on his reading of the dispensary idea, and Tillman gave it his full endorsement. Evans's bill was offered as an amendment to the House prohibition bill, so as to obviate the need of the three required readings of a new bill. Sensing a rat, ten senators argued that the amendment was not germane to the original bill, and when they were overruled, they filibustered. As night gave way to morning, the filibuster continued, until finally, under increasing threats from Tillman, the senators abandoned their opposition at 7:00 a.m. and the dispensary bill passed. The following evening the amendment was sent to the House with the instructions that either it or nothing would be approved by the governor. Arguing that this bill was in essence a prohibitionist bill, inasmuch as it closed saloons, Tillman and his allies succeeded in getting the measure passed on the last day of the state legislative session.

When South Carolinians opened their newspapers on Christmas Eve 1892 and read the text of their new "Act to Prohibit the Manufacture and Sale of Intoxicating Liquors," many were likely astonished that in fact the law had created not prohibition but instead a statewide monopoly of the liquor traffic. Assessing their early holiday "gift," prohibition supporters celebrated the dispensary with one leader, exclaiming: "Governor Tillman, in closing the bar rooms of the state, has done a great work, for they were the great boulders in the way of prohibition. ... Our soul sings out glory to God in the highest for it." Others, including the editor of the *State,* saw the dispensary more as the proverbial lump of coal: "Some silly prohibitionists have supported this measure. Believing the sale of liquor to be criminal they have made the state and themselves partners in the alleged crime. Believing that men ought not to be allowed to drink they have aided in directing that the state shall sell them all the liquor they can pay for. Believing the profits of liquor selling to be the wages of the devil they have made a bid for a share of the profits. ... It is a scheme to fill an empty treasury. That's all."[9]

DEFENDING THE DISPENSARY

In the immediate aftermath of the law's passage, Tillman and his supporters offered many defenses of the system that quickly became identified as "Ben

Tillman's baby." Although the governor acknowledged the dispensary did not offer the ideal solution to a complex problem, it was, by his lights at least, "the best method of controlling the evils which are inherent and inseparable from the intemperate use of liquors." Fifty dispensaries would displace the more than 613 saloons and the 400 drugstores selling liquor. The element of profit was destroyed, thereby removing the most powerful motive for stimulating sales. Pure and unadulterated products would be ensured by a system of chemical analysis. Restrictions preventing drunkards and minors from purchasing liquor and prohibiting drinking on the premises would limit sales to those thought most vulnerable to alcoholic enticements. It was also hoped that the prohibition of consumption within or near the dispensary would limit the practice of "treating" to drinks that reformers were convinced stimulated excessive consumption. Men compelled to buy liquor during the day and "go elsewhere to consume it will be likely at home and be within the restraining influence of that charmed circle." Saloons as centers of gambling and prostitution would be destroyed, as would the political influence of whiskey rings, resulting in less drunkenness and crime as well as greater peace and social order.[10]

Other observers agreed with Tillman's analysis. One commissioner of the system argued that it "especially commended itself to the women of the cities . . . because it has done away with the saloons and their attendant crowd of loafers who stood around the front doors and ogled women as they passed."[11] Guaranteeing the purity of the alcohol sold "minimized the effect of liquor drinking" on the consumer's body. Moreover, the lack of credit at the dispensary meant that "workmans' wages were not dissipated by credit drinking at a saloon before payday comes."[12] Summing up these views in an 1895 article in the *Arena*, R. I. Hemphill noted: "The dispensary is a great improvement on any solution of the liquor question that has ever been known in this section of the country. It had diminished drunkenness, decreased crime, reduced court expenses, promoted morality, rescued many of the fallen and restored happiness to many homes. . . . It is one of the coming reforms and South Carolina is leading it."[13]

Tillman and his supporters hoped an additional benefit of the dispensary would be the removal of the most disruptive force in South Carolina politics: black voters. Tillman shared the conviction of many South Carolinians that politicians in the past had been tempted to buy black votes and that little could be expected from blacks themselves when offered free whiskey but to vote as they were instructed. For Tillman the dispensary stood as a bulwark against "the probability of a desperate political struggle between prohibitionists and anti-prohibitionists two years hence with an appeal to the Negro as the balance of power."[14] In previous local option elections at the town level, Tillman asserted, "this has been the effect and when applied to the state, we must look for a like result."[15] Thus, Tillman argued the dispensary would eliminate the divisive effect of the liquor issue and keep South Carolina politics the sole province of white men.

Tillman also had a ready response for critics that labeled the dispensary as nothing more than "an easy way to spin straw into gold," that is, a scheme to meet the state's financial obligations without violating pledges to reduce taxes. He argued that such practical considerations were "not to be despised." Rather than agree with those "fanatical unreasonable people who cry aloud against the iniquity of a government's sharing in the blood money from husbands and fathers addicted to whiskey,"[16] Tillman pointed out that all branches of the United States government had for quite some time shared in the profits of alcohol through the license system. "It is far-fetched, unreasonable, then—hypocritical in fact—to pretend that any disgrace can attach to the revenue feature."[17]

STARTING UP

Once the law was passed, the state had six months to prepare for the opening of its dispensaries on July 1, 1893. Tillman himself visited brewers and distillers to arrange for the initial shipments to lay in a supply with which to begin the system. The act establishing the dispensary appropriated $50,000 ($1.25 million in today's dollars) as initial capital, and when this proved inadequate to supply the whole state, Tillman arranged with the distillers for a line of credit. In Columbia a building near the State House was set up as a bottling plant so as to comply with the law's insistence that "every package of liquor must be sealed and bear a certificate that it was bought by the commissioner."[18]

While the state board of control (governor, attorney general, and comptroller general) busied itself with procuring supplies and establishing a constabulary to enforce the law, county boards of control (three-member panels appointed by the state board, with recommendations from representatives and senators from the corresponding county) began scouting locations for their local liquor outlets. The state law mandated one dispensary for each county to be located in the county seat. The lone exceptions to this rule were Charleston and Richland Counties, where extra dispensaries were permitted to allow for the convenience of Charleston and Columbia residents. If desired, counties could add dispensaries, with "the place of business of each to be designated by the County Board, but the State Board of Control must give consent." When such a designation was made, "twenty days public notice shall be given [and] it shall be competent for a majority of the voters of the township in which the Dispensary is located to prevent its location by signing a petition or petitions requesting that no Dispensary be established."[19] Alternatively, citizens in any town might obtain a dispensary through a majority vote in an election that the county board was bound to honor. As they divined the political will among their citizenry, county boards were remarkably restrained in adding new liquor outlets. When the state system was established, the dispensary closed some 613 barrooms in South Carolina; at its most expansive the state dispensary had only 146 outlets spread across South Carolina's forty counties, roughly four liquor stores per county.

Despite all the confident prognostications from its supporters, preparations for the dispensaries' opening were not made without opposition. The most troubling question to arise was that of dealers' licenses for the first six months of 1893, during which time saloon activity was still permitted. Most dealers applied for licenses for the whole of 1893, reasoning that full-year licenses might allow them to circumvent the law. The saloonkeepers of Chester brought a test case before the South Carolina Supreme Court, petitioning for a writ of mandamus that would compel the town of Chester to issue and honor these yearlong licenses. Once this suit was denied by the Supreme Court, towns that had previously issued yearlong licenses were forced to rescind them and refund the difference to their respective barkeepers.

On the last day of legal sale great quantities of liquor were purchased as consumers took advantage of liquor dealers who soon would be targets of the law if they did not unload their goods. Some customers laid in stocks that would seemingly last for months; others drank as if they would never have an opportunity to taste liquor again. The dispensary began business on July 1. From all over the state reports began to come in that all was quiet, even in the city of Columbia, where the *State* noted: "The jag last night was very mild. Even the opening of a new era could not intoxicate a phenomenally sober population."[20] In many places, according to the paper, "liquor dealers will keep their places open. They will keep their stocks on the shelves with a sign upon them 'these liquors are not for sale.'"[21] All seemed to be going according to plan.

OVERCOMING LOCAL RESISTANCE

Flushed with pride over what seemed to be the dispensary system's success, Tillman proudly proclaimed to a group of anti-liquor activists, "I . . . contend that prohibition does not prohibit, cannot prohibit, and never will prohibit; and to tell you that we in South Carolina have found a plan that utterly destroys the saloons."[22] Other commentators surveying the situation in South Carolina thought Tillman was being too hasty in pronouncing victory. The *New York Times* pointed out that while a prohibition on saloons might be easily monitored by dispensary constables, "is it [not] likely that the bringing of liquors into the state for private consignee could be prevented. They would take all manner of disguises . . . and there could not be a search of every box and bale of merchandise for contraband liquors, even supposing that interstate commerce were subject to state supervision and regulation."[23]

As the state dispensary system's constabulary force never amounted to more than a few hundred members, prohibiting illegal liquor consumption and sales required the cooperation of local officials. If Tillman had counted on such support, letters from local liquor boards and dispensers shortly after the onset of the dispensary would likely have persuaded him otherwise. "The police chief announced a raid for the next day to the county dispensary board to ask them to come along," a board member in Orangeburg county informed Tillman, "but the dispenser here told me that had had been informed by one of the police force that the raid was a put-up job, that the saloon men had all been notified that the raid would take place."[24]

Writing from the upstate town of Union, the local dispenser urged Tillman, "I think it would be better for you to send the Attorney General up to prosecute the case for you can't get anyone here to prosecute it that would do justice as all the lawyers in town are opposed to the law."[25] In Anderson a liquor board member described the complete disregard for the dispensary law shown by local officials: "A word now as to the city authorities helping enforce the law here, they are simply not doing it, the blind tigers are selling more liquor here than last year and are bolder at it. They seem to think their lawyers can pull them through any emergency, they have employed the best ones here and plenty of them. So far they have won every case against them. In my opinion the only way here to get the Council's assistance is to withhold the cities part of the profits and this summer they will elect a council that will help enforce the law. The present Mayor belongs to the whiskey crowd in full."[26]

In response to these developments Tillman urged his constabulary to be ever more vigilant, vowed to stand behind them foursquare in the prosecution of lawbreakers, and threatened towns across the state with withdrawal of their dispensary funds if they refused to enforce the new law. "The people," opined the *State,* "will now know that if the Governor's armed spies enter their homes, insult their women and shoot down their sons or brothers, they will be promptly pardoned" by Tillman,[27] and across the state there was increasing talk of armed resistance to Tillman's perceived tyranny and the constables charged with enforcing it. Even Tillman's brother urged the taking of arms, remarking "I'll be a — if I don't shoot the first spy who enters my residence and opens my package of goods."[28]

With what seemed like the entire state whipped into a revolutionary fervor, events in Darlington provided the spark for armed resistance to the dispensary.[29] In late March 1894 constables conducted a raid there under the increasingly watchful eyes of the local population. The tension surrounding the constables' activities was palpable, as reported to Tillman by the local dispenser:

Constables Meekin, Swan, Pepper, McClellen-Cain and one other officer whom I do not know came in town today to raid several places where whiskey has been sold. The first place visited was J. M. James on the public square . . . they found not more than one flask of whiskey, but was compensated for their trouble for a few minutes after they had gone in the building, a steady stream of whiskey came pouring out the drain pipe. It seems that the officers were this time a little too soon for the James crowd and to save themselves they had to dump the liquor out the best way they could. . . . There were other places raided. . . . We were sure there was whiskey at every place but as soon as the first raid was commenced everyone at once went up to their places so when the constables came up all was as clean as a pin. All the time the constables were doing their duty there was a howling crowd of men and boys armed with pistols, shot guns, sixteen shooters and Winchester rifles, hissing, cursing, and threatening the officers in the discharge of their duty. Coupled with this and to make matters worse the rest of the crowd who did not have a gun and could not get any went to the Darlington Guards Armory and ... marched up to the Public Square. ... I suppose there was over one thousand people on the street and they all seemed to be trying to do all they could to molest the officers.[30]

The constables concluded their activity without incident, yet tensions remained high until the next day, when the constables, set to leave town, got into a fight at the Darlington train station—a fight that resulted in the deaths of Constables Pepper and McLendon as well as Darlington residents Frank Norment and L. S. Redmond. The Darlington crowd quickly reassembled, and by the end of the day newspapermen reported that "one and fifty mounted men are scouring the woods for the constables, who are armed with their rifles and will fight for their lives."[31]

Faced with a direct challenge to his authority, Tillman declared Darlington County to be in a state of insurrection and ordered that all rail and telegraph lines to the town be cut off. He further ordered five companies of the state militia to advance on Darlington. All five refused to comply. "No company of this command will sustain the constabulary in their methods of enforcing the Dispensary law," wrote the brigadier general of the Charleston militia. "This brigade will uphold and defend the honor of the State but will not lend itself to foment Civil War among our brethren."[32]

Tillman responded by calling for volunteers "among the sturdy farmers, mechanics and clerks. If we can't get the city companies to enforce the law, their arms will be taken from them and given to those in the country who will see that they are properly cared for."[33] Tillman's supporters across the state responded to the call from their governor. In the next two days eight companies of volunteers, close to five hundred men in all, assembled in Columbia and were ordered to march on Darlington. As they approached the town, they learned that members of the posse pursuing the constables had returned home, unsuccessful in their search to ferret out Tillman's spies. Shortly afterward, the fugitive constables reported unharmed to the governor, and Darlington again became quiet. The five or six days of excitement known as the "Dispensary Riot" were over.

Determined to avoid another whiskey rebellion, Tillman quickly canvassed local officials, demanding each town weigh in on the status of enforcement and threatening again to cut off funds for those places that refused to express fealty with his orders: "Your attention is directed to the following extract from Section 10 of the new dispensary law: All profits, after paying all expenses of the County Dispensary, shall be paid one-half to the County Treasury and one-half to the municipal corporation in which it may be located, such settlements to be made quarterly: Provided, that if the authorities of any town or city which in the judgment of the State Board of Control do not enforce this law, the State Board may withhold the part going to the said town or city and use it to pay state constables. There are ample provisions in the said Act giving policemen and marshals necessary power, without regard to any restrictions which may be in your charter. We shall be glad to have your cooperation and assistance and will expect an answer indicative of your purpose."[34]

Some mayors, fearful of their towns becoming another Darlington, replied conciliatorily: "The governor threatened Florence with withholding of funds. I write to ensure we get these back now. All citizens bow to the law. I have spoken to the Sheriff and Chief of Police. I have given them positive and unequivocal instructions that all will back officialdom and that any failures will be reported immediately to Tillman."[35] Others, acknowledging Tillman's political power, if not its legitimacy, were indignant: "This ordinance will be enforced just as all other ordinances of this City . . . and you will pardon me for suggesting that we have heard of no complaint against this administration for failure to enforce the City ordinances."[36]

Although most town leaders wrote expressing loyalty with Tillman and promising strict enforcement of the dispensary law, local dispensers cautioned Tillman to expect that such words would likely not be supported with action. "In answering your letter in regard to the city officials carrying out the dispensary laws," wrote Columbia's Fourth Ward dispenser, J. W. Roach, "I can say that I believe that the city officials are not trying and don't intend to carry the Dispensary laws out if possible. There are few of the city police who would carry out the law if they were not afraid of being discharged from the force."[37] Writing from Summerville, the local dispenser informed Tillman that although "the Mayor . . . authorized the clerk to refuse all license to barkeepers and gave instructions to the police to enforce the dispensary law, in my opinion there has not been an effort to enforce it."[38] In Blacksburg the county dispenser's warnings were even more dire: "It is the impression of the people here that a great more is sold outside the dispensary than in it. There used to be liquor sellers and they averaged about $10,000 per month in sales, the highest sales I have ever had was $5,000 a month. Send an officer!"[39]

Although dispensers' reports of mayoral lip service to the dispensary were undoubtedly troubling, even more so were the responses from town leaders openly hostile to Tillman's aims. Several mayors spared no vitriol in making the governor aware of their position. Predictably, one of the most recalcitrant cities was Charleston, which not only refused to enforce the law but took Tillman to task for making the request for enforcement in the first place: "Your communication asking our cooperation in the enforcement of that portion of the State law familiarly known as the Dispensary Act was duly received and has been carefully considered. Our self-respect compels us to state that the inquiry made in the said communication is not only without precedent, but that it is highly objectionable."[40] Equally hostile in questioning Tillman's intent as well as the dictatorial nature of the state board of control in determining the status of dispensary funding was the mayor of Newberry:

> You will observe that the Statute leaves this question to the judgment of the State Board of Control, without prescribing the method by which a judgment is to be formed. It gives Municipal authorities none of the safeguards of an ordinary judicial investigation. One must look to the character of the board, and not to the law, for any guarantee that the rights of the town will not be determined by mere caprice. Our desire is to find out what the board will regard as an enforcement of the law and by what rules they will be guided in reaching a conclusion. The first duty of the town authorities is to the town. And it is the primary duty of the town marshals to enforce the town ordinances for the protection of life, limb and property and the preservation of the public peace and good order. The promise of an uncertain revenue would not justify us in requiring our small force of Marshals to devote special and unusual zeal to the enforcement of any particular statute law, at the risk of impairing the general efficiency of the police service of the town. For this reason we ask whether you intend to hold the municipal authorities to a stricter enforcement of this statute than is required in the case of other penal statutes or the town ordinance. Our custom has been to instruct the Town Marshals to report violations of the Criminal Statutes of the State within their jurisdiction and to this custom we will adhere.[41]

As it became clearer that Tillman was going to get at best little help from the various municipal leaders across the state, he increasingly sought to place men he could trust in key positions within the dispensary system. As none of the 384 jobs within the dispensary system carried with them civil service restrictions, Tillman was free to appoint those loyal to him both as dispensers and constables. "Party exigency was the father of the dispensary act," noted one observer, "and party welfare demanded its growth and nurture in the face of the bitterest opposition."[42]

While the *State* and other newspapers hostile to Tillman condemned the appointment process as consisting "everywhere of scuffling and grabbing and snatching for these jobs, with log rolling and wire pulling as accompaniments,"[43] Tillman continued to make appointments on the advice of local dispensers and constables, who were encouraged to weigh in on an applicant's willingness to support the dispensary system. In Charleston one such Tillman supporter was the chief of police, who candidly evaluated three of his officers appointed to dispensary posts, describing them as "in sympathy with the enforcement of the law. They say that they will use every legitimate means if appointed to assist you in its enforcement. I candidly think that the three mentioned are as suitable men as you will be able to find, but of course I don't expect any Regulars to fight for *us* particularly."[44] By 1897 the state board came under the General Assembly's control, but little changed except the head of the patronage pyramid. The dispensary became a potent source of campaign workers and campaign contributions, in short "a magnificent political machine."[45]

CONFRONTING THE COURT CHALLENGE

As the dispensary gradually took hold in the localities across the Palmetto State, it confronted another challenge, this time from the courts. Charles S. McCollough, a resident of Darlington, brought a suit against Joseph Brown, the local dispenser, the aim of which was nothing less than a direct test of the constitutionality of the Dispensary Act. Specifically, McCollough argued that the law violated those sections of the state constitution that guaranteed that no persons would be deprived of their liberty or property. Ultimately, the case made its way to the state supreme court, which was then composed of three judges, Chief Justice Henry McIver and Judge Samuel McGowan, both Anti-Tillmanites, and Judge Y. P. Pope, a Tillman supporter.

Predictably, the court decided in favor of McCollough and against the dispensary. In rendering the majority opinion, Justice McIver wrote, "The Dispensary Act was intended to put the manufacture and sale of liquors within the limits of this state, for any purpose whatsoever, in the hands of the state officers, and for the purpose of realizing a profit to the State . . . through such monopolized traffic."[46] The law's intent put it in direct violation of the South Carolina Constitution, which provided that "every person has the inalienable right of acquiring, holding and disposing of property, of which right he may not be deprived . . . by the law of the land."[47] By reading the Dispensary Act as a measure designed to generate revenue rather than as a prohibition law and in seeing the statewide dispensary as a monopoly created primarily for the purpose of the state's financial benefit, the court concluded that "the conceded right of a State to prohibit the sale of intoxicating liquors as injurious to society does not give to the State the right to take for itself a monopoly of the liquor traffic within its territorial limits."[48]

Based on this decision, all dispensary activities were suspended on April 21, 1894. Although Governor Tillman declared the decision to mean nothing more or less than free liquor and that anybody could open a barroom anywhere, the state supreme court stated that under the law there was no authority invested with the power to grant licenses for the sale of liquor. Thus, prohibition was the law of the state, but its general enforcement was not attempted by Tillman. The governor stated that he had no authority to enforce prohibition because "sheriffs are under-officers" and he "no longer had control of the police force, as the necessity for that was not now at hand."[49] The constabulary, it was said, had been appointed to enforce the dispensary law only, and without dispensary funds it was unclear if or how they might be paid for their services. In the absence of state enforcement, liquor sellers sprang up across the state. Between April and August 1894 no less than 1,174 United States taxes were paid by liquor dealers in South Carolina, a clear sign of virtually unregulated liquor traffic in a supposedly prohibition state.

It was not until July that Tillman made his next move. In a campaign speech delivered that month, Tillman announced the reopening of the dispensaries to begin August 1. In setting aside the supreme court decision, Tillman argued that it only applied to the Dispensary Act of 1892, rather than the slightly amended one passed a year later. As stunned observers marveled at Tillman's moxie, the governor made clear his reasoning, stopping just short of gloating in a speech before the House: "I fully anticipated a case being brought under the act of 1893, and a decision of like nature to the first . . . although I felt, as did most people, that the decision was an outrage, and the result of partisan bias . . . I knew . . . that the same general principles underlay both Acts and that if one was unconstitutional the other must be also. . . . But . . . I resolved to thwart the court if I could; and every effort was put forth to prevent the act of 1893 from coming before the court as it was then constituted. . . . The Act of 1893 had been ignored by the court in two cases, and a change in the court made me feel it a duty to revive the act of 1893, and test the question of its constitutionality once and for all. So, on July 22, I issued a proclamation ordering the dispensaries to be reopened August 1st."[50]

The change in the court to which Tillman alluded was brought about by the retirement of anti-dispensary judge Samuel McGowan on August 1, 1894 (not coincidentally, the day Tillman selected to reopen the dispensary). Ensuring that his handpicked appointee, Eugene B. Gary, would fully support the dispensary, Tillman now had a majority on the court. Another test case of the dispensary's constitutionality quickly made its way through South Carolina's judicial system, and on October 9 the court pronounced the 1893 Dispensary Act constitutional. "I propose," Tillman crowed, "to make the enemies of the Dispensary get out of the road and obey the law. . . . It has come to stay, and the sooner this fact is recognized by the whiskey people and the other opponents the better it is for them."[51]

Pressing this advantage, Tillman's successor, John Gary Evans, the senator initially responsible for drafting the Dispensary Act, asked for further amendments to it during the 1895 session, all of which strengthened the governor's hand in running the dispensary. These included enabling the governor to remove any delinquent officer immediately concerned with the enforcement of the law; procedural changes in liquor cases whereby they may be given to rural juries that Evans hoped might bring more convictions of violators; increasing the penalties for violation of the law; increasing the number of officials available to prevent violations; and allowing dispensary officials half of the proceeds from their sale of confiscated liquors.[52] Evans further encouraged enforcement by establishing a reward of twenty cents per gallon for informers if their information led to the confiscation of liquor.

The power of Tillman and his acolytes within South Carolina was enough to keep the dispensary "in the saddle," but beyond the state legal trouble was also brewing as petitioners began questioning the conflict between the Dispensary Act and interstate commerce provisions laid out by the federal government. Early in 1895, Judge Nathan Goff issued a temporary injunction restraining "all State authorities and their employees, officers and agents from interfering in anyway with liquor shipped into the State from points outside the State either in transit, at the point of destination, or in the hands of consignee."[53] Governor Evans declared that Judge Goff's injunction would be disregarded and sent state constables instructions to be particularly vigilant to catch any package not bearing the proper certificates issued by the state board of control.

This disregard of Judge Goff's authority was halted by federal circuit court judge Charles H. Simonton. His decision in the case of *Donald v. Scott* declared null and void that portion of the dispensary law prohibiting the importation of liquor for personal use. Simonton concluded that the sale of liquor was "beyond the scope and power of police laws" and that "the dispensary law was neither a prohibition law nor a law for the inspection and was not enacted in the lawful exercise of police power and was therefore invalid as to imported liquor."[54] This ruling, alongside a later one that held the provisions of the Dispensary Act that prohibited the taking of orders for liquors to be shipped into the state to its citizens to be unconstitutional, allowed traveling salesmen of liquor dealers outside South Carolina to come into the state to take orders and to fill them by interstate shipment. In an attempt to evade Simonton's rulings, Evans instructed the legislature to amend the Dispensary Act to make it read as a public health measure, requiring that "all liquors entering the State be purchased by a board of control to be elected by the Legislature for the term of five years and that such liquors as entered the state be tested by the state chemist for purity."[55]

Angered by Evans's impudence, Simonton struck down the new dispensary law, asserting that "any State may, in the exercise of its police power, forbid the manufacture, sale . . . or use of spirituous liquors. . . . But when a state recognizes and approves . . . and encourages the manufacture and sale . . . it is not a lawful exercise of police power to forbid the importation of such liquors . . . for personal use and consumption." Simonton concluded that "the Dispensary Act . . . inasmuch as it approves the purchase and manufacture of alcoholic liquors for the state and provides for the sale of such liquors as a beverage in aid of the finances of the State are in conflict with the laws of interstate commerce, and therefore to that extent, void" and that "residents of South Carolina had a right to order from any state and to receive it without having it interfered with in any manner."[56]

Once again, it seemed the dispensary was dead. Governor Evans issued orders to constables to make no more seizures until the case could be appealed to the U.S. Supreme Court. Liquor forces rejoiced, believing they had found the long sought for loophole that would render the Dispensary Act null and void. As dealers from outside the Palmetto State set up "original package" stores in South Carolina cities and towns, the state dispensary, eager to compete with the new sellers, also established beer dispensaries, dividing them with flimsy partitions into two rooms and outfitting the back room tables and chairs, whose purpose was clear. Not only did these beer dispensaries defy the spirit of the original dispensary law; they did little to help the state stores compete with outside dealers.

Then, just when it seemed the dispensary was on its last legs, it was granted another life. On May 8, 1898, the U.S. Supreme Court overturned Simonton's ruling. The Court held that under the Wilson Act of 1890 Congress had adopted the laws made or to be made by the states on the regulation of the liquor traffic as its own and to that extent had granted to the states power to regulate interstate commerce as it applied to intoxicating liquors. This being the case, no state law passed by South Carolina could in any way be construed to stand in violation of federal interstate policy, and the state was free to resume its monopoly on the liquor trade.

THE DISPENSARY IN POLITICAL CAMPAIGNS

The failure of both armed insurrection and court challenges to the Dispensary Act left its opponents only one more option for overturning it—the ballot box. The Tillman machine made this avenue seem initially unlikely, as Tillman's successors John Gary Evans (1894) and William Ellerbe (1896) encountered little opposition in their campaigns for governor. The passage of the 1895 state constitution, which eliminated African American voting rights and also consolidated the Democratic Party's hold on the state, gave prohibitionists new hope. Reformers believed it was possible to challenge the dispensary without risking white political hegemony, and prohibitionists, accordingly, began to mobilize.

Their first effort was a petition to the legislature. Signed by close to twenty thousand people across the state, the petition urged the South Carolina General Assembly "to enact such legislation as will prohibit the manufacture and sale of intoxicating liquors as a beverage," as these were believed to be "the source of pauperism, slavery and crime . . . a positive hindrance to all material and industrial prosperity, and a foe to morality and religion."[57] When bills introduced in both 1897 and 1898 failed to gain support, dry campaigners vowed to get behind legislators who would support their cause.

In the campaign of 1898 they put out a ticket headed by Claudius Cyprian Featherstone, an upstate lawyer and also an ardent prohibitionist. Allowing that "the [dispensary] law has some good features" and that "some dispensary officials are good men who are seeking to do their full duty," Featherstone assailed the system for containing within it "a large percent of rottenness and corruption." Although preferring prohibition, Featherstone promised that if elected without a corresponding dry legislature, he could nevertheless tame the dispensary system by having it "enforced by men who will make its management clean and honest—who will not use it as a political machine and to further their own private ends."[58]

As the campaign reached its height, Featherstone brought forth specific instances in support of his charge that "the dispensary system . . . had been used as a political machine. First. A box of whiskey [samples] was shipped to Laurens . . . from a house in Philadelphia from which the dispensary buys liquors. . . . On the day of the campaign meeting it was . . . handed out to those who were thirsty and who belonged to the faithful. Second. At Spartanburg, on the day of the campaign meeting . . . I discovered that a quantity of stuff was on hand and being used. . . . It had been shipped there a few days before by representatives of certain whiskey houses who had either sold or hoped to sell to the dispensary. . . . How the whiskey could have been shipped in open violation of the dispensary law, without somebody being arrested and punished, can be readily surmised. It is the system and the manner in which it is enforced."[59]

Featherstone's case was strong enough that even with Tillman's support William Ellerbe, the current governor and dispensary candidate, made a secret deal with N. G. Gonzales, the editor of the *State*. In return for that newspaper's endorsement against Featherstone, Ellerbe agreed to dismantle the statewide dispensary system and in its place pursue the policy that Gonzales favored, allowing counties to decide the liquor question for themselves in a series of local option contests. Ellerbe defeated Featherstone by roughly five thousand votes. But upon reelection Ellerbe did not keep his promise to Gonzales, instead holding fast to the dispensary system under the formidable compulsion of Tillman.[60]

W hen Ellerbe passed away, in 1899, Miles McSweeney became the new governor and, as Evans and Ellerbe had before him, promised to "administer the law according to your [Tillman's] specifications."[61] Responding to charges of dispensary corruption, Tillman demanded a complete financial investigation of the dispensary system, drafted a bill aimed at making the dispensary's operations more transparent, and then embarked on a public relations campaign defaming prohibition as "an impractical and undesirable ideal." "I am proud to believe," Tillman added, "the Dispensary law is much better in its practical results than Prohibition could possibly be."[62]

In the 1900 gubernatorial campaign McSweeney (backed by Tillman) was challenged by James A. Hoyt, an Upcountry Baptist minister who "wanted the dispensary wiped out and prohibition put on the books." "The dispensary," Hoyt claimed, "has some good features but they are not enforced and [instead] is used to supply the blind tigers in order to increase the sale of liquor."[63] Across the state Hoyt was supported by a chorus of sermons, editorials, and letters published in newspapers that condemned the dispensary as an institution dedicated "to break[ing] the hearts of wives and daughters, to blacken and ruin homes and to make vagabonds and outcasts of sons."[64] Opponents charged that the "great moral institution" "had put illegal sale of liquor as well as legal sale in excess; that the dispensary law had always been and would continue to be unduly violated; that dispensers' salaries, being proportioned to the volume of sales, offered an incentive to push sales; and that the dispensary failed to give promised returns in revenue and should, therefore, be replaced by a more satisfactory system."[65]

Mindful of the close call in the 1898 election, Tillman (though now a senator running unopposed for reelection) canvassed the state in defense of his "baby." As had been the case for the past decade, Tillman quickly became "again the centre of attractions—he does his best to revive the old spirit in favor of the dispensary."[66] He warned his fellow countrymen: "You are mighty prone to go to sleep and if I can keep your eyes open it is my duty. . . . It is my duty to point out wherein and why certain advocated policies ought not to prevail and I am present in defense of my administration." Reminding his listeners that "if a majority had voted for prohibition in 1892 he would never have stood against it" and that "he certainly needed no political machine now, as no one would run against him," Tillman insisted he came before them only as an interested observer to discuss what course the state best ought to take with regards to the liquor question.[67]

Attacking his opponents, Tillman argued: "The ministers are good men but they are wrong up here (pointing to his head). Prohibition will not do because of the Old Adam in us. . . . You love your liquor just like you do your girls." To support his point, he reminded his listeners that drinking was countenanced by the Bible and that prohibition had also failed in recent history during "the free liquor and prohibition period, while the dispensary law was suffering from the interregnum. That is such prohibition as will come."[68] Tillman also took aim at Marlboro County (*Marlboro* and *Marlborough* were used interchangeably as spellings of the county name), one of the two that had never adopted a dispensary: "Marlborough is a model county, they say. They have never sold whiskey by law. Oh you hypocrites! When I was Governor I heard of wagons coming down there from North Carolina. Where do you get your liquor? I know you drink it. You love it. You go down to the depot on Saturday evening and you will find a whole express car loaded with jugs and demijohns."[69] With the failure of prohibition patently obvious, Tillman wondered aloud about the source of such recalcitrance in the face of what any man could see was the preferred system of liquor control. He mused that "prohibitionists have half a loaf yet they want all or none," a sure sign that "there is an unholy alliance of preachers and barkeepers led by Colonel Hoyt."[70]

This last remark was quickly attacked as slanderous. Bishop William W. Duncan condemned this "reckless statement of Tillman," calling it "an outrage and disgraceful," and Baptist reverend Charles S. Gardner of Greenville contended it was " a mean and contemptible effort to break the force of the almost unanimous advocacy of Prohibition by the preachers, and served its author as a good occasion also to throw contempt upon a class of men for whom he has in many other ways expressed contempt."[71] The state Baptist newspaper agreed, adding that Tillman's use of the Bible to justify drinking "puts him down as a far worse man than his most ardent enemies have ever branded him. . . . We do not believe His Satanic Majesty is capable of handling God's Word more perversely and irreverently than Senator Tillman does."[72]

For his part Tillman was content to let the people judge between him and the preachers. As he toured across the state, his addresses were greeted with enthusiasm, complete with the "old-time whoops." His campaign culminated at Greenville, where Tillman refuted point by point Reverend Gardner's sermon "amid a raising of hands which proved that the accusation about an unholy alliance between clergy and barkeepers was widely believed."[73] McSweeney ultimately defeated Hoyt in the governor's race by the safe margin of roughly fourteen thousand votes; once again, the dispensary system was safe.

2

THE ECONOMIC CONTEXT OF THE DISPENSARY

A longside Tillman's political acumen, the primary reason for the dispensary system's continued existence lay in its economic benefits. Between 1893 and 1907 the dispensary generated over 9.7 million in profits, roughly $465,000 annually, which more than doubled the 1892 revenues generated from license fees. The state and localities split these revenues evenly and both benefited greatly. Towns and cities found that their dispensary funds offset lost license fees, and as neither the state nor the counties received revenue from saloon license fees, their portion of dispensary profits was extra revenue.

This extra revenue arrived at a moment when it was sorely needed. Progressive leaders and New South advocates, eager to develop their towns and rural districts, had identified massive deficiencies in the state's road and school systems and argued forcefully for their immediate redress. Unfortunately, little money existed for such projects because South Carolina's tax system rested too heavily on property taxes, which were under-assessed and often resisted. To bridge the gap between widely agreed-upon public needs and severe shortfalls in funding necessary to meet them, state and county officials made liberal use of dispensary profits.

Yet not all counties across South Carolina benefited equally from the dispensary. Because its profits were split between the state and each county individually, each county received half of the profit made in a given year. The dispensary school fund, which was statewide, was apportioned first on the basis of need, and therefore the counties that had the fewest resources received more dispensary funds. In addition to these distinctions, the contribution of dispensary money to each county's budget depended on how much money a county raised from taxes; thus, counties with larger tax bases found the dispensary contributed less to their bottom line. Ultimately, these factors had a hand in counties' deliberations once they were given the option of continuing their dispensaries or adopting countywide prohibition.

TAXES AND REVENUE IN SOUTH CAROLINA

"Government has no right to take more from the people than is absolutely necessary for a wise and economical administration of the affairs of the State, and it should be so taken that the burden will bear evenly on all property. It is the duty of every citizen to contribute his portion to the support of the government in proportion to his ability."[1] These words, spoken by Governor Miles McSweeney in 1901, echoed the three basic principles most South Carolinians believed should govern the state's taxation system: equality of assessment, full contributions from all, and a minimal use of funds granted to the state. In practice such lofty goals were rarely met, and it is the violations of these core principles that formed the backdrop of dispensary economics.[2]

In the early twentieth century South Carolina, unlike most of its southern neighbors, derived the majority of its revenue from two sources: personal property taxes and the state dispensary (table 2.1). Reliance on the property tax in South Carolina, as elsewhere, developed in an era when farmland was the chief source of productive wealth, and aligning taxes with property values made intuitive as well as financial sense. As the country developed, this system increasingly violated the principle of assessment equality. As Janet Hudson notes, "Industrialization and urbanization shifted populations from farms to towns and consolidated wealth in industry and commerce rather than exclusively in land.... Moreover, professionals and white-collar workers could earn large salaries without owning large amounts of productive property.... By the twentieth century, levies on property alone no longer were a fair and equitable means for taxing wealth in South Carolina."[3]

Not only did South Carolina's tax system not bear its burden equally on everybody, citizens, aided by overworked local officials, often violated the principle of full contribution by all members of society. "If all property were returned honestly and fully at its just valuation the tax problem would be solved, but so long as human nature is frail and the impression prevails that it is not expected to return property at its value, we may not expect this result," wrote Governor McSweeney, who asked the legislature to consider a more

Table 2.1. State revenue sources, 1903 (dollars)

State	Total revenue receipts	Property tax revenue	Liquor revenue	Other revenue
Kentucky	4,816,593	3,373,919 (70%)	333,275 (6%)	1,109,399 (24%)
Virginia	3,960,752	2,000,849 (50%)	293,317 (7%)	1,666,586 (43%)
Georgia	3,716,443	2,249,631 (65%)	149,834 (4%)	1,316,978 (31%)
Louisiana	3,565,975	2,268,492 (63%)	—	1,297,483 (37%)
South Carolina	3,533,434	1,028,702 (29%)	2,282,293 64%)	222,439 (7%)
Alabama	2,882,199	2,035,557 (70%)	166,633 (5%)	680,009 (25%)
Tennessee	2,632,386	1,401,139 (53%)	—	1,231,247 (47%)
Mississippi	1,972,852	1,358,995 (68%)	—	613,857 (32%)
North Carolina	1,700,551	898,533 (52%)	6,432 (3%)	795,586 (45%)
Arkansas	1,436,417	1,122,908 (78%)	113,333 (7%)	180,176 (15%)

Source: U.S. Bureau of the Census, *Thirteenth Census*, vol. 2: *Wealth, Debt, and Taxation.* The specific information in this table is found in table 7, 38–39.

centralized system of taxation to remedy the highly localized system that was in place. He explained that according to the current way of doing things, "returns are made [by individuals] to the county auditor [and] a township board of assessors which meets . . . and undertakes to go over all of them in one or two days. . . . All of this is done in a perfunctory manner and accomplishes little or nothing in securing an equitable assessment of property." The result of this haphazard work could be felt across counties in the state "in which some of the land is assessed at one-third or one-half its actual value, while other land is assessed at its real value. In fact, there may be two adjoining plantations, the one worth twice as much as the other, and yet under our system each is assessed for taxation at the same price per acre."[4]

As the legislature was slow to alter the state's tax system and the feeling persisted across much of the state that others were not honoring their fair share of the tax burden, citizens increasingly pressured their representatives to make good on the final principle outlined in Governor McSweeney's 1901 inaugural: that the state undertake a wise and economical use of tax funds, and ensure that only those truly necessary state functions be fulfilled. "I have not presumed to lecture you on economy, for I feel sure that you realize as fully as I do the needs of our people and will be as economical in the expenditure of public money as is consistent with efficient service," McSweeney's successor,

Duncan Clinch Heyward, reminded legislators in his 1906 annual address. "If you find that in any department the expenditures can be cut down without hurt to efficient service it is your duty to cut them down. Useless and extravagant appropriations should under no circumstances even be considered."[5] That such messages were taken seriously is borne out in table 2.2. Aside from basic government functions, state institutions, and the retirement of state debt, the only significant spending South Carolina engaged in was to support the one group most of its citizens agreed were worthy of some state resources, Confederate veterans.

Support for Confederate veterans was so freely granted in part because of the intimate connection between Confederate veterans and the cult of the Lost Cause, which had thoroughly permeated southern life by the early twentieth century. This southern civil religion, through song and story, poem and monument, honored both the war effort and the Old South it had defended, elevating the status of the war's veterans in the eyes of their southern neigh-

Table 2.2. South Carolina state budget expenditures, 1899 and 1905 (dollars)

	1899	1905
Administrative		
Executive	62,499	100,245
Judiciary	62,410	75,339
Legislative	43,589	42,761
Tax	27,279	61,644
Social services		
Mental hospital	108,800	163,746
Public health	18,205	12,020
Penal institutions	5,800	6,100
Higher education	97,685	140,842
State militia	8,000	15,000
Confederate pensions	100,598	199,647
Sinking fund	0	20,000
Debt interest	287,749	304,439
Other expenses	43,870	70,314
Total	866,484	1,212,097

Sources: South Carolina General Assembly, State Comptroller General, *Annual Report, 1900,* 9–32; *1906,* 35–49.

bors. As southern soldiers had already demonstrated "great sacrifice and self-denial . . . never more cheerfully made in any cause . . . than in this struggle," it was easy to cast Confederate pensions as payment due for services rendered rather than an outright gift. Summing up these sentiments, Governor Heyward defended the continued rise in pension costs as "our duty to take care and provide for those who are in need of our help."[6]

While some viewed the veterans' war sacrifice as sufficient to merit state support, equally important were the former soldiers' continued good behavior. The Lost Cause mythology cast an image of veterans as honorable self-sacrificing individuals; accordingly, potential recipients had to continue to demonstrate these qualities. Having a high moral character and honorable habits were essential to be eligible for aid; no insane men or drunkards were permitted in Confederate soldiers' homes, and often such bad habits excluded veterans from receiving their pensions. Green points out that "recipients had to pass a means test before qualifying for state support, leaving no doubt that this was a welfare program. No matter how meritorious a veteran's war record might be, he would not receive a pension if he could not show need."[7]

Confederate pensions also served the political agenda of white supremacy following its re-enshrinement in the 1895 state constitution. By making honorable service a prerequisite for eligibility, pensions could be doled out to poor whites and denied to poor blacks without having to resort to fraud or intimidation. Green further notes that "Confederate veterans and their families, the recipients of both welfare benefits and automatic voting rights, would likely be among the most loyal Democratic voters from the non-elite classes. The combination of pensions and the vote served to tie those families to the state, the Lost Cause, and the Democratic Party simultaneously."[8]

Sadly for southern reformers, none could make the broad cultural and moral claims that veterans' advocates had marshaled so successfully. No other group could claim their activity would benefit the entirety of (white) South Carolina as the former soldiers had; no other cause could ask recompense for a job already completed. As any other claims on the public coffers ran the risk of benefiting some while taxing others, the state passed these choices to the county and municipal levels, arguing that it was there that taxpayers could best guarantee they would get what they paid for. Among South Carolina's counties operating budgets were tied to local property taxes, and as a result, local political leaders were as reticent to take on extra projects as the legis-

Table 2.3. Average South Carolina county expenditures, 1905 (dollars)

Item	Average cost per county
Criminal justice	10,444
Road construction and repair	7,002
Tax personnel	2,610
County poorhouse	1,555
Other expenses	723
Total	22,334

Source: South Carolina General Assembly, State Comptroller General, *Annual Report,* 187–232.

Note: I calculated the average county expenditure from the county reports submitted to the comptroller general.

lators in Columbia. As table 2.3 demonstrates, most local budgets addressed only those issues deemed necessary: the administration of criminal justice, local tax assessment, and the maintenance of county poorhouses.

Such tightly restricted local spending did not go unchallenged, as reformers across the state persistently championed a variety of causes. The two that made the greatest headway were the push for better roads and efforts to improve schools. Similar to the discussion surrounding Confederate pensions, most South Carolinians agreed these were causes worthy of greater financial support. Unlike the Confederate pension movement, roads and schools were understood to be local political issues reliant on local taxes. Further, while all South Carolinians were theoretically bound to honor the veterans' sacrifice for their state, not all citizens saw it as their responsibility to pay for better roads or schools if they themselves did not benefit directly from these services.

THE GOOD ROADS MOVEMENT

Shortly after its founding in 1898, the South Carolina Good Roads Association released its initial survey, in which it painted a grim picture of the Palmetto State's roadways.[9] "We find that there are about 50,000 miles of roads in South Carolina," the association's vice president, F. H. Hyatt, concluded. "There is not over 20% that we would call in good shape at this time."[10] Likely few across the state were surprised by these revelations; newspaper columns around the turn of the century consistently pointed out the woeful condition of their local roads. "There can scarcely be found a good road in this county when the best of weather prevails, and during a rainy period ... the roads are almost impassable," fumed the *Manning Times* in 1903; "we wish the Legislature could spend a few days in this county just now and attempt to drive over any road. We believe that every member ... would go back to Columbia ... determined to take some action looking towards road improvement."[11]

This deplorable state of affairs was taken up as a Progressive cause, as it impinged upon the state's development in multiple ways. Chief among them were economic benefits to rural residents. Arguing that "fully ninety-nine percent of the agricultural products have to be moved over public highways" and that in their present condition "the greatest distance a farmer can afford to haul his product to the railroad station over current roads is twenty miles," good roads advocates offered multiple ways in which better roads would improve the farmers lot.[12] In May 1901 the *Edgefield Advertiser* urged its readers, "We can agree that a good road will (1) economize time and force in transportation between farm and market (2) enable the farmer to take advantage of market fluctuations in buying and selling, regardless of weather conditions (3) permit transportation of farm products and purchasing during times of comparative leisure (4) reduce the wear and tear on horses, harness and vehicles (5) enhance the market value of real estate throughout the entire county."[13]

In addition to economic improvement, good roads also promised that to "diffuse light in dark places is to bring the dark places within easy reach of the light" by increasing rural school attendance.[14] Greater access to markets, school, and church would ultimately mean the continued maintenance of the rural way of life, as "good roads will keep the farm boy and farm girl by the farm home and put a stop to the congregation in cities."[15] Summing up these arguments, Governor Heyward lectured the legislature in his 1906 annual message: "There is no subject of greater importance and that will affect more people than that of good roads. The tendency has been for the county population to move into the cities and towns in order to secure the advantages of church and school. . . . The condition of the roads at certain sessions of the year makes it almost necessary that country people should be denied school, church and special privileges. If this continues, the county districts will become depopulated. . . . The country is the preserver of true manhood and the foster father of manly independence. Nothing will contribute more to its development and desirability than the building of good roads."[16]

With "the whole country . . . aroused as never before over the subject of better roads [and] the necessity for such improvements . . . everywhere admitted . . . the agitation of the question may now be directed to some feasible plan for obtaining money to make good roads."[17] This financial piece would prove to be the biggest stumbling block to further road construction. Nearly every observer agreed something needed to be done, but few could agree on who should pay for road improvement. Most often, the answer was somebody other than the person doing the speaking.

In his 1902 message to the legislature Governor McSweeney pointed out that "to build roads will require money and in order to secure money there will have to be a provision for raising it by taxation." Following a resolution passed by the Good Roads Association, McSweeney requested that "each county be given the privilege to determine by election the right of such county to levy a tax . . . and that such counties as desire to do so be given authority to issue bonds to construct and maintain their public highways."[18]

With the question of good roads now squarely at the county level, South Carolinians fiercely debated how, or if, to fund further improvements. Predictably, the proposal to levy further taxes aroused great consternation. For every enthusiastic advocate of good roads who asserted that "a property tax is the right and proper method of securing the money" and suggested that "this would not be a tax in the ordinary sense, but an investment that would pay good dividends to those who would be called to pay it,"[19] there was a detractor countering in equally vociferous terms: "The road tax has not made much headway in making permanent roads. It has made more mud, but fewer better roads. . . . A different plan of finance is what is wanted. Not more taxes. Not more money."[20]

In between these extremes were those who threw barbs at groups perceived as not doing their fair share. For some the wealthy were to blame. "The farmers alone have had to build country roads without assistance from the cities, from wealthy corporations or from the state. Every citizen will be benefitted by the construction of good roads, directly and indirectly, and every taxpayer should contribute his share to their cost. No wonder the farmer opposes the good roads movement, if he alone is to stand the expense," declared the editor of the *Abbeville Press*.[21] For others it was the poorest citizens who needed to contribute more. "What you need is a commutation tax," asserted a reader of the *Newberry Herald and News*. "There is a certain class of citizens (referring to Negroes) which you can't reach with a property tax. Then, if you want to do it, and I say you ought to do it, vote upon yourselves a separate tax for good roads."[22]

Others argued that if a locality showed good faith in taxing itself, it might credibly request federal funding for road improvement projects. After all, one state representative pointed out, "the United States government has appropriated millions to build good roads in the Philippines and Puerto Rico . . . if we can pay taxes to build good roads in a foreign country we might build them at home and keep our money."[23] Even within the United States, some speakers asserted, it was time for South Carolina to step up and ask for its fair share: "South Carolina has got nothing from the government compared to the vast amounts appropriated to other states for river and harbor improvements, to the west for land irrigation, to the Mississippi levees. It is right and just for South Carolina to get this aid and in order to get it you will not be forced to pay a cent more tax than you are paying now."[24]

THE NEEDS OF THE SCHOOLS

Standing apart from the state and county budgets, but nonetheless intimately bound up in them, was the question of funding for South Carolina's free public schools. The years during which the dispensary was in operation saw multiple efforts to improve school conditions across the state, which virtually every commentator agreed were far below any appropriate standard. But these efforts ran headlong into South Carolina's extreme political localism and resistance to taxation, making meaningful progress difficult, if not impossible.

The themes of educational necessity and financial probity were clearly struck by Governor Tillman during his first inaugural in 1890, in which he wrestled with the competing mandates he felt had been signaled by the voters. "Our task," he told the gathered legislators, "is to give the people better government, and more efficient government, as cheaply as possible." Such improvements began with "the improvement of the free school system and the wise adjustment of means to ends . . . so as to obtain the best results. These demand your best care and prompt attention." Tillman exhorted his listeners, reminding them that "the education and proper training of the voters who must choose the public officers to carry on the State's affairs is . . . a sacred duty which cannot be neglected without injury to the State and to society."[25]

In this sacred trust, as in so many other areas Tillman had campaigned on, he found previous efforts sorely lacking. "Are we doing all we can to educate our youth and fit them for the duties of life? I answer unhesitatingly, no!" Tillman declared. Staying loyal to his largely rural constituency, Tillman decried the imbalance in the free school system: "In our towns and villages, by reason of supplementary taxes . . . the schools are fairly good. Among the farmers in the country, the good school is the exception, while inferior schools, which run three or four months, are the rule." He concluded by saying: "We spend in round numbers for free common schools per annum about five hundred thousand dollars. . . . This allows less than two dollars to each child of school age," a sum Tillman considered unacceptable.[26]

Even as Tillman railed against educational inequities and urged legislators to repair them, he was also mindful of his consistent campaign promises to alleviate his constituents' tax burden as well as the deep and abiding concerns South Carolinians had against overreaching state legislative activity. Pointing out the "popular demand that the State . . . shall make the system effective or do nothing, and abolish the two mill tax, leaving education altogether to the people themselves," Tillman proposed no increase in state education taxes, instead "allow[ing] voters in each district to levy at their option . . . a supplementary tax . . . with the privilege for each taxpayer to designate the school to which this additional tax should be applied."[27]

School Finances

With less than 4 percent of the entire public school revenue derived from the general treasury, school districts were forced to rely almost entirely on local and county sources of taxation.[28] At the county level the three-mill constitutional tax supplied the bulk of school revenue. Collected and disbursed in accordance with section 6, article 11, of the 1895 constitution, the proceeds were to be apportioned on the basis of enrollment, thus favoring larger schools located in towns. At the district level the poll tax and dog tax were applied to local schools and throughout the first decade of the twentieth century accounted for roughly 10 percent of total school revenues. School districts could also vote in a tax to raise district school revenues, although these tax hikes were far from common. Janet Hudson points out that "town districts primarily levied these optional taxes to enhance their schools with longer terms and more and better-qualified teachers, and districts with a railroad, public utility, or a power plant benefitted tremendously from levying the special taxes."[29]By 1909 the state superintendent reported that only "six hundred and fifty-six of the eighteen hundred and thirty-three districts ... are now supplementing by this means their apportionment of regular school funds."[30] Table 2.4, which shows the amount per capita spent on South Carolina schools over the first decade of the twentieth century, attests to the results of such penury.

With such minimal financial support South Carolina schools, and their students, predictably suffered. The yearly reports of the state superintendent of education to the South Carolina General Assembly served as constant reminders of the deplorable conditions, beginning with Superintendent John McMahan's summary judgment in 1900: "It is a misnomer to say that we have a system of public schools. In the actual working of the great majority of schools in this state, there is no system or orderly organization. Each county supports its own schools with practically no help from the state. Each district has as poor schools as its people will tolerate—and in some districts anything will be tolerated."[31]

As the twentieth century dawned, a third of the state's citizens were illiterate, and the small country schools that served the majority of the pop-

Table 2.4. Per capita expenditure on South Carolina schools, 1899–1909 (dollars)

Year	White	African American	Average of both races
1899	4.98	1.42	2.69
1900	5.55	1.30	2.93
1901	5.82	1.30	3.37
1902	6.01	1.53	3.82
1903	6.11	1.45	3.96
1904	6.88	1.47	4.08
1905	7.49	1.51	4.31
1906	7.83	1.47	4.41
1907	7.93	1.57	4.50
1908	9.00	1.60	4.99
1909	10.34	1.70	5.67

Source: South Carolina Secretary of Education, *Annual Report*, 21.

ulation were woefully inadequate. "This schoolhouse must be the poorest in the county," wrote an observer describing conditions at an Anderson County school in 1903. "It is a frame building with one room about twenty or thirty feet, having a fireplace in one end . . . made of rough stone. It had been planned to have a fireplace at the other end, but it had never been placed there, and the opening was covered with a few rough planks with large cracks between them. How the unsealed room was kept warm in the winter is a mystery to me. Slab benches served as seats. The one blackboard in the room was less than a yard square."[32]

The lack of funding for common schools also impacted the quality of instruction. "A large percentage of teachers are young people who cannot pass our grade school examinations," observed Mayre R. Shelor as he toured Oconee and Pickens County schools in 1905, "yet the teachers are permitted to shape the destiny of the country."[33] Across the state, in Marion County, Penelope McDuffie noticed the same thing: "The teachers are fresh from the schoolroom themselves, or quite often town girls who teach for diversion and a salary. Obviously, there is no professional spirit and no attempt to increase the efficiency of teaching." Although clearly unimpressed with the background of rural schoolteachers, McDuffie understood that impediments to better hires lay in part in the facilities provided for them and their students: "It is almost inconceivable how a self-respecting teacher can remain in a bare shelter, lighted except for one glass window, minus three-fourths of its panes, and without any desks. I presume the children learn to write on slates—certainly there are in the four of the schools just visited no arrangements for writing any other way."[34]

Pressed to take some action, the South Carolina General Assembly responded with the 1907 High School Act, which included a fifty thousand–dollar state appropriation providing a matching funds incentive designed to push local investment in high schools. The law mandated that high schools would have at least two teachers with top-grade certificates and be in session thirty-two weeks. The state's approach reflected the self-help reasoning of education reformers: the state would help those who first helped themselves. As state funding was tied to local governments' ability to raise money, it did little to aid the state's poorest districts.[35] Not only did their residents have few resources; local tax increases were difficult to extract from recalcitrant farmers, who were "slow in realizing the value of a high-priced teacher. It seems that the only salaried people with whom they have to deal is the farm laborer, they, in all their comparison, use this as the standard, and thereby form the opinion that teachers are paid too much salary already."[36]

The results were predictable and, to the educational leaders of the state, increasingly maddening. "Time and again I have sat in school rooms watching the blind blunderings of teachers plodding through recitations without ever getting hold of a teaching fact or teaching principle until my heart ached in sympathy for the children who had to endure it all," reported state high school supervisor William H. Hand in 1909. "Why are so many incompetent teachers employed? Such teachers can be had cheap. When a school board goes out to find a cheap teacher, it usually succeeds in getting a cheap one in every sense."[37]

THE DISPENSARY AND THE BUDGET

While refusing to improve funding for the state's roads or common schools directly from taxes, state and leaders were willing to tap the dispensary systems' increasingly vast profits for this purpose. As the dispensary was responsible for roughly two-thirds of the state's revenue (see table 2.1), it offered a way forward for legislators hoping to mollify both Progressives requesting greater funding for roads and schools and taxpayers who argued that these social issues should not require more financial obligation on their part.

The state dispensary system offered two potential revenue streams to South Carolina's counties and common schools. The larger of the two came from the distribution of dispensary funds to the various counties and municipalities that hosted liquor shops. The initial dispensary law, as well as all its subsequent iterations, provided that all profits be split evenly between the state and counties, with the local portion to be divided between the county and the municipality in which the dispensary was located. Although counties were given some discretion in how their local funds were used, the pattern quickly adopted across the state divided local liquor funds into three equal parts—one each for the county, the dispensary towns, and the county schools.

The smaller portion of dispensary revenue came directly from the state to its common schools and promised aid to those in rural areas. Consistent with Tillman's desire that liquor profits not be the sole (or primary) province of the cities, as was the case under the license system, the dispensary law mandated that "all net income derived by the State from the sale of liquors in this State, under the Dispensary Law, shall be apportioned among the various counties of this State, for the benefit of the common schools, in proportion to the deficiencies existing in the various counties of this State, after the application of the three-mill tax and the poll tax to run the public schools for . . . [three months]; and if there shall be a surplus remaining of such net income after such deficiencies have been equalized, it shall be devoted to public school purposes and be apportioned among the counties in proportion to . . . enrollment."[38]

Because county budgets and school systems could grow and shrink based on the success of the dispensary, each county liquor board came under increasing pressure to boost sales. The persistent need for dispensary revenue collided with the dispensary creators' assurances that the system would bring about a meaningful reform of the liquor problem. The idea, so common among its proponents, that the dispensary would reduce inducements to drink because the dispenser as paid employee had no incentive to push greater consumption the way saloonkeepers would, overlooked the larger financial climate in which the dispensers worked. Although it was true that individual dispensers might not feel the need to increase sales to maintain their own livelihood, county liquor boards, which often found their chief justification for the system lay in its profits, could ill afford an unprofitable dispensary.

No Customer Left Behind

As county liquor boards worked to increase contributions to their county's bottom lines, the strategic location of dispensaries was their most important decision. Each county was initially granted one dispensary in its county seat, and county boards were encouraged to seek out other sites for liquor stores should they deem it necessary. In their bid to ensure that no potential dispensary customer was left high and dry, the boards sought expansion most often in counties where the population was widely dispersed beyond the county seat. In these counties populations were "widely scattered . . . [over] magnificent distances . . . and communication from the county seat is difficult. So far as these points are concerned, to confine the sale of whiskey to the county seat might as well be a prohibition law."[39] Table 2.5 bears out this trend; as of 1895, when the initial expansion of the dispensary system was completed, only those counties with better than nine hundred square miles had at least three dispensary towns.[40]

Table 2.5. Number of South Carolina dispensary towns by county size, 1895

County size (square miles)	No. of dispensary towns		
	1	*2*	*3+*
400–650	5	2	0
651–900	11	6	0
901–1,150	1	0	5
1,151–1,400	1	0	5

Source: South Carolina General Assembly, State Dispensary Auditor, *Annual Report,* 9–10.

In those counties where dispensary expansion was deemed wise, potential dispensary locations were carefully vetted with an eye toward maximizing the number of people each liquor store could potentially serve. Accordingly, county liquor boards considered three factors in their selection of dispensary towns. The first was the size of the town. As the most likely customers were in-town residents who lived near enough to make frequent purchases, larger towns and cities were often the first sites of dispensary expansion, when they were not already county seats. Of the twenty-three South Carolina cities and towns with populations above two thousand, all but one had a dispensary by 1895, and all continued to operate until the end of the state system in 1907 (table 2.6).[41]

A second factor considered by county boards was whether a potential dispensary town had a railroad stop. This point was especially critical for towns with less than two thousand residents, where a dispensary could be profitable if it could draw customers from the surrounding rural area. Reasoning that these customers were most likely to be farmers seeking the nearest train depot from which to ship their crops, county liquor boards were encouraged to find locations "somewhere on the Railroad where crowds would likely gather on market days."[42] County boards took this advice seriously; among towns with less than one thousand residents, all that featured dispensaries had railroad depots (see table 2.6).[43]

The third factor used in county board deliberations was the distance of a potential new dispensary to those that already existed. It made little sense to expand if it seemed likely that profits garnered at a new dispensary would only be registered as losses in an already existing liquor shop. Of the state's sixty-four towns with populations under two thousand that also had railroads

Table 2.6. Factors determining location of South Carolina's dispensary towns in 1900

Town characteristics	Dispensary in town
Population above 10,000	yes 4, no 0
Population 2,000–10,000	yes 18, no 1
Population 1,000–1,999	yes 17, no 3
Population below 1,000	yes 46, no 97
Town had railroad	yes 46, no 64**
Town had no railroad*	yes 0, no 33

Sources: South Carolina General Assembly, State Dispensary Auditor, *Annual Report,* 8–9; U.S. Bureau of the Census, *Twelfth Census;* Report of State Officers and Committees to the General Assembly, 148–56.

* This category includes only the 143 towns with populations under 1,000.

** Of the 64 towns with populations under 1,000 with railroads, 61 were located within twenty miles of an existing dispensary town.

yet did not house a dispensary, all but three were located within twenty miles of an already existing dispensary in a town with a larger population, making an increase in overall profits unlikely (see table 2.6). With a couple of exceptions, then, the dispensary system in every county had expanded as far as it could to gain the maximum profits.[44]

Once a town had been selected, the dispensary law gave the county board authorization to select and rent the particular site of sale. Eager to draw as many customers as possible, county boards sought locations in the center of towns nearest the courthouse or markets, where most citizens would be doing business. These sites were most often available in county seats; in towns outside the county center, dispensaries were usually established close to the railroad so as to take advantage of the foot traffic near those locations. Sanborn Fire Insurance Maps made from 1895 to 1907 show that in every one of the eighty-five dispensary towns, the liquor shop was in one of those two locations.

THE ECONOMIC IMPACT OF THE DISPENSARY

The state dispensary system was responsible for the lion's share of the state's revenue (see table 2.1). Offsetting the potential profits, however, were the system's operating expenses, including the cost of liquor, county liquor board dispenser, and constable salaries as well as the inevitable extra costs brought about by breakages and grafting that ran throughout the system. During the 1890s, when resistance to the dispensary system was at its peak, the costs of running the system often outweighed its profits, a condition that was especially acute after the circuit court ruling permitting original package stores to set up shop legally in South Carolina. Surveying this state of affairs in his 1898 address to the legislature, Governor William Ellerbe warned that "the finances of the state are in a very unsatisfactory condition. . . . The levy for state purposes will be high but you must remember that we have a deficit of $100,000— not of our making—to be provided for and that the state will no longer receive any revenue for current expenses from dispensary profits."[45]

The tide quickly turned after the legal challenge was overcome. Beginning in 1899, the dispensary system consistently turned a profit, eventually reaching $870,318 by 1905.[46] Based on this windfall, Governor Heyward, in his 1906 remarks to the state legislature, proudly proclaimed that the dispensary was without doubt "the best solution of the liquor question yet to be devised." Pointing to information from the 1905 annual dispensary report, Heyward noted that "profits will be much larger than in any previous year." Seeking to assure voters concerned about the rise in drunkenness, he added, "This does not necessarily mean that the consumption of whiskey has increased, but rather argues that less whiskey was shipped in the State for personal use and the blind tigers have decreased."[47]

The dispensaries' significant contribution to the state coffers also led the governor to cast aspersions on prohibition as being "very nice in theory but in existing circumstances and conditions I do not believe it would be practicable. Extraordinary machinery would be necessary to enforce it, and there would be no means with which to employ the machinery except by additional taxation."[48] As South Carolina politicians became more acclimated to employing dispensary funds (see the figures for 1899 and 1905 in table 2.2), prohibitionists increasingly despaired of ever turning back the tide. "If whiskey is to be shaken out of South Carolina politics," one dry observer wrote, "the people are going to have to use heroic measures to administer the cure to the body politic. If this great political machine is to be broken, there are innumerable indications which point to the conclusion that the people will have to more than hint . . . that political death awaits the man who stands in the way."[49]

THE IMPACT OF THE DISPENSARY IN THE COUNTIES

While the dispensary system emerged as a consistent source of funding for the state's counties and common schools, its impact varied considerably across the state. This disparity rested primarily on the ability of each county to turn a profit once the state had taken its share of dispensary revenue. The profitability of a county's dispensaries was largely dependent on its population. Those with few incorporated railroad towns outside of sparsely populated county seats saw few customers, while Charleston and Richland Counties drew on their urban populations to sell much larger amounts. Within these extremes the main determining factor in a county's dispensary sales was the percentage of its population residing in dispensary towns. Although rural residents frequenting dispensaries on their trips into town certainly aided liquor shops' sales, it was the in-town repeat customers that formed the bulk of their customer base.

These dispensary profits are only half the story when considering the impact of the dispensary on each county's financial situation. The other part is the amount of taxable income each county had to draw on. Here, as with dispensary sales, county fortunes varied widely, with rural, sparsely populated counties having assets less than one-tenth as large as the state's most affluent county. Taking these two sets of data together allows an assessment of the relative impact dispensary funds had on each county's budget (see table 4.1).[50] The counties that made the most of dispensary funds typically featured dispensary profits enhanced by one good-sized town surrounded by a few smaller towns that contributed little to the overall tax base (e.g., Florence, Orangeburg, and Sumter). Of special note here is Georgetown County, which had both a profitable dispensary housed in its county seat and virtually no population to draw on beyond that, meaning that dispensary profits were of considerable importance to the county's operation.[51]

In the richest dispensary counties the amount of liquor money coming in became an important argument for continuing the state system. "The revenue from the dispensary in this county is certainly a valuable consideration amounting to a sufficient sum to keep all the county affairs and schools . . . on a cash basis [meaning no debt]—a condition that the people in the city and county certainly appreciate," wrote a Georgetown newspaperman, while the editor of the Bishopville (Lee County) newspaper observed: "There is . . . a business side to the matter, which may be sneered at by the super moral element, but which to the sensible, certainly must have weight. The dispensary paid . . . for the eight months from October 1, 1904 to June 1, 1905, nearly $10,000. . . . Should the dispensary be abolished and this source of revenue eliminated—where would we be?"[52]

Dispensary profits were so great in some instances that they managed to turn what was originally seen as a disreputable system into one with a great number of supporters. The state dispensary auditor's report in 1905 cited the case of Sumter County, where "the dispensary system was forced in over the protests of the majority of the people, today there is no serious or organized opposition to the system in this county. . . . The profit features of the dispensary unquestionably have much to do with the kindly feeling toward the system that now prevails."[53] Meanwhile, in the state capital, where "Richland County has never favored the dispensary system and while it may not be altogether pleasant to record the fact, its hold is largely through the money influence—that is the $50,000 in profit and the saving of that much in taxes. The city of Columbia last year derived $22,356.69 net from the dispensaries . . . and with the extravagant expenses in the city of Columbia and the disposition to keep on spending, the people are not disposed to cut off this money . . . and pay for it in additional taxes. . . . It is simply a case of dollars and cents between the dispensary and prohibition in this county."[54]

While South Carolina's wealthiest dispensary counties rejoiced in their abundant riches, other counties had to make do with far less. The counties that benefited the least were those in which the only dispensary was located in a small county seat with no other viable place to expand (e.g., Pickens, Horry, Saluda, and Newberry). In these instances the amount of revenue generated by liquor sales was so minimal that it made the dispensary a poor economic bet. "As for the dispensary helping the taxpayers," wrote one angry citizen in Pickens County, "I have not been able to see the help yet and I know that the levy for State taxes this year is one-half mill higher than it was when the dispensary was enacted. The dispensary sells $3,500,000 worth of whiskey a year and turns the profit over to the State, and yet taxes are higher; where does the help come? Has anybody's taxes been reduced? If so, I would like to hear from it!"[55] As citizens in these counties saw their taxes rise with minimal improvement in their public services, they began to question the wisdom of a system that "from the standpoint of morals . . . is the most iniquitous thing in the history of men." "Last year the county levy was 3 mills and the state 5 mills," the *Newberry Herald and News* calculated for its readers. "This year the legislature with all its dispensary money had raised the state levy to 5 and a half mills while the county levy was 3 and a half mills." Not only had the people "paid more taxes last year than in 1902," former Newberry mayor George B. Cromer reminded his fellow citizens, but "we are in no better fix as to public roads etc *sic*] . . . than we were before."[56] Such sentiments threatened the dispensary; if citizens gained little economically from liquor sales, then their focus would increasingly turn to the social harms associated with the state's liquor shops.

3

THE SOCIAL COSTS OF THE DISPENSARY

The ever-increasing amount of money flowing into South Carolina's schools ensured the dispensary's popularity among many South Carolinians, particularly among the state's politicians. This popularity kept the dispensary alive, especially during Tillman's time as governor and even for some years after his influence on South Carolina politics began to wane. But these forces could not dissuade the dispensary's enemies, who pointed to the central contradiction in the statewide system—that it did not advance the reforms proclaimed by its creators.

Tillman and other dispensary proponents had continuously held that the dispensary, because it was not run by the drink industry, would not seek to make a profit. With the profit motive removed, the state liquor board would harbor no allegiance to the "liquor trust," nor would county dispensers feel compelled to induce their fellow citizens into consuming liquor. The results would be a state relatively free of drunkards, destitute families, and liquor-related crime. As the dispensary system's economic imperative became more pronounced, opponents pointed to its increasingly cozy relations with the drink industry as well as its failure to drive out inducements to drink and the alarming rise in poverty and crime that seemed to plague the state since the dispensary's adoption. In short critics argued that the dispensary was a false reform.

The subject of prohibition sentiment in South Carolina is well-trod territory; many excellent monographs exist that detail the social location and motivations of prohibitionists across the state and the South as a whole. Moving beyond the important yet simplistic equation of evangelism and prohibitionist sentiment, recent scholarship has coalesced around a view of southern prohibitionists as earnest, middle-class progressives proposing a logical way to deal with the myriad social problems caused by excessive alcohol consumption. These problems were understood to begin in the home, where money spent on alcohol squandered family finances, putting wives and children at risk. As such, dry campaigns often aroused the interest and participation of women, especially the Woman's Christian Temperance Union (WCTU), providing one of the first platforms for their political participation. Beyond the home progressives linked drinking to social disorder on the part of African Americans (although recent monographs also demonstrate that many blacks supported the dry cause), by the nascent southern working class, or by rural whites on their frequent sojourns into town. Finally, scholars also emphasize that these sentiments, though widely held, required political organization to gain legal victories. The Anti-Saloon League (ASL) is credited with being the organization most responsible for dry success, although the degree to which the ASL influenced the course of events in the South has been questioned by some scholars.[1]

Within South Carolina it has been well established that the Progressive movement in general and prohibition in particular owe much of their impetus to the fears of townspeople in the new Upcountry mill counties. Faced with the seemingly sudden appearance of mill towns in their midst, Upcountry leaders determined to do something about what came to be known as the "cotton mill problem." This concern, writes David Carlton, "untied ministers, journalists, teachers, club women, and businessmen in both a common desire for a more stable and better organized society and a common perception that one of the major barriers to its realization was a 'shiftless' undisciplined operative class."[2]

Previous scholarship makes it possible to investigate differences across South Carolina's counties that would likely influence their attitudes toward prohibition. Such differences did not result from disagreements about prohibitionists' assertions regarding the effects of alcohol on their communities. Religious South Carolinians were no different than other southern evangelicals in abhorring drink and its negative effects on individual souls, families, and communities. South Carolina progressives were no different than those across the region who warned about the influence of the whiskey trust on local and state politics. Nor were Palmetto State residents different from other southerners in worrying about drunk African American's ravaging white women or the baneful effects on social order should white mobs, also under the influence, retaliate.

Instead, differences between South Carolina counties' willingness to embrace prohibition lay in the degree to which these potential problems associated with alcohol actually occurred in local communities. True, dispensaries across the state tempted the young into lives of drunkenness and despair, and most struck deals with the liquor traffic that made increased sales more likely. Where counties differed was in the social class of dispensary customers as well as the amount of crime that seemed to spring from dispensary sales. It is those local conditions that separate the counties that adopted prohibition from those that did not.

THE SOUTHERN EVANGELICAL ATTITUDE TOWARD DRINK

Any discussion of the social problems South Carolinians related to alcohol use must be set against the backdrop of southern evangelicalism. Evangelical Protestantism emerged in the South during the late eighteenth century along what was then the frontier of Tennessee and Kentucky. Through revivals Baptists, Methodists, and Presbyterians spread their message, and by the late nineteenth century evangelical Protestantism was the dominant religious tradition across much of the region.[3]

Evangelical southerners believed that life at its most basic level required a series of choices between right and wrong behavior—decisions that reflected one's relationship with God and therefore spoke to the quality of one's salvation. Although all life choices were theoretically free, evangelicals took a dim view of human nature, believing that humans were inherently sinful. Consequently, if left to their own devices, most people were apt to sin. Accordingly, the central theme of evangelical Protestantism was to stress the need for individuals to "get right with God" through conversion, only after which a moral life was possible.

This view of sin and salvation, according to Ted Ownby, "dominated the cultural horizon of most Southerners. For some, it connected everyday life with the heavens, giving a joy and satisfaction to otherwise routine activities. For others, it set goals for behavior that were high and sometimes frustratingly out of reach. For still others, it loomed dark and threatening, inducing guilt and insecurity and working against the pursuit of pleasure. For almost all, it was an extremely powerful influence in setting the standards for personal behavior."[4]

Of course, not all southerners followed these standards, and chief among the violators were those who consumed alcohol to excess. Enumerating the host of problems associated with drunkards became commonplace for evangelical commentators, as, for example, the North Carolina preacher in 1905 who warned that "alcohol undermines the health, enfeebles the will, makes the mind coarse and the tongue vulgar, brings discord to the family, deprives children of their rights, lowers the standard of morals, corrupts politics, fills prisons and asylums with human wrecks, mocks religion and ruins immortal souls."[5]

In addition to these individual and social costs, the evangelical cosmology identified public liquor sales as a source of temptation whose negative impacts were felt by individuals, families, whole communities, and the state. This concern was in keeping with evangelicals' observation that even those who had been saved nevertheless existed in a world of sinners, whose actions could be the undoing of even the most pious individuals. These themes harked back to the earliest biblical stories, which, according to one preacher, cast "a clear light on the nature of sin. It began in temptation—the suggestion of the serpent. . . . The first sinner, Eve, became an agent of sin and of evil. She who had been only good to Adam now became the agent of his ruin. That history is repeated daily. If you sin, you are apt to induce others to sin."[6]

Applying this lesson to the drunkards and dispensaries in their midst, South Carolina evangelicals worried that weaker souls would be tempted by those they respected into adopting the drink habit for themselves. Seen in this light, it was easy for Rev. W. R. Richardson of Greenville to assert that "the dispensary, selling as it does intoxicating liquors as a beverage [rather than as sacrament] is making drunkards of our young and perpetuating drunkenness by gratifying the appetite of inebriates . . . and binding the chains of the drink habit more securely around those who are already enslaved."[7] Compared to barrooms, the dispensary system was even more likely to tempt the young into drink, Yorkville reverend W. C. Ewart noted, because "the use of liquor money for education" would influence "children who received its benefits . . . [to] conclude the traffic was all right and . . . evil effects ensue."[8]

Once the first drink was taken, turning back was virtually impossible; the only road left was toward ruin. "Jewels the most valuable that men possess, purity, integrity, intellectuality, moral and physical manhood are . . . slowly dissolved by intemperance," cautioned Rev. R. S. Truesdale of Columbia.[9] This being the case, "drunkenness has become disreputable . . . and in all callings of life, from the highest to the lowest, sobriety is more and more at a premium."[10] With increasingly less ability to work and ever more in need of drink, a man would slowly slide into destitution, dragging with him "the patient mother, wife or sister toiling for the protection of home and provision of the inno-cent."[11] The pitiful end would likely come sooner rather than later, as "in gen-eral it can be said that hard drinking can rarely be carried on for more than 20 years and regularly brings the victim to grief at about the age of 40."[12] Given this tragic course of events, Rev. F. C. Hickson of Gaffney urged his follow-ers to abstain, reminding them that "the Bible says no drunkard shall enter the kingdom of heaven. It classes drunkards—those who would use liquor as Mr. Tillman would allow—with liars, murderers, whoremongers and harlots."[13]

Given the universal threat posed by liquor sales in their midst, evangelicals were among the most vociferous opponents of the dispensary system, casting its supporters as a threat to home and family. "Why do they seek to perpetu-ate such an institution," asked one preacher "from which is sold that vile stuff which dethrones reason, debases character, kindles in the crazed brain of the drunkard the desire to commit murder, destroys the virtues of our daughters, and . . . brings upon the human race those hell-born pangs known only to the mother, wife and sister of a debased drunkard?"[14]

Against such implacable foes seeking only to line their pockets, Baptist and Methodist church leaders were among the earliest to advocate for prohibition, each adopting it as part of their official temperance policy. According to one Methodist leader: "The church has spoken in no uncertain tones on the sub-ject, and her standards must be maintained. There can be no compromise, no letting down of the standard. There is no middle ground. There is no place for casuistry. Other may argue, if they wish, as to the best method for controlling the liquor traffic. With us, it is not a question of control, but of complete pro-hibition."[15] The Baptists spoke with equal fervor: "As regards whiskey-selling, a Christian should stand only upon a prohibition platform. It is his duty to re-move evil temptations wherever he can, and so he should vote to remove in-toxicating liquors as a constant source of temptation to the weak. He should be a prohibitionist."[16]

Although church leaders appealed most directly to men, as they alone held the vote, the South Carolina WCTU, although small in number, also agitated for the cause. "There should be a general uprising of women in the defense of home and temperance," implored one member. "You may do much to elevate the dear old mother State to its former noble position in the world."[17] Another prohibitionist sought to involve whole families in the movement, as it was the entire family who stood to suffer if liquor shops won out: "Fathers and mothers, do you wish to see that manly son ruined by the curse of drink? If not, vote, work and pray against it. Sisters, do you wish to see your brother become a drunkard, ruined in this world and the next? If not, won't you help the cause of prohibition? Young ladies, you who have selected your ideal from among mankind, do you want to see your ideal shattered and realize that from this ideal has come a beast? If not, throw your influence—you have much more than you think—on the side that is striving to keep him away from the vile stuff that causes it."[18] By the early 1900s South Carolinians across the state had grown accustomed, both within church and outside it, to hearing invocations such as one entitled "To All Church Members":

Let us rise like Christians, brothers, Let us rally at the polls,
For the votes that we are casting, Fix the destiny of souls . . .
Can you lead the struggling brother, Whom your master came to save,
Step by step away from Heaven, Down into a drunkard's grave . . . ?
Think! The eye of God is on you, He each secret action notes,
You who praise Him in your churches, Will you shame Him by your votes . . . ?
Take the Savior with your brother, Let his will your motive be,
Say as close beside He standeth, Lord this vote I cast for thee . . . !
Vote today as Christ would have you, Let your vote for Jesus tell,
Some poor reeling ruined drunkard, You may save from death and hell.[19]

Such invocations and arguments were rarely contested in debates about the dispensary. Outside of Charleston, the only place in the state where evangelical Protestants were not the majority, few questioned the self-evident facts that drunkards put themselves and their families at risk and that the presence of liquor sales increased the likelihood of drunkenness across the state. In fact, the creator of the dispensary system, Ben Tillman, said as much in his message to the legislature asking them to sign off on the statewide liquor system. Neither he nor anyone else expected the dispensary to prevent such misfortunes. But then again, they argued, neither did prohibition. As an outright ban of liquor sales could not be enforced, such action offered little protection from the misfortunes of the drunkard and his family.

THE DISPENSARY AND THE LIQUOR TRAFFIC

Where dispensary proponents did expect their approach to improve on other systems of legal sales, and perhaps perform even better than prohibition might, was in controlling the conditions under which liquor was sold. These interventions might not save every drunkard, but they could prevent the worst abuses of the liquor traffic and in the process reduce the number of men suffering from alcohol abuse. For more secular critics of the dispensary system this bold claim that the dispensary could tame the business of drink was the system's signal failure. By creating a state monopoly over liquor sales, opponents argued, the government of South Carolina became a client of the beer and hard liquor industry, rather than a regulator of those retailers. The pressure to make money and stay in the good graces of citizens and political leaders ultimately made the dispensary less a reform measure than a naked attempt to fill the state's coffers. Of course, this was not necessarily the intent of those who made the dispensary law. To understand the slow slide from reform to business venture, we need to start with a look at the liquor trade as South Carolina's leaders found it in 1893.[20]

In the years before prohibition Americans bought two types of whiskey. As K. Austin Kerr explains: "There were firms in Kentucky and Pennsylvania, making bourbon and rye whiskey . . . that distilled grain mash, aged it in wooden casks for a period of years, and sold it under brand labels. This so-called straight whiskey was not, however, the common product. Americans drank mostly rectified whiskey in their saloons, a product made by a two-stage process. First, a distiller produced alcohol from grain . . . and then sold the alcohol either for industrial or beverage purposes. For drinking, the rectifier diluted the alcohol with water and flavored it in one of several ways: with aged whiskey or even fruit juices. . . . He sold his products to wholesale firms that in turn distributed them to retail outlets."[21]

After the Civil War increased competition, prompted by both changes in federal tax policy as well as a growing market, encouraged greater consolidation within the distilling industry. By 1891 distillers located in Illinois, Kentucky, Ohio, and Pennsylvania accounted for nearly 85 percent of the industry's capacity. Eager to gain every possible advantage in the market, these distillers formed pools, offered illegal rebates, attempted price manipulation, and in one spectacular instance attempted to dynamite a competitor's plant. This higher concentration in turn spurred competition among wholesalers, as a host of middlemen fought for the right to market distillers' output.[22]

Further competition for the distillers came from the rapid rise of breweries. During the fifty years after Appomattox the average per capita consumption of distilled spirits declined from 2.1 to 1.2 gallons. Consumption of beer, by contrast, rose from 3.5 to 20.2 gallons during the same half-century. Part of this increase was due to scientific and technological developments. Lager beer required fermentation and shipping at cool temperatures. Mechanical refrigeration reduced brewers' dependence on natural ice and made possible cooler freight cars for shipping to distribution centers. Beginning in the 1880s, brewers initially located in midwestern cities with limited markets—Anheuser-Busch, Pabst, Schlitz, Miller—took advantage of technological developments to bolster their distribution to other cities across the country. As they expanded, these "nationals" encountered increasing numbers of local brewers attempting to gain a foothold in their respective cities, where the influx of European immigrants created concentrated spaces of potential consumers.

To reach these growing markets, distillers and brewers began to finance local saloons. In return for a brewer financing the mortgage and providing all the fixtures and furniture, a saloonkeeper agreed to market a particular brewer's product exclusively. The low initial startup costs meant even relatively poor immigrants could establish saloons, and not surprisingly, these liquor shops quickly proliferated across American cities. The new saloonkeepers quickly found themselves squeezed between brewers' insistence on steady profits and consumers' many choices for where to purchase liquor.

Accordingly, saloonkeepers resorted to all sorts of inducements to attract new clients and turn them into regulars. The inducements could be fairly banal—for example, free lunches and music to entice new clients or credit for regular customers. To continue to keep ahead of the competition, many liquor retailers also engaged in minor violations of the law, such as selling to drunkards and minors and increasing business hours beyond those proscribed by local regulations. The most bold (or most desperate) liquor sellers provided illegal inducements such as gambling or prostitution. Such violations put saloonkeepers at risk of legal trouble and therefore required liquor sellers to seek the protection of the police and local politicians, thus turning many of them into cogs in larger urban political machines.

THE DISPENSARY AND THE LIQUOR BUSINESS

Various abuses in the liquor industry were well known to South Carolinians when they opted for prohibition in 1892. In setting aside the voters' mandate, Tillman promised he could do better—he would provide South Carolinians with legal liquor and do so without being corrupted by the system of liquor sales that had trapped so many retailers into making deals with the devil. At the very beginning this kind of reform seemed possible. Upon making his initial order for the dispensary, Tillman received a rebate from the "whiskey trust" (the so-called cabal of wholesale liquor dealers that dominated the market)—which he promptly declined. Sadly for the dispensary system, its future leaders would not be so high-minded.

Similar to other liquor retailers across the country, the dispensary's primary suppliers of both spirits and beer were the large liquor trusts and national brewers, whose competitive advantage meant they could undercut more local dealers on price. By 1904 dispensary ledgers showed the dominance of these national producers, with Schlitz, Anheuser-Busch, and Pabst, accounting for 61 percent of the $126,665 the South Carolina Dispensary spent on beer.[23]

Faced with being completely cut out of the potentially lucrative South Carolina market (one that had been a major source of income prior to the establishment of the dispensary system), brewers in Georgia and North Carolina resorted to increasingly desperate measures. One of the most common was to offer bribes and illegal rebates to local and county dispensers in the hopes that they would press the state to order their brands. To disguise the free liquor they received in each shipment, local dispensers' monthly reports often listed "shortages," bottles they had ordered but not received, or "breakages," bottles for which there had been no sale but the contents were nevertheless lost. While some human error in shipping was expected, the increasingly large amounts of shortages reported by some dispensers raised red flags when reported in the *Augusta Chronicle* in July 1897 (the dollar figures represent the value of shortages then and in today's dollars):

August 1896, T. A. Scott, Columbia: $4,920.20 ($123,005)

August 1896, Wade Lamar, Aiken: $252.92 ($6,323)

August 1896, R.F.D. Holzclaw, Greenville: $1,301.34 ($32,533.50)

April 1896, B. O. Evans, St. Matthews: $1,708.70 ($42,717)

November 1895, A. F. Dixon, Camden: $938.84 ($23,371)

June 1895, G. M. Langston, Laurens: $674.71 ($16,867)[24]

Later that year the *Chronicle* reported on Florence dispenser H. D. Williams, who had constructed an even more elaborate scheme to hide his illegal profits: "He some time ago claimed his dispensary had been robbed by burglars and $480 worth of goods carried away. The assistant attorney-general was asked to investigate it. He reported today that so far as evidence went there was nothing to show that there had been any robbery. An affidavit was submitted with the report signed by Clerk Martin, of this particular dispensary, in which Martin swears that for two years he has been falsifying the reports of stock on hand at the orders of his superior. He also tells how his superior drew about $40 a month for clerk hire and paid the clerk $17.50, and gives numerous instances of the doubling of expense accounts. The affidavit was very damaging."[25] Other brewers, liquor dealers, and wholesalers who sought greater influence within the dispensary set their sights higher, reasoning that gaining the favor of those making the statewide purchases would eliminate the need to go hat in hand to each county dispenser. The files of Tillman and subsequent governors are filled with such appeals, and many indicate that they came with further inducements. "I have taken the liberty of having my neighbors and friends, James Clark and Co. send you a sample of 'Mountain Dew' distilled under the direction of an old Virginian and ex-Confederate soldier," wrote one hopeful liquor dealer. "I feel that I am a judge of this product of our mountains and considering it is excellent, trust that your excellency will enjoy it."[26]

Other local brewers appealed to the previous connections they already had within South Carolina. "For the past eight years I have supplied the towns of Beaufort and Port Royal with beer . . . and have located at that point a branch house under the management of Mr. Charles F. Cohen, *whom I know to be a friend of yours,*" wrote wholesaler George Meyer to Tillman. He then made clear that he "would not lose the business we get from that section under the new Dispensary law. We are fully prepared to make your prices . . . and uphold your law."[27]

Such pleas, no matter how common, paled in comparison to the efforts of the liquor trust to gain favor with state dispensary commissioner F. M. Mixon. Inviting his son to their headquarters in Cincinnati, "where he had been royally entertained by the distillers and given thousands of dollars as commissions and brokerage fees," the distillers pressured Mixon to pay "higher prices to one house of liquors than others had been offering the same grade for. Mixon subsequently resigned.... In the end, he became a salesman for a liquor house with South Carolina as a territory."[28]

Even setting aside the most overt attempts at bribery, dry campaigners' concerns that the dispensary would become nothing more than a cog in the liquor trust, with the state playing middleman, proved accurate when it came to the volume of liquor sales. When the dispensary opened in 1893, the state had on hand one type of beer and four types of whiskey carrying no brand name—instead labeled *X* to *XXXX*. As the liquor business gradually gained a foothold in the state system, dispensers were compelled, both by consumer demand and liquor dealers' largesse, to increase their stock lists. By 1905 the state dispensary stock directory listed 24 separate types of beer and 211 different brands of wine and hard liquor.

These additions greatly expanded dispensary profits after the turn of the century. In 1900 the state's dispensaries sold a total of $1,350,634 worth of nonbrand items (*X* through *XXXX*), and $978,046 worth of brand-name liquors. By 1905 sales of non-brand liquor had increased slightly, to $1,458,251. Brand-name liquor sales, by contrast, more than doubled across the entire state, totaling $2,098,460.[29] The greater penetration of brand-name liquors was virtually statewide. In 1900 brand-name liquors accounted for more than half of total sales in seven South Carolina counties; by 1905 thirty of the state's then thirty-eight counties derived more than half of their sales from brand-name products. Only two counties across the entire state saw declines in their percentage of brand-name sales relative to the state products between 1900 and 1905.

For South Carolinians opposed to the dispensary, the sight of "dispensers making constant efforts to increase sales in order to get more profit and keep their dispensaries from being closed by the state liquor board" and stocking "fancy brands of liquor to entice the unwary ... in all dispensaries so that new and young customers are continuously being roped in"[30] stood as the critical indictment of the system. "Alcoholic sales are increasing in South Carolina at a rate of more than $45,000 per year," noted Rev. Joel E. Brunson of Greenville. "The above figures ought to convince any fair-minded man that the dispensary is, in no sense of the word, a temperance measure. Its object is not to control but to increase the sale of whiskey," Brunson argued, and therefore the dispensary ought to be eliminated.[31]

The state's cozy relationship with liquor dealers also alarmed critics concerned about dealers' impact on the state's politics. "The air is offensive with rumors of all kinds of dishonest practices in the conduct of the dispensary; there are rumors of newspapers being bought and sold and subsidized," wrote one observer.[32] In a climate in which the state press could be controlled by outside money, the *Newberry News and Observer* wrote, "if the dispensary continues much longer, with its debauching and corrupting influence, not only the office of liquor and beer dispensers will be bought and sold, but every other office in the state, from Governor down."[33] The editor of the *Beaufort Post* was not the least surprised and in fact argued that "the dispensary situation . . . might have been expected, and naturally exists in the establishment of great big speculative concerns." After all, the dispensary was just an extension of the whiskey trust and therefore subject to "the gigantic frauds and rascalities of the big trusts that are committed every day. See the Equitable and other big insurance companies that are swindling the public every day, and are rich enough to defy the law and its consequences. The State went into the liquor business for the profits," the author concluded.[34] To expect any other outcome than fealty to the source of those profits would be incredulous.

Summing up these arguments, and noting the disgust of many citizens, the *Darlington News Era* asserted: "We do not oppose the dispensary simply because it is the dispensary or because we wish to give Tillman a black eye. We oppose it because there is inherent corruption in the system; because it is a huge political machine; because it opens wide the door to graft; because it has neither curtailed the sale nor restricted the use of whiskey; and because it has contaminated every man who has touched it."[35]

THE SOCIAL HARM FROM DRINKING

Another set of concerns for dispensary opponents were the social disorder and crime that were said to be the inevitable result of alcohol use. Across South Carolina, according to the *State*, "it is generally admitted that three-fourths of all crimes committed by our people are directly due to the drinking of liquor."[36] This fact caused few to raise their eyebrows; as the *Spartanburg Herald* pointed out, the link between liquor and crime was manifest for all to see: "Give men that which deprives them of reason and conscience, and then expect acts of folly and lawlessness. Let the State continue to sow the seed and we shall have no lack of a harvest of death."[37]

At the time of its founding, dispensary advocates had promised that their system would reduce the amount of crime. Yet six years into the dispensary experiment, the *State* surveyed the state's crime statistics for its readers, concluding, "If the dispensary system, operated as is claimed by those who are maintaining it to check the crimes which are generated by liquor selling, and it is an improvement in that respect over every other plan to regulate the traffic, how happens it that in the last six years . . . it not only does not show some decrease in crime, but there is an actual doubling of crimes . . . ?"[38]

The initial dispensary law specified that every purchaser had to make a written request for liquor, each person's name was to be recorded by the dispenser, and the buyer had to sign to indicate he had received the request. These provisions had the potential to reduce (legal) consumption, both through dispensers denying the requests of drunkards and minors and through the potential social stigma a repeat buyer might face by his neighbors seeing his name so frequently on the dispenser's customer list. Each of these innovations, it was thought, would aid in keeping liquor from those least able to control themselves while under its sway.

These stipulations would quickly become the first casualties in the dispensary's drive for profits. Within the first month of their opening the state board issued a revision: "County dispensers are not required to enter individual names in the Dispenser's Record Book of Liquors sold. . . . All that is necessary is to enter the aggregate number of names of persons who have bought liquors . . . the kinds of liquors sold, the quantity kind, number of packages of each kind, amount of money received thereof and the amount of stock on hand."[39] As the Fairfield County Prohibition Committee pointed out, this ruling made clear that "instead of decreasing the consumption of liquor and lessening the evils of intemperance . . . the effort of the dispensary authorities has been to sell all the liquor possible, thus raising larger revenue."[40]

Indeed, far from discouraging liquor consumption, the Anderson County

Prohibition Committee argued that "the officers whom we have put in charge of the dispensary to see that the law is enforced, instead think that we put them there to ply a commercial venture . . . to push the sale of poisonous liquors among her young men and among the helpless victims of the fatal habit, and to fatten the state's treasury at the cost of those whom the State should be most solicitous to protect."[41] The result, argued the Fairfield Prohibition Committee, was that while "the State Board of Control, in its annual report to the Legislature, has congratulated itself on the increased sale . . . the records of crime during these years in murders, manslaughters and assaults, a large majority of which are directly traceable to the dispensary, is the blackest in the history of our state."[42]

As the years wore on, far from discouraging drinking, liquor advertisements became more frequent in South Carolina newspapers, as liquor manufacturers hoped to entice consumers with new product lines that might also boost sales. These advertisements, although proscribed by law, clearly had the dispensary board's blessing. "We are sending you by express package a certain advertising matter," the director of the Atlanta Brewing Company wrote to dispensary head M. H. Mobley. "We would thank you to distribute same among the different people connected with the dispensary."[43]

Threats to a dispenser's bottom line became more acute after the 1897 federal court rulings allowed the sale of imported liquor in South Carolina if it was sold at original package stores. These establishments not only threatened to undercut the dispensary's prices; they also offered inducements that the state system legally could not, including operation at night and on-premise consumption. To win the price war, the state liquor board introduced a new grade of liquor, the "80 percent brand." Aimed at the state's poorest citizens, this cheap liquor was cut with 20 percent water and was priced to undercut any full-strength liquor. To compete with package stores' promise of onsite consumption, the state board authorized the opening of beer dispensaries, which permitted drinking on the premises.

Even after the state's supreme court victory eliminated the threat of package stores in 1898, both innovations in stock and practice that had been done in the name of competitive expediency remained in place. Although the state officially banned drinking on the premises across all of its dispensaries, the practice continued. One dispenser explained: "We claim that it is not on the premises. I can only rent the front part of my place, and the landlord reserves the back part. . . . It is left vacant and if they want to drink back there it is none of my business."[44]

These adjustments in dispensary practice brought forth further negative commentary, this time from reformers worried about the social disorder that seemed to surround the state's liquor shops. As a Columbia preacher commented in a 1902 sermon: "Those gamblers there that night in that den on Main Street almost surely they were drinking men, as certainly as they were profane men; beyond doubt one of them had murder in his heart and a weapon in his hand, while the bullet was in another's heart. These things naturally go together and you know it, and yet no effort is made to shut up such a place."[45] Rural counties, too, struggled with the social disorder associated with the dispensaries. In 1903, fed up with conditions near their only county liquor shop, Saluda citizens petitioned for its removal, painting a graphic picture of the damage it had wrought: "A man from the country would go into a bar-room and buy drinks, but when he buys a bottle, he does most of his drinking on the way home and commits acts of lawlessness beyond the reach of police protection. . . . On every public day the town is taken possession of by drunken men, and the danger to officers is so great that they can get no one to perform the duties."[46]

Such bad behavior was generally associated with one of two groups: African Americans and poor whites, especially those increasing employed in South Carolina's textile mills. In the Black Belt and Lowcountry counties, it was taken as an article of faith that "but for the extensive patronage of the negroes the dispensary would not fare well financially," and Lowcountry planters complained that African Americans "went to town on Saturday evenings" and drank so much that "I'll be d— if I can get my darkies sober before Wednesday."[47] Beyond labor concerns whites were generally concerned with policing the state's color line, dramatically reinstituted in the 1895 constitution, which deprived African Americans of their civil rights. This "need to keep the negro under" acquired particular force as fears grew of a black crime wave that was supposed to include theft, arson, murder, and rape, "those horrible crimes that almost every day are committed somewhere by the villainous black tramps who are to be found in every community."[48]

In the Upcountry commentators were more likely to associate the dispensary with working-class customers, many of whom were accused of participating in lynchings of the very same African Americans who had run afoul of the law. Fearful of a burgeoning race war between the most backward of both races, "enlightened" progressive South Carolinians sought out liquor control as a way to end attacks by whites on both blacks and each other. One citizen, who called himself "Studious Juris," suggested that "the governor be authorized by the legislature to use the dispensary fund in the counties where lynchings occur in apprehending and punishing the lynchers." He further asserted that this was "a good idea and retributive justice, the lynching class being the largest patrons of the State's saloons."[49]

A more prominent example of this thinking comes from a speech by Joseph A. McCollough, a Greenville lawyer and Methodist layman, in a 1904 address he gave to the Greenville Club of Thirty-Nine, a group of businessmen, doctors, college professors, and lawyers who met to discuss matters of public concern. In his address, entitled "Lawlessness in South Carolina: Its Causes and Remedies," McCullough attributed the rise in lawlessness to the "temper of our people and a too liberal indulgence in intoxicating drinks," but he was quick to confine this cause only to whites, who, he claimed, "are naturally high-spirited, quick tempered and of a restless and nervous temperament." Among this group there had been "31,516 quarrels [leading to homicide] . . . at least 75 percent of them are super-induced by intoxicating drinks." Based on these numbers, McCullough offered a prescription: "I believe . . . that the State should go out of the liquor business; should prohibit its sale as a beverage by others and do all in its power to discourage the traffic." This would "considerably lessen the consumption of alcoholic liquors, and this would result in fewer quarrels and less frequent homicides."[50]

THE DISTRIBUTION OF SOCIAL HARM

The fears that prohibitionists stoked of black aggression and social disorder and working-class whites' propensity toward violence were likely taken as truth by the majority of South Carolinians. Whether these potential threats were seen as actual social problems depended on the town one lived in. Communities across the state varied considerably in three characteristics, each of which might shape the local view of the dispensary: the amount of alcohol consumed by the less fortunate; the actual degree of violence; and the possibility of future acts of aggression. How locals calculated these risks influenced their view of the dispensary.

With regards to liquor sales, it is of course impossible to know with any great accuracy the social status of dispensary customers. Had the original law requiring each person to sign individual request forms been followed, this information would have been available, but without such signatures, our best guess lies in the type of liquor bought and particularly its cost. The 80 percent brand piloted by the state to undercut competitors during the original package store period offers the best chance at calculating such an estimate. Because the 80 percent brand was by far the least expensive alcohol that could be purchased, and because it was likely not all that flavorful given its mixture of 80 percent liquor with 20 percent water, we can perhaps assume that only those who could afford no other liquor would have continuously purchased this product. If that is the case, 80 percent brand sales give a window into the

Table 3.1. Average percentage of 80 percent liquor sales, by county, 1905

County and average percentage of 80 percent sales to total sales	
Edgefield 15	Chesterfield 2
Georgetown 12	Colleton 2
Horry 11	Greenville 2
Saluda 10	Hampton 2
Union 10	Laurens 2
Darlington 8	Beaufort 1
Cherokee 7	Clarendon 1
Marion 7	Oconee 1
Lexington 6	Orangeburg 1
Spartanburg 6	Abbeville 0
Williamsburg 4	Barnwell 0
Anderson 3	Fairfield 0
Berkeley 3	Florence 0
Chester 3	Kershaw 0
Dorchester 3	Lancaster 0
York 3	Newberry 0
Aiken 2	Pickens 0
Bamberg 2	Sumter 0

Source: Reports of the county dispensers, 1905.

Note: County dispensers' reports were submitted quarterly to the state. The yearly average is taken by adding the percentage of 80 percent sales in each quarter and dividing that total by four.

poorest class of dispensary customers, the very same people whose overconsumption of alcohol most worried South Carolinians.

The 80 percent brand started out as a consistent seller for the dispensary, accounting for nearly 11 percent of all liquor sold in 1900. As the popularity of brand liquors from outside of South Carolina increased, the 80 percent brand, like all of the state stock, saw a steep decline in its sales. By 1905, 80 percent liquor accounted for only 3.6 percent of the state's liquor sales, yet this percentage varied considerably by county (table 3.1).[51]

With regards to the actual amount of violent crime, the South Carolina Attorney General Reports provide the best resource. Table 3.2 shows the distribution of murder by county from 1900 to 1905. If commentators of the time

Table 3.2. Murder rate in South Carolina counties, 1905

County and murder rate per 100,000 population	
Greenville 43.7	Aiken 20.5
Laurens 37.9	Newberry 20.4
Oconee 35.2	*Bamberg 20.2*
Cherokee 35.1	**Spartanburg 18.8**
Barnwell 33.8	Dorchester 18.4
Chesterfield 33.4	Georgetown 18.5
Lancaster 28.1	Williamsburg 17.3
Pickens 27.5	*Edgefield 17.0*
Darlington 26.2	*Berkeley 15.8*
Union 26.1	*Lee 14.8*
Fairfield 26.0	Lexington 14.6
Orangeburg 25.7	**Richland 14.2**
Charleston 25.5	**Anderson 14.0**
Hampton 23.8	Florence 14.0
Saluda 22.8	Kershaw 13.4
York 22.3	*Clarendon 12.4*
Chester 20.9	Abbeville 11.9
Marion 20.7	Horry 11.4
Colleton 20.6	*Sumter 9.7*
	Beaufort 9.4

Source: South Carolina Attorney General, *Annual Report*, 291–320.

Note: Counties in boldface type had heaviest concentration of mill villages; counties in italics had heaviest concentrations of African Americans.

were accurate, the counties with the heaviest concentrations of mill villages would be those with the most murders. The data support the contention in some counties, though not all, and thus go some way toward explaining mill county Progressives' persistent attacks on the dispensary.

Beyond a specific counting of homicides (the details of which citizens might have had only vague familiarity with) there was a growing sense that something had changed both in the patterns of violence and in their location. Stephen A. West discusses this shift at some length, pointing out that by the early part of the twentieth century, the pistol had become the weapon of choice in the majority of killings. "Knowing that their opponents might be carrying a weapon," West argues, "many men dispensed with the rituals that had once channeled violence, and fights often turned into a race to see who could draw his weapon first. Once such behavior and expectations became commonplace, they permanently altered practices of violence."[52]

This upsurge in violent confrontations occurred at the same time that the textile mill industry was expanding in the South Carolina Upcountry, drawing into the villages thousands of white southerners, many of whom brought their pistols as well as new norms surrounding their use. While patterns of violent behavior resembled those in the countryside, West argues that the mill village multiplied the occasions for violence. "The villages crowded together thousands of strangers and brought them into a kind of daily interaction unknown on the farm, providing countless possibilities for disputes and misunderstandings."[53] When alcohol was added to this mix, the potential for violent encounters grew even more acute. Townspeople increasingly looked with trepidation at the large concentrations of men from nearby mill villages who descended on the local dispensary carrying their pistols, their unresolved disputes, and their weekly paychecks with which to buy liquor. The result was, on Saturday nights in particular, scenes of "drunkenness and rowdyism" across the Piedmont towns and mill villages.[54]

As was the case with the murder rates, communities were not all equally at risk of experiencing such episodes. Alcohol was available (if only illegally) outside of the dispensary, and as dispensary law forbade the establishment of rural liquor shops, mill villagers located some distance from county seats could seek out moonshiners to supply them with liquor. For mill villagers living in or around the Piedmont's larger towns, the dispensary provided the most direct source of liquor, and thus it was in those towns that residents might have most likely feared violent confrontations. Table 3.3 gives a sense of which counties might have felt themselves most at risk, as it shows the percentage of mill villagers in dispensary towns.

In contrast to Upcountry counties struggling with the influx of white millworkers, the South Carolina Midlands and Lowcountry were predominantly African American. For white citizens inclined to believe the worst, liquor was linked primarily with two crimes, rape and murder. With regards to the first, rape charges were exceedingly rare in South Carolina during the first five years of the twentieth century, at least as counted by the attorney general. Annual reports for the years 1900–1905 show only seventy-one total rape charges, an average of roughly twelve per year for the entire state com-

Table 3.3. Percentage of millworkers in dispensary towns, 1907

County and millworkers in dispensary towns (%)	
Union 81	Abbeville 16
Greenville 72	Edgefield 16
Chester 69	Clarendon 13
Lancaster 67	Orangeburg 11
Pickens 66	Barnwell 2
Spartanburg 65	Charleston 1
Anderson 63	Sumter 1
Oconee 53	Aiken 0
Cherokee 47	Beaufort 0
Darlington 47	Berkeley 0
Laurens 41	Chesterfield 0
Lexington 37	Dorchester 0
Newberry 36	Fairfield 0
York 30	Florence 0
Richland 28	Georgetown 0
Marion 24	Hampton 0
Kershaw 23	Horry 0
Bamberg 21	Lee 0
Colleton 17	Saluda 0
	Williamsburg 0

Sources: Kohn, *Cotton Mills of South Carolina;* South Carolina General Assembly, State Dispensary Auditor, *Annual Report,* 1905; South Carolina General Assembly, State Comptroller General, *Annual Report,* 1905.

bined. The counties with the most charges, Aiken and Clarendon, each totaled only six rape charges, an average of one per year. With regards to the murder rate, table 3.2 shows that the counties with the largest African American populations (over 60 percent) were not well represented among the state's most violent.

As was the case with town residents in the Piedmont, Black Belt and Lowcountry planters might nevertheless have felt themselves at risk from black crime and linked this risk to their local dispensaries if they reasoned the state liquor shops served as meeting places for black men bent on doing harm. The specter of a large number of African American men gathering at a Lowcountry dispensary was quite a bit more remote than that of white millworkers congregating at a Piedmont liquor shop, as black South Carolinians were spread out among several sparsely populated towns across largely rural counties, while the millworkers tended to gather near towns, close to where the mills were located. All this is not to say that fear of black crime was not at all in evidence but, rather, that its impact across South Carolina's Black Belt would have been felt with less urgency.

Not surprisingly, the counties that experienced the most social disorder were also the sites with the most highly organized protests against the liquor system. Both C. C. Featherstone and James Hoyt, who had run for governor, hailed from the Upcountry, as did the few anti-dispensary legislators. The different dispensary experience of South Carolina's counties would, in 1905, lead dry advocates to pursue a strategy of local option, whereby they sought to win the right to eliminate their local liquor outlets while leaving untouched liquor shops in counties that relied heavily on profits from the sale of alcohol.

4

FROM STATEWIDE DISPENSARY _TO_ LOCAL OPTION

B y the beginning of 1903, the state dispensary system had fought off both legal and extralegal challenges and was seemingly a permanent fixture in the lives of South Carolinians. The lion's share of credit for the system's continuation lay in the unwavering political support given by Ben Tillman and his handpicked successors in the statehouse. Any favorable feelings toward the dispensary among most South Carolinians were likely due to its economic advantages, especially in those counties with poverty-stricken schools and barely functioning roadways. There were still a sizable number of opponents to the dispensary, and this antipathy was especially acute in the Upcountry, where dispensary liquor was said to fuel disorder and lawlessness among mill operatives.

Looking at the situation in early 1903, it would have been hard to fathom that within a year one-third of South Carolina's counties would be scheduling referenda aimed at removing their liquor shops and within four years the state dispensary system would cease to exist. This rapid transition from statewide dispensary to a county option system was due primarily to two factors. The first was pressure from a new organization, the South Carolina Temperance Law and Order League (SCTLOL). Unlike previous anti-dispensary groups, the SCTLOL sought not to replace the state dispensary with prohibition but, rather, to give voters the option of deciding for themselves the best liquor policy in their counties. This more moderate reform placed the SCTLOL squarely within the mainstream of the state's political culture, which preferred local control over state intervention. The second factor contributing to the dispensary's downfall were revelations of widespread graft and corruption throughout the system. As these abuses became public, South Carolinians moved to dismantle the state dispensary.

Even with anti-dispensary feeling on the rise in South Carolina, there was still little appetite for statewide prohibition. The continued existence of blind tigers in rural areas across the state convinced many voters that prohibition could not stop the sale of liquor or at least would do no better than the dispensary had. With a choice between two flawed systems of liquor control, voters in counties reaping large profits kept their liquor shops, while counties that had recently adopted prohibition breathed easier in the knowledge that town life was safer.

THE TEMPERANCE LAW AND ORDER LEAGUE

The entirety of the dispensary system's existence was marked by sporadic attempts to organize and dislodge it, each appearing for a short time and receding when it became clear the battle was lost. Late 1903 saw the emergence of another attempt, one that would ultimately succeed in part of because its goals were far narrower in scope than those of previous anti-dispensary campaigns.

The source of the latest protest was Saluda County, one of the several across the state where the dispensary had made little headway or profit because of the largely rural population. Having adopted the dispensary some six years earlier but now realizing that it was causing more trouble than it was worth, Saluda townspeople petitioned their local liquor board for their dispensary to be closed: "Before the establishment of the dispensary here there was no legalized place for the sale of whisky in this whole county—not even within the present bounds of the county—and while we do not mean to say there was no whisky drinking on the part of our people, yet we do say that since the establishment of the dispensary here the drinking has wonderfully and dangerously increased among our people.... After seeing the demoralizing effect that the sale of liquors in our town is having upon the town and the surrounding country, we prefer to assume the burden of town taxation for current expenses and also meet the indebtedness, than to see ruin which is coming to our town and county."[1] The county dispensary board refused to comply with the petitioners' wishes, as there was no provision in the state dispensary law for the removal of a dispensary once it had been created.

Saluda citizens responded by planning to petition the state legislature to change the dispensary law and in so doing sparked public meetings across the state. Sensing an opportunity, James A. Hoyt, the 1900 prohibitionist candidate for governor, brought together these disparate groups, forming the South Carolina Temperance, Law and Order League. At its inaugural meeting in October 1903, Hoyt asked his new membership "to initiate some practical measures of non-partisan and non-political lines to improve the present condition of affairs in our state, and to concentrate into some kind of organization all the elements that are willing to work for the destruction of those forces that tend to perpetuate and enlarge the sphere of intemperance and the reign of crime in South Carolina."[2]

The newly appointed executive committee responded to this call with an address to the people of the state, in which they not only took on intemperance directly but also cited the negative social consequences they saw flowing from it. "It is sufficient to call attention to the fact that 180 homicides are reported in the daily papers as committed in this state . . . to show that a terrible lawlessness exists and to justify the most earnest and strenuous efforts on the part of law-respecting citizens to correct it. . . . The laws of God and man are violated with impunity as witnessed by . . . scenes of drunkenness, disorder and bloodshed, the violations of criminal law, and the shameful violation of the dispensary law in all its restrictive and prohibitive provisions." Laying much of the blame for this urgent state of affairs at the foot of the dispensary, the executive committee concluded by requesting "the legislature to enact such legislation as may be necessary to give the voters of a municipality the right to vote a dispensary out of their community."[3]

Empowered by this new organization, anti-dispensary forces introduced the Brice bill in February 1904. In bringing the bill to the floor, Senator John S. Brice admitted that he had initially supported the dispensary as the surest method of combating the liquor trade but that his observations of its operation had now convinced him otherwise. He derided the dispensary system as "the worst idea ever conceived by man," condemned the widespread corruption it brought, and reminded his colleagues that since the dispensary was instituted, its profits had been used to complete state projects rather than lower taxes.[4]

Further support came from citizens' petitions, some asserting that "whatever the dispensary has done for other communities, we know it has proven a curse and not a blessing to our community,"[5] and others asking, "Who is the best authority for knowing what would be best for the city? Those who live there or those who are there now and then?"[6] Moved by these requests, the legislature overwhelmingly passed the Brice bill, allowing any county to hold an election at which time they might vote out their dispensaries. As they did so, the legislature protected state finances by requiring prohibition counties to forfeit their share of dispensary profits and levy a special tax of a half-mill to aid the state in prohibition enforcement.

In making it possible to close existing dispensaries, the state legislature effectively made South Carolina a local option state and at the same time "put the [legislative] body in accord with the sentiments upheld by the State Temperance Law and Order League . . . the State Baptist Convention and South Carolina conference of the Methodist Church. It is the opinion of . . . many straight out prohibitionists, that the most satisfactory regulation of the liquor question in this state can be secured by local option."[7] The legislature's decision also fell in line with much existing sentiment across the state that insisted that important county affairs be settled at the county level.

THE DISPENSARY CORRUPTION SCANDAL

In granting the local option on the dispensary question, the legislature was not only responding to prevailing opinion on county prerogatives. Such localism had been present since the birth of the dispensary a decade earlier and had been rebuffed, at least as far as the liquor question, the entire time. Counties pleas for self-determination in 1903 greatly benefited from the increasing awareness that those who ran the dispensary were men who deliberately and fully violated the mandates of the law they had sworn to uphold.

South Carolinians had by this time grown accustomed to a dispensary system that looked only vaguely like the one initially enshrined into law by Tillman in 1892. Most citizens understood the state was in the liquor business, and as with all businesses, certain allowances needed to be made to secure a profit. Thus, if a county dispensary did not take the names of its customers, advertised its wares in the local newspaper, or permitted some drinking around the back of its establishment, most citizens were prepared to look the other way if it meant better roads, longer school years, and, most important, less taxes. Of course, there were some prohibitionists who pointed to the folly of all this, and in counties where the profits were too small or the public nuisance too great people might squawk, but on the whole South Carolinians had accepted the dispensary for the business it was—that is, until it became clear that it was also the site of an enormous government scandal.

As often happens with political scandals, the uncovering of dispensary corruption began with rumors of handsome presents to state administrators, samples of fine liquors sent to county dispensers, and rebates from liquor companies accepted by public officials. All of these were common practices of the liquor industry in other places; in fact, they were the very reasons offered by Tillman for the establishment of the dispensary system, which proponents claimed could, and would, avoid such snares.

Rumors gave way to hardened inquiry on January 31, 1905, when a resolution was passed by the assembly providing for the appointment of three senators and four members of the House "to investigate the affairs of the State Dispensary." Giving the committee complete subpoena power over officials and dispensary documents, the legislature charged its members with investigating the financial aspects of the system, looking especially for incidences of graft by the state board of control, the dispensary commissioner, and the county boards and dispensers.

These positions were targeted because each was an overtly political appointment, each paid its occupant precious little salary, and each had almost daily contact with liquor dealers and middlemen anxious to sell their wares. The three-man board of directors was elected by the legislature at a salary of four hundred dollars per year (equal to ten thousand dollars today) and tasked with purchasing all dispensary liquors and supplies. The dispensary commissioner was also elected by the legislature and was paid a salary of three thousand dollars a year (seventy-five thousand dollars today). From his location at the dispensary warehouse in Columbia, he received the liquor bought by the board, rebottled it when necessary, and reshipped it to local dispensers. County board members were appointed by the state board on the recommendation of the legislative delegations of the respective county. Paid only with a per diem of two dollars a day for a maximum of thirty days, they were responsible for locating the dispensaries as well as selecting and prosecuting county dispensers. The dispensers selected by the board members conducted all the business at the site of sale, making them potential targets of liquor dealers eager to avoid the state board.

The committee—composed of Senators Coleman Blease, Niels Christensen, and J. T. Hay as well as Representatives T. B. Fraser, A. L. Gaston, J. Fraser

Lyon, and D. A. Spivey—began its investigation in August 1905 and continued through January 1907. Some of the delay was due to the nature of the work. Historian Ellen Alexander Hendricks writes: "The intention of the legislature had leaked out and the majority of the dispensers were prepared. Persons who were called as witnesses in a number of cases were advised as to what course to take and were obstinate about bringing out facts that would prove violators guilty. . . . Those who attempted to bring out the truth about the grafters were threatened with violence."[8] The primary reason for the lengthy investigation was the volume of both the original findings (which came to over two thousand pages) and their substance; the misconduct associated with the state dispensary system, according to John Evans Eubanks, represented "one of the most amazing and revolting scandals that has ever blackened the history of any state."[9]

Graft was found throughout the system, starting with the board of directors. The committee spoke with one former board member who had refused reelection because, he said, "the general impression was that it was not an honest place, and I did not want people to suspect me" and heard another relate a story of a successful board candidate who reportedly told legislators: "You prohibitionists say you want someone who will discredit the dispensary by continuing the stealing. Then elect me for I'll promise to steal everything in sight."[10] Such revelations led Senator Christensen to lament, "No man who values his reputation will become a candidate for a position in which men get rich on $400 a year."[11]

The key to getting rich for board members lay in their control of liquor purchases for the entire system, a position that made them the target of solicitation by liquor dealers across the country. The back room negotiations, one informer testified, took place in a hotel room. "It was a private room, hired by the liquor drummers—Room 12 at the Columbia Hotel. The state board of control was in session. I saw money change hands between members of the state board and liquor drummers. I have seen members of the state legislature come up into these rooms and participate in the liquor and cigars. As soon as the legislature would adjourn, about mid-day, they would always go up to the hotel. That was headquarters, and always had plenty of champagne and liquor and cigars."[12] Predictably, instances of graft followed: "Much 'Old Joe' whiskey was bought from an Atlanta concern in carload lots for $36.00 a drum, whereas the same goods were sold in single drum lots to Atlanta saloons for $28.00.

This firm made a 'Christmas present' to a member of the Board of a carload of very handsome furniture worth about $1,500 [$37,500]. Labels which could be bought for $8,000 were purchased for $35,000. An Augusta brewery, after a long failure to secure orders, put its business in the hands of a friend of one of the dispensary board of directors. At the direction of their representative the brewery raised the price $125 per car, which amount was paid to the agent to be divided, as understood, with the director. The price to the state was subsequently reduced and the commission cut off, whereupon the business stopped."[13]

The commissioner's share of the plunder was founded on his power to push favorite brands. With so much extra liquor bought (and profits pocketed by) the state board, the commissioner ran a warehouse in which, increasingly, virtually anything could be had for a price. A letter written to a liquor house in Louisville, Kentucky, sums up the situation: "Dear Sirs, Do you want to sell goods to the S.C. Dispensary? . . . My uncle, Commissioner—, has a salary of $3,000, quite insufficient for his needs. My father is a dispenser at $1,200 annually, selling $52,000 to $60,000 a year; he could use at least $20,000 to $25,000 a year in 'Ripple Creek' for a small substantial inducement. . . . My uncle, the commissioner, will not accept a check, but as his agent, I can do some business for him and for you, as nearly, in fact, all whiskey concerns, as you know, are paying for their trade with a small rebate."[14]

County boards, too, got considerable kickbacks. "In Spartanburg County, beer dispensers and their breweries paid members $450 for an appointment as dispenser for a one-year term." After his appointment one dispenser reportedly asked the county board chairman for instructions on how to run his dispensary. He was told, "Don't mind instructions; make every dollar you can; you will need it for your next election." In Greenville County a beer dispenser wrote to a brewer asking for help paying the latest installment for his appointment: "Gentlemen: The second call is made on me by the grafters for $200, so I will have to call on you again for $100. This settles up everything for that three."[15]

In addition to paying off county board members, local dispensers were also beholden to the state board and as such became handpicked political operatives. In one such instance a state board member wrote (on official letterhead) to a dispenser: "Dear sir: I feel a deep interest in the success of my friend ——, in his race for Governor, and take the liberty to write you in his behalf. If you have no particular choice in the matter I assure you I will appreciate anything you can do for him. If you can support him, please endeavor to get his friends to the polls at the various boxes in your county."[16]

Local dispensers were well recompensed for their efforts. County and state board members were especially lenient with those who supported them, as Niels Christensen reports. "One dispenser wrote to ask whether he could receive rebates in the shape of empty cases returned, and permission was cheerfully given. A liquor dealer asked whether Christmas presents to dispensers would be objectionable and the reply was 'Dear Jim . . . will say that I can see nothing unlawful or improper in sending Christmas gifts to your friends.'"[17] Freed from any restraints, liquor dealers favored dispensers with all manner of gifts, as seen, for example, in this letter from a Louisville whiskey dealer: "Dear Sir: It is a well-known fact that only sober gentlemen are in charge of the dispensaries, yet we doubt not that every last one of them will partake of an occasional thimbleful 'for the stomach's sake.' Desiring to contribute something toward good cheer for the holidays . . . please accept them with the compliments of the season, and in the hope that whenever you partake of these liquors you will give us a kindly thought. . . . Thanking you for preference shown all our brands."[18]

The graft of local dispensers having been provided for, requests flowed to dealers across the country, such as one to a New York whiskey house: "Dear Sirs: . . . The advertisements are posted, but this will accomplish nothing unless you can get the county dispensers to handle the goods . . . if you want the goods sold communicate with the county dispenser of each county and let him know what he may expect, if anything, for special courtesies. It is an old proverb as true as holy writ: 'Whose bread I eat, whose song I sing.' The county dispensers order what they want and sell what they get. A hint to the wise is sufficient, and this is given confidentially. . . . We can handle the goods all right if the proper quid pro quo is forthcoming."[19]

In many respects the operations of the dispensary revealed by the committee were no different than business as usual in the liquor industry. Cozy relations with board members and dispensers were certainly akin to those that dealers formed with saloonkeepers, and even at its worst the dispensary system kept dealers at a distance farther removed than might have otherwise been the case. Taken in the context of promises repeatedly made by dispensary advocates of a system devoid of corruption, they generated deep shock and disappointment among the people of South Carolina. Perhaps equally problematic was the amount that graft had cost the state. An audit undertaken by the American Audit Company in early 1907 revealed "invoices aggregating over $200,000 [$5 million] omitted from the books with intent" for the year 1905 alone.[20] As the magnitude of the huge losses of money and public trust became public, South Carolinians faced important decisions about the future of their liquor policy, first at the local level and then statewide.

THE 1905 LOCAL OPTION CAMPAIGN

As they undertook a reevaluation of local and statewide liquor policy, South Carolina citizens faced two grim realities. The first was that the dispensary did not work. In addition to the abundant graft throughout the state system that perpetuated "corrupting influences tainting the very fountain of good government,"[21] local reporters observed that even when the management of dispensaries was exemplary, the system had failed to curb illegal sales. Surveying the situation across the state, the *Charleston News and Observer* reported, "A number of correspondents speak of illicit sales in the rural districts, and while the information as to them is not definite, it is sufficient to indicate ... that the dispensary sales ... lead to retailing by the drink by negroes when the packages have been carried out of town."

The existence of these "blind tigers" was reported across the state. In the Lowcountry a Georgetown County observer noted, "No doubt there are a few negroes who sell whiskey and beer ... but it is carried on in such a quiet way ... that it is often hard for the police to get any inkling of it." Farther west, in Orangeburg County, a reporter remarked about having heard "recent rumors ... of the operations of blind tigers ... operating over the county, as well as outfits in operation for the making of 'tussick' whiskey." Upstate in Union County another observer wrote: "Blind tigers are reported to be at work all over the county. All efforts to trap and punish the offenders have proved to be unavailing." In the far west of the state "a division chief constable resides in Greenville and with him in this city are five constables and a Federal officer. They are constantly catching blind tigers and illicit distilleries are cut up almost every week."[22]

The second grim reality facing Palmetto State residents was that even though the dispensary failed to curb liquor sales and consumption, prohibition seemingly fared no better. "Were absolute prohibition possible," wrote a

Lee County newspaperman, "the county would no doubt be carried in its favor. ... But having had the experience of living in a so-called dry town and knowing that prohibition simply means the flooding of the town and county with wretched liquor [many remained in favor of the liquor shops]."[23] Barnwell County's brief flirtation with dry laws had yielded similar results. "Prohibition did not prohibit; but the drug stores became improvised bars to which the traffic from the saloons was in many instances transferred; blind tigers were all over the county, numerous cases of violation were brought up for trial before the various courts and in very few instances were any convictions had."[24] Comparing the current prohibition counties with their recent experiences under the dispensary proved no better, at least in terms of curbing illegal sales. "It is true that some blind tiger liquor has been sold here since the closing of the dispensary," admitted a Pickens County observer. "It is equally true that blind tigers plied their trade to some extent in the palmiest days of the dispensary."[25]

Caught between the devil and the deep blue sea, voters employed calculations other than likely sales and consumption in determining whether to remove their county liquor stores. Perhaps the most important of these calculations was financial. Such profits were necessary for county governments, which found themselves squeezed between two constituencies with rather different concerns. The first were landowning farmers, a constituency whose primary concern was South Carolina's heavy reliance on the property tax, which placed the fiscal burden of financing county initiatives disproportionately on them. Any talk of new county projects, such as roads or new schools, meant tax increases, which "fell heavily on this group and ... had a multiplying effect because every government entity in South Carolina—state, county and municipality—depended heavily on this tax."[26] While landowning farmers carefully counted their share of the county's income, urban progressives interested in social uplift and civic boosters seeking notoriety sought for their cities and towns "anything deemed progressive and modern: banks, hospitals, schools, parks, skyscrapers, colleges, churches and hotels."[27] City planning and beautification also typically included technological advances (e.g., electric lights, trolleys, and telephones), each of which cost money.

Squeezed between these twin imperatives, dispensary advocates aimed to convince voters to retain dispensaries, as their profits could further progressive goals without having to raise the taxes (and ire) of their rural citizenry.

"If the dispensary were voted out," argued a Beaufort County commissioner, "$12,000 a year would have to be raised or the county will have to cut off all extraordinary improvements such as shelling of roads, building bridges and the like. In addition ordinary expenses for road repair would have to be cut down by at least $6,000."[28]

Undoubtedly, the social institutions that benefited most from dispensary sales were local schools. The dispensary law mandated that one-third of dispensary profits be earmarked for school funds, and in many counties this windfall enabled "the schools [to] operate for six or seven months, rather than the three or four months before the Dispensary was established. Further, "the Dispensary has also brought higher teacher salaries, improved school houses and improved equipment."[29] Although anti-dispensary campaigners urged voters not to "poison the fountain your boys and girls are drinking from" and instead to "go down in your pockets to get money to send them to school,"[30] one local editor wondered if people would be willing to pay taxes to "make up for the loss of town and county income if the Dispensary were voted out": "Could the schools continue to operate for the usual time? And what about decreased receipts and increased expenditures if the county has to enforce prohibition?"[31] That some counties took these arguments seriously is illustrated in table 4.1. Taking the percentage of county revenue contributed by the dispensary in 1905, those with the most to lose elected to keep their liquor shops.[32]

Another consideration for voters was the issue of public safety and the disorder, drunkenness, and crime that were said to plague dispensary towns. Although any drunkenness was understood as problematic, most discussions of public safety centered around two groups, African Americans and millworkers. Of these the millworkers seemed to have caused the greater consternation, if only because of their concentrated numbers in particular towns. By 1900, historian George Tindall notes, "of the total Negro population, only 10.8 percent were residing in towns, and many of these towns were so small ... as to be semi-rural in nature."[33] The 1905 census confirms this calculation, showing only four South Carolina cities that housed more than twenty-five hundred African American citizens.[34] Millworkers, and the villages that housed them, were another matter entirely. By the early 1900s such villages were common across the Piedmont region of South Carolina, and as the mills they labored in were often located nearby towns with dispensaries, so, too, were the millworkers and their families.

Table 4.1. Contribution of dispensary revenue to each county's bottom line, 1904

County and percentage of dispensary income to expenditures

Georgetown 34.5	Darlington 19.8
Orangeburg 32.4	**Charleston 19.7**
Sumter 31.6	Oconee 19.7
Lee 30.1	Cherokee 19.2
Florence 29.0	Anderson 18.4
Bamberg 28.4	Marion 17.8
Chesterfield 28.2	Laurens 16.8
Richland 26.6	Union 16.7
Chester 26.0	Spartanburg 16.4
Kershaw 25.7	**Colleton 16.1**
Clarendon 25.2	**Berkeley 15.8**
Barnwell 24.5	Hampton 13.2
Williamsburg 24.4	**Fairfield 11.7**
Dorchester 21.1	Newberry 11.1
Beaufort 20.9	Edgefield 10.4
Lancaster 20.6	Horry 9.4
Abbeville 20.5	Saluda 8.5
Aiken 20.1	Pickens 5.3
Greenville 20.0	**Lexington 5.1**
	York 3.6

Sources: South Carolina General Assembly, State Dispensary Auditor, *Annual Report,* 9–10; South Carolina General Assembly, State Comptroller General, *Annual Report,* 287–314.

Note: These figures were calculated by dividing each county's dispensary intake by the total the county paid for roads and schools. Counties with the most to lose (shown in bold) elected to keep their liquor shops, a process that will be discussed further in chapter 4.

The social ills associated with the dispensary varied by county. Table 4.2 shows the impact of these combined factors on prohibition adoption across South Carolina's counties in terms of excessive lower-class drinking (as measured by the percentage of 80 percent alcohol sales), the murder rate per 100,000 residents, and the percentage of mill villagers residing in dispensary towns.

Taken together, the twin impacts of financial dependence on dispensary funds and social concerns brought about by the combination of dispensaries and "dangerous drinkers" account for the election decisions taken by most of

Table 4.2. Relationship between social ills, dispensary profits, and prohibition adoption, by county, 1905

3 Social ills	2 Social ills	1 Social ills, little profit	1 Social ills, large profit	No social ills, little profit	No social ills, large profit
Cherokee	Greenville	**Anderson**	Barnwell	Abbeville	Bamberg
Darlington	Lancaster	**Edgefield**	Chester	Aiken	Clarendon
Union	Laurens	Fairfield	Chesterfield	Beaufort	Florence
	Lexington	**Horry**	Georgetown	Berkeley	Kershaw
	Oconee	**Marion**	Orangeburg	Charleston	Lee
	Pickens	Newberry		Colleton	Richland
	Spartanburg	Saluda		Dorchester	Sumter
		York		Hampton	Williamsburg

Source: South Carolina General Assembly, State Dispensary Auditor, *Annual Report*, 9–10; South Carolina Attorney-General, *Annual Report*, 291–320; Kohn, *Cotton Mills in South Carolina.*

Note: Greenwood and Marlboro Counties were already under prohibition. The number of social ills refers to how many of the conditions (amount of 80 percent liquor sold, number of homicides, percent of mill villagers in dispensary towns); see tables 3.1–3 for specific data on each county. Bold type represents those counties that adopted prohibition in 1905.

South Carolina's then thirty-nine counties. The thirteen counties with dispensary profits close to or above 25 percent of their county budgets all opted to retain their liquor shops. Conversely, six of the seven poorest dispensary counties opted to eliminate their stores, with voters reasoning that there was no need to continue a corrupt and unprofitable system. Fifteen of the counties suffering from some combination of poor drinkers, millworkers, and a crime wave voted out their dispensaries; six of them also featured very small liquor profits.

Of the remaining eleven counties eight had little in the way of dispensary profits or social ills that might move voters firmly into the dispensary or prohibition camp.[35] All eleven of these counties retained their dispensaries—a result due more to indifference about calling an election than it was strong support for liquor stores. "The dispensary question . . . is in a state of quiescence in Clarendon County," wrote a columnist there, while a Berkeley County newspaperman threw up his hands in frustration when asked to describe the dispensary issue: "As there is no agitation on the question in this section, your correspondent does not know what to write as to the dispensary. There are some people opposed to the dispensary and there are some in favor of it, but who are in the majority no one can say as the matter is very little discussed." In Aiken County a local reporter described the issue there as "non-agitating . . . the people generally not wishing the excitement of an election as to dispensary or no dispensary." The cause of this ennui, it was explained, lay in the fact that "a large part of the county being connected with the city of Augusta . . . which affords an open bar-room where liquors can be bought cheaper than at the dispensaries and to these people it matters not whether there be prohibition or the dispensary."[36]

Settling the dispensary status at the county level did not mean the end of South Carolinians' wrestling with the liquor question. The Brice Act, which enabled county option in the first place, had not yet been put to the voters, and as such it was still possible South Carolinians might yet judge that the best solution lay with the state, either through resumption of the statewide dispensary system or the enactment of statewide prohibition. All citizens, then, looked toward the 1906 campaign, as the voters' choice of the next governor and composition of the legislature, it was thought, would go a long way to determining the path next taken.

THE 1906 CAMPAIGN

The success of the 1905 county referenda convinced local option advocates that bigger gains were possible in the 1906 election cycle. If a local option governor and legislature was sent to Columbia, they reasoned, it might be possible to do away with the state dispensary entirely and leave each county to determine its own dispensary policy. As the gubernatorial contest took place amid continuing revelations of wrongdoing by state dispensary officials and a growing sense that "gross corruption fosters everywhere; it is too palpable and too imprudent," the hopes of any anti-dispensary plan seemed buoyed. After all, to "prattle of cleansing and rehabilitating this thing, born as a make-shift and a subterfuge, nourished for partisan advantage, and through all its years reeking with ever increasing offense, is to trifle with facts, deny the obvious, and to fight on the side of public crime."[37]

Of course, local option was not the only option for responding to the continuing dispensary revelations, and such questions consumed both the public's attention and that of the eight candidates for governor, each of whom developed "a platform . . . hatched up out of the murky, fuming stinking odors arising from the seething cauldron of corruption on the banks of the Conga-ree, known as the State dispensary." In contrast to campaigns fought over the previous decade, in which there were often two candidates, "one each chosen by two factions of the Democratic party . . . Tillmanites and anti-Tillmanites . . . of the eight candidates for Governor, only one, Mr. Blease, was distinctively aligned with the Tillman forces . . . [and] neither he nor anyone else during the campaign has thought it worthwhile to refer to his record in this respect."[38]

Tillman's waning influence, coupled with widespread dispensary malfea-sance, would seem to have offered a golden opportunity for prohibitionists to make their case anew to the people. Dry leaders, most affiliated with the Tem-perance, Law and Order League and the Baptist or Methodist churches, were largely content with the recent gains made in creating a local option. Although some argued for nominating a slate of prohibition candidates for statewide of-fice, the consensus reached at a statewide meeting in mid-June 1905 elected "not to put into the field a ticket for political offices . . . taking the position that the fight should be for the cause of prohibition and that to connect it with any man would weaken its chances for success."[39]

Not all prohibitionists agreed with this strategy. Among the most vocif-erous advocates for a statewide prohibition candidacy was Joel Brunson. "Throughout the fall and winter [of 1905]," Brunson informed his colleagues, "I have done the best I could to aid in giving the prohibitionists . . . an oppor-tunity to name their own candidates." By May 1906, with the gubernatorial campaign well under way, Brunson wrote informing dry leaders of his plan to campaign alone if need be: "It is now too late to get an organized conven-tion of the prohibitionists . . . we have now reached the point where someone must take up the work and press it vigorously. . . . When the campaign opens I shall be there upon a clean prohibition platform as a candidate for Governor of the State."[40]

Joining Brunson on the campaign trail were seven other contenders, a field that quickly became whittled down to three viable men, in addition to the drys' standard-bearer. The most prominent was Richard Manning, a state senator from Sumter who had in the most recent session cosponsored a bill to signifi-cantly reform the state dispensary by providing fewer opportunities for graft and greater state oversight. Also prominent in the fight was Coleman Blease, a former Tillman lieutenant who was for the continuation of the state dispen-sary with as few alterations as possible. Rounding out the major contenders was Martin Ansel, a Greenville lawyer and former state representative who was known as favoring local option.

With the four major candidates each offering different ways forward on the liquor question, South Carolinians spent the summer of 1906 weighing the views of each. Speaking for the prohibition platform, Brunson repeatedly reminded listeners of the "ruin and damnation upon the home of the poor drunkard," often regaling them with a tale of "a fellow who in need of a quart-o-licker cut another fellow across the face with his knife. . . . Now the fellow had a wife and six little children . . . and they took him to jail . . . [where] they tried him, convicted him and sentenced him to death." After this tale Brunson often concluded by "begging the men on election day to take their little boys on their knees just before going to the polls, and, when they vote, vote for those little boys," whom he claimed he alone represented.[41]

Anxious to support their champion, other prohibitionists attacked the dispensary system more directly, arguing that the source of the problems within the system was the inevitable result of a morally wrongheaded decision. "To say that the system has been tried and found wanting is to confess that we did not know it to be a bad thing from its very inception," the *Baptist Courier* wrote. "The wonder is that anybody ever advocated it as a contributor to public morals. . . . To expect moral success from moral blunder is to defy common sense, good conscience and divine law." Given the inevitable failure of the dispensary and the mountain of evidence showing it to be "morally bankrupt and unable to fulfill its promises," the *Courier* concluded, "the only course of action left was clear—it ought to be dissolved."[42]

For those voters not swayed by such moral reasoning, there was the experience of the fifteen newly prohibition counties to serve as a potential harbinger of how such a program might work if adopted statewide. Here the results were decidedly mixed. In the mill counties the conditions were said to be improved, with the Oconee County police chief reporting that "law and order and sobriety have increased 80%" and Spartanburg mayor John Floyd stating that there was "no comparison between the number of drunks and disorderlies which come before him now and the number that came up during the dispensary regime. . . . The general condition of the town in regard to law, order and sobriety is much better than when the dispensary was in Spartanburg."[43]

The rosy picture in the towns, of course, did not mean complete prohibition had been achieved in the rural areas. "There has been some whiskey sold," allowed Anderson chief of police L. M. Murphy, "but this has been in small quantities and from jugs shipped here to individuals." In Greenville federal revenuers continued their work, although they noted "less illicit distilling in the Dark Corner section of the county now than during dispensary times." Such violations were to be expected, as "there are parties who will have liquor and do get it, and there are many who got it when the dispensary was here, and who could ill afford to buy and drink it." Despite these exceptions, the consensus in the mill counties was that "county officials are doing all they can to suppress the liquor traffic and are meeting with success."[44]

If the areas just outside mill towns gave potential dry voters reason to pause, conditions in those counties that had discontinued liquor stores largely because of their unprofitability were truly of concern. "I could not say whether there is more or less drinking in the county at large but I do believe there is more illicit whiskey handled," admitted a Saluda County official. "In my opinion, the people of the county prefer the legal sale of whiskey to the illicit sale of it and would rather have the dispensary purged of rottenness and graft than blind tigers."[45] Even more disconcerting was the situation in Horry County. There, Sheriff B. J. Sessions reported, "I can't say that I see any appreciable change in the citizen's observance of law and order . . . since we voted out the dispensary. The jug trade is enormous, liquor is ordered in larger quantities, and they seem to have just as much. I can't say that there are any blind tigers, but I have every reason to believe there are, and that they are more plentiful now than they were before the dispensary. Candidly, I believe, from the expressions I hear throughout the county, that in the light of present conditions, if the vote were ordered again, the people would vote to reopen the dispensary."[46]

The mounting evidence that prohibition could not prohibit set it closer to equal footing with that of the obviously flawed dispensary. For the three gubernatorial candidates that supported the continuation of alcohol sales (Ansel, Blease, and Manning), this provided an opening, as long as they could convince voters that some version of a reformed system was possible. Of the three Blease had the hardest case to make, as it was abundantly clear the dispensary was in need of reform, yet he refused to specify how (or if) he would undertake such a task. Instead, Blease attacked both prohibition and a proposed county dispensary system as unworkable. He was especially hard on the prohibitionists, refusing to tone down his rhetoric when he campaigned in dry counties. At a campaign stop in Lancaster, "a strong prohibition county," according to the *State Leader,* "Blease made a vigorous attack on prohibition which he claimed was a humbug and farce. You got a barroom down here in the express office and you know it. . . . There's more liquor drunk in Lancaster county now than there was before you voted out the dispensary!" Reporters traveling with the campaign suspected Blease indulged in such tactics just to be sure he had the people's attention, at which point he could launch into his main complaint with a county dispensary scheme: "If you can't control three men in Columbia [the state liquor board] how are going to control 120 men scattered all over the state?" Given the unworkability of either alternative to the state system, Blease argued that, warts and all, it remained the only appropriate solution to the state's liquor problem.[47]

Making a similar argument far less stridently, Manning (the other state dispensary advocate) pointed out, "We all know the liquor is an evil, but if there are people enough in South Carolina to drink up three or four million dollars worth of it annually besides that which they get from the jug trade and from blind tigers, is it reasonable to suppose that people will give up their taste?" With liquor consumption on such a grand scale a seeming inevitability, Manning argued, those who would do away with the state system "should offer something practical in its stead." Hearing none from any of the system's detractors, Manning argued that any "calm dispassionate consideration of the liquor problem . . . [would make it obvious that] the dispensary is the very best solution of the liquor problem *for every county.*"[48]

Standing alone in favor of dismantling the state dispensary and installing a county system was Martin Ansel. In addition to appealing to the desire for "each county to have the privilege of deciding by popular election whether they shall have a county dispensary or prohibition," Ansel argued that "if the people are capable of managing their own affairs in respect to other matters, they ought to be able to do it with respect to this."[49] In this argument Ansel was supported by J. Fraser Lyon, candidate for attorney general and a man whose position as lead investigator of the state dispensary gave great credibility to Ansel's opinions. "County dispensaries could be managed better than a state dispensary because they would be right under the eyes of the people, and graft could be prevented," remarked Lyon, who then added this extra incentive for those considering county liquor stores: "Each county, then, would get all the money accruing from its dispensary and there would be no necessity of division [with the state]."[50]

This possibility of doubling their liquor profits was seized upon by other commentators, though few made it as forcefully and openly as the editor of the *Aiken Journal and Review:*

As to the revenue feature, the results which have been obtained in Georgia and North Carolina afford an index to what could be accomplished here. There are several counties in these two states in which the county dispensaries pay all expenses, no taxes being levied at all. That Aiken county could derive from the county dispensary a great deal more than it now receives from the State dispensary is believed by all who consider the question. The investigating committee has shown that the liquor dealers in Augusta purchase liquors cheaper than the state dispensary and Aiken county should be able to do as well as the dealers in Augusta. . . . On all sales in this county 10 percent goes toward paying the expenses of the dispensary in Columbia which would be saved by the county dispensary. The amount Aiken County received last year was but a mere bagatelle. . . . Clearly from a business standpoint the county dispensary is better than the state dispensary.[51]

As for the current prohibition counties that would lose school funding should the statewide system be abandoned, one "reader" of the *State* had a simple solution: "Do you want good schools? Well pay for them. You have the right to insist upon other counties selling sufficient whiskey to pay for your good schools, or for a part of them. Do you think that you are under some obligation to weak counties of the State to assist them in the matter of education? Well, reach down in your pocket and make the contribution. You have no right to say you will help the weak counties and then insist upon other counties selling sufficient whiskey to make up your contribution."[52]

The 1906 South Carolina Democratic primary proceeded in two phases. In the first Ansel, who favored local option, was the winner, with Manning, who had advocated the reinstatement of the dispensary system across all counties, garnering enough votes to force a runoff. Brunson, the prohibition candidate, finished a distant fourth, with slightly more than 10 percent of the total vote. In the runoff election Ansel maintained his lead over Manning, and his victory ensured that whatever form the dispensary might take in the future, it would not be forced upon those counties that did not want it. A closer analysis of the voting results makes clear this was the deciding factor in the campaign—

Ansel enjoyed an advantage of only 700 votes in the state's non-mill counties, whereas in the mill counties he outpolled Manning by over 9,729 votes.

THE DEMISE OF THE STATE DISPENSARY

When the state legislature reconvened in January 1907, its members brought with them to Columbia a mandate from the people to pass a local option bill that would do away with the state dispensary once and for all. Governor Ansel had run on a local option platform, and it was known that if such a bill were passed by the legislature, he would support it. Within the legislature things were a bit less clear. While opponents would "have a substantial majority in the . . . House of Representatives,"[53] the Senate featured few changes in its membership, given that so many of that body had run unopposed for reelection. As the Senate had been understood by all to have a small majority in support of the statewide system, it was not clear whether a local option majority could be created in that chamber.

It fell to two upstate House delegates, "Mr. J. P Carey of Pickens and Mr. T. P. Cothran of Greenville, two of the ablest lawyers in South Carolina . . . to study out the situation and draw a bill that will stand the test of the Courts . . . [and] abolishes the State dispensary which is the mandate of the people."[54] The resulting Carey-Cothran bill did just that, proposing to shut down the state dispensary system. "The chief advantage of their bill," argued Mr. Carey in the *Charleston News and Courier,* "is its placing the power outside of the hands of the State and under the control of the individual counties. . . . There is much less opportunity for graft because the counties will overlook the management, and it will be on so much smaller scale that they will be able to do so. It means prohibition where it is wanted, for the county that desires it will see to it that the law is enforced. . . . However, where the dispensary is voted in, it will mean revenue to the county, and, for this reason, the county will guard very strictly against blind tigers."[55]

The bill proposed to close the state system and eliminate all state officials, save for an auditor appointed by the governor. Each dispensary county would continue to conduct its own system under the same regulations as before. So as to diffuse the concentration of political power in dispensary counties, the three-member county board of control would now consist of one man each appointed by the governor, the county legislative contingent, and the county board of education. These adjustments aside, the bill essentially froze in place operations as they were currently being conducted around the state. Those counties with dispensaries would keep them in place until "a special election to be held in such County on the first Tuesday following the first Monday in November of any year in which a general election for State and County officers is to be held."[56] Current prohibition counties would remain dry for the same period. Profits were to be divided equally between the dispensary town, the county, and the county school fund.

Although there was general agreement on the principles outlined in the original draft, many individual legislators initially balked, with the result that the final measure included over one hundred amendments to make it palatable to representatives and senators who were wrestling with local conditions. These amendments generally came from three sources. The first came from political leaders wishing to retain power over dispensary appointments. Pushed by these legislators, the final bill was amended so that in several counties the process by which county liquor board members would be selected was concentrated in the hands of legislators and less with the governor or county education boards.

The second source of amendments were prohibitionists, who viewed the bill as "a step in the right direction. . . . It will break up the great central machine into its component parts and expose each to the immediate scrutiny of a grand jury." But, drys wondered, why not go a step farther and make the bill a true local option measure? Noting that any current dispensary would continue operations until an election could be scheduled to remove it, dry forces asked: "Is this fair? Suppose in such a county there is a community which now has a dispensary and does not want it?"[57] To provide remedy to such instances, the bill was amended to give certain individual communities and counties the privilege of scheduling elections on the dispensary prior to the next statewide election cycle in November 1908.

The third set of amendments was initiated by those counties and towns unhappy with the allocation of dispensary funds initially provided. Arguing that local conditions should be dictated by local preferences, legislators introduced a slew of amendments that allocated dispensary funds according to the current whim of their population. To allow for constantly changing local preferences, pro-dispensary voters were given an option at all future dispensary elections: "Every voter who may be in favor of the application of one-third of a Dispensary profits to the County School Fund shall cast a ballot in the box . . . upon which shall be printed the words, 'For School Fund'; and every voter in favor of its application to roads and bridges shall cast a ballot in the box, upon which shall be printed the words, 'for roads and bridges.'"[58]

Having altered the general bill to fit the peculiarities of their local constituencies, most legislators happily endorsed the final measure, which gave both prohibition counties the opportunity to eliminate liquor sales and dispensary counties the ability to allocate profits as they saw fit. The final tallies in both chambers gave overwhelming support: in the House the vote was sixty-eight to twenty-eight in favor, and in the Senate the vote was twenty-three to eight in favor. As a measure of both general statewide support for local option as well as the good politicking done by Carey and Cothran, there were no county delegations in which a majority of both House and Senate members opposed the bill. The liquor question, it seemed, had been settled.

PART II

THE DISPENSARY IN AIKEN AND NORTH AUGUSTA

L ike several other South Carolina counties that kept their dispensaries in 1905, Aiken County did so without any rancor or for that matter any discussion. This acceptance of liquor sales did not signal strong support for the dispensary system at the state level, as Aiken, too, had seen its share of political shenanigans within its own county liquor board. Instead, Aiken County residents felt little compulsion to do away with their liquor stores because the dangerous drinkers in their midst typically frequented the saloons across the river in Augusta, Georgia. With little social disturbance arising from liquor sales, the dispensary issue, which consumed so much attention in other mill counties, initially aroused little comment in Aiken.

Two years later, when Georgia adopted statewide prohibition, the situation dramatically changed. With Augusta now dry, the forty thousand residents of that city turned to Aiken County's dispensaries in search of legal liquor. On the one hand, this development promised great profits, especially if a dispensary could be placed in North Augusta to cater to Augusta's drinkers. On the other, North Augusta's residents saw great peril in a new liquor shop, as it likely meant being overrun by all manner of drunken debauchery that their town would have to endure.

The suddenness with which Aiken's citizens, who were unmoved by the dispensary question in 1905, began to fight it vigorously two years later highlights the importance of local conditions, specifically profits and social disorder, in accounting for the development of anti-alcohol legislation. This case reminds us that researchers have to go beyond the usual discussions about prohibition that emphasize demographic groups (e.g., religion or class) and instead see anti-liquor sentiment as more fluid—people can at times come to care deeply about an issue they had previously ignored. In Aiken County's case financial considerations trumped concerns about social disorder, and over the next several years both North Augusta and Aiken County reaped substantial benefits from their liquor shops.

Augusta's status as a dry city was quickly altered when city leaders took advantage of two legislative dispensations permitting cities to license and tax social clubs that kept alcohol for their membership and saloons that served supposedly nonalcoholic "near beer." As Augusta went about regulating these new businesses, it created a situation virtually identical to what had been in place prior to the onset of prohibition. While Augusta was recouping its losses with new liquor money, fewer customers had a need to frequent the North Augusta dispensary.

This back-and-forth jockeying for liquor revenue by local governments was common during the years 1907–13, as several other southern states initially followed Georgia's lead and adopted statewide prohibition. When these states went dry, counties and municipalities along their borders acted much as North Augusta and Aiken did, opening up liquor stores to take advantage of a suddenly new customer base. In reaction newly dry states followed Georgia and Augusta's lead in rolling back prohibition statutes or finding loopholes that permitted them to relicense dealers on their side of the border and take back lost revenue.

5

AUGUSTA, AIKEN COUNTY, AND NORTH AUGUSTA

Located at the southwestern edge of Aiken County, the town of North Augusta rests on a series of five gradually terraced bluffs overlooking the Savannah River, which separates the town from Augusta as well as the states of South Carolina and Georgia. North Augusta's location next to the Savannah as well as its position on the fall line made this area an attractive one for settlement. Despite these advantages, previous attempts that had been made to build a commercial hub on the site failed due to competition with Augusta. By the late nineteenth century what is today North Augusta was still undeveloped, save for the former plantation home of Mattie Butler Mealing situated at the very top of the five bluffs. It was not until 1890, when Augusta stockbroker James U. Jackson bought up much of Mrs. Mealing's property, that North Augusta was developed as a suburb catering to Augusta's new commercial elite.

In building their new community, North Augustans often found themselves caught between two competing centers of power. On the one hand, Augusta's commercial development led to the creation of North Augusta, and Augusta's citizenry made up the entirety of its newest suburb's population; therefore, events in Augusta inevitably influenced North Augusta as well. On the other hand, North Augusta was politically part of Aiken County and the state of South Carolina, meaning that it was also impacted by events in both the county seat of Aiken and the statehouse in Columbia.

AIKEN COUNTY

The only South Carolina county founded during Reconstruction, Aiken was also the scene of some of that era's most significant and brutal racial confrontations.[1] Republican legislators saw the creation of Aiken in 1871 as the establishment of a political base. Much of the area's population was African American and featured some of the party's strongest personalities. By 1876 whites in Aiken and neighboring Edgefield Counties had organized militias intent on reclaiming power, if necessary, by force. Seizing on an incident in the Aiken County town of Hamburg, in which two white men were rebuffed when they requested a black militia company make way for them to pass through town, members of the Edgefield and Aiken "Red Shirts" marched on Hamburg, killing five members of the militia and "redeeming" the town for the white population. Two months later a similar action was undertaken by white insurgents in Ellenton; this time the death toll was estimated at between twenty-five and thirty African Americans.

Attempts to bring the perpetrators to trial failed. South Carolina governor Daniel Henry Chamberlain appealed to the United States government for help and was rebuffed. Emboldened by the lack of federal intervention, South Carolina Democrats, led by former Confederate general Wade Hampton, adopted a policy of outright intimidation of African American and white Republican voters during the 1876 election, a strategy that eventually resulted in the Democratic takeover of power and the installation of General Hampton as governor.

Virtually overnight, Aiken County's white insurgents became its new ruling elite, participating in all levels of state and federal government and helping to frame the South Carolina Constitution, which fixed white supremacy firmly across the state in 1895. As many of these men were relatively young when Reconstruction ended, they continued to hold power in Aiken County for the next several decades, and in a more immediate sense than most local political rings, this group was seen as the literal founders of the county, at least by white citizens. Aiken's political elite also had connections well beyond the county, chief among them Governor Tillman, who proudly claimed membership in the Edgefield Red Shirts and whose chosen successor, John Gary Evans, hailed from Aiken. Tillman's connections with Aiken were so strong that when his nephew stood trial for shooting a political opponent, Tillman called on Aiken attorney T. G. Croft to act as defense council.

By the early years of the twentieth century few challengers to this political elite had emerged across the county, and any dissatisfactions with their decisions were often wiped away by the retelling of the glorious campaign of 1876.

At a time when Confederate reunions were common across the entire South, such stories of the "trials of the men who redeemed the state from the rule of the alien" still held enormous sway.[2]

AIKEN'S GEOGRAPHY AND AGRICULTURE

The county over which this ruling elite presided is located about fifty miles southwest of the state capital, Columbia, along the Savannah River, which forms the southern border of both Aiken County and South Carolina. Founded from parts of its neighboring three counties (Barnwell to the east, Lexington to the north, and Edgefield to the west), Aiken is shaped like a rectangular diamond seemingly perched upon its southern tip, with its western and eastern boundaries each roughly forty-five miles long and both its northern and southern boundaries about twenty miles long. Aiken, the county seat, is located a few miles southwest of the geographic center.

In 1900 the entire county north and southeast of Aiken town (population 3,414 in 1900) was agricultural. These three-quarters of the county together had only five incorporated towns, and all were barely more than glorified train depots—none had a population of more than three hundred. The southwestern quarter of Aiken County, by contrast, was increasingly dominated by the city of Augusta, Georgia, which lay just beyond the state line at the county's southwestern corner. As Augusta's importance as a textile center grew in the late 1800s, its industrial elite expanded across the Savannah, creating an industrial colony of mill towns in the Horse Creek Valley that occupied the seventeen miles from Augusta to Aiken.[3]

As was the case across the South, railroads in Aiken County were built with an eye toward connecting people and shipping freight between larger cities. Smaller towns then grew up around these existing rail lines. Aiken County's location near Augusta meant it was well endowed with railroads, even though they were largely concentrated between Aiken and Augusta in the Horse Creek Valley. The Southern Railroad operated three rail lines that ran through Aiken County. The Charleston-Augusta line entered the county from the east, passing through the rail depot at Windsor (population 103) before heading to Aiken and then southwest through the Horse Creek Valley to Augusta. The Columbia-Augusta line entered Aiken County in its southwestern quarter, again passing through Horse Creek Valley to its final destination in Georgia. The Southern Railway also created a branch off of its Charleston-Augusta line toward Columbia; this branch passed through the northeastern corner of the county, where three small railroad towns sprang up: Salley (population 241), Perry (population 76), and Wagener (population 192). A fourth line operated by the Charleston and Western Railway hugged the Savannah River from the coast up to Augusta, passing through Aiken County's extreme southern tip at the rail town of Ellenton (population 252).

In 1900 the agricultural portion of Aiken County's population stood at 27,618, almost 70 percent of the total number of people living in the county. Half of Aiken's rural population was African American. Like most of rural South Carolina, Aiken County featured two systems of farm tenancy in the years following the Civil War, sharecropping and renting.[4] Under sharecropping arrangements the landowner maintained ownership of the entire crop. The sharecropper provided labor, while the landlord provided nearly everything else necessary for the land to be worked, including draft animals, tools, seed, feed, and fertilizer, along with the house in which the sharecropper lived. At harvest the crop was split between landlord and sharecropper. In contrast, renters actually leased the land they worked and thus gained ownership of the crop they produced, some of which was then paid to the landowner as rent. Both croppers and renters could secure furnishings or advances against the unharvested crop from the landowner. Landlords typically charged between 10 and 20 percent interest on these advances. When the crop was brought in, accounts were settled, often to the detriment of the cropper or renter, who was left with little cash, forcing them again to seek advances with which to acquire the everyday necessities for the coming year.

The tenancy system focused on the production of cotton, which in Aiken County accounted for 42 percent of all the improved land use. Cotton's predominance as a cash crop meant it brought farmers the best chance of securing short-term profits with which to get through the winter to the next planting season. The expansion and improvement of rail lines continually promised easier shipment and greater profits although such visions often proved a mirage. Unlike the Sea Island cotton grown in the South Carolina Lowcountry, which consistently fetched high prices, Aiken's upland cotton prices rose and fell unpredictably on commodities markets. Often a rise in price was quickly followed by an increase in acreage planted in cotton, which in turn flooded the market, causing the price to drop dramatically. At least eight of these cycles occurred between 1890 and 1928, one of them in 1905, during which time the *Aiken Journal and Review* despaired: "As much as we would like to believe otherwise, it must be admitted that . . . the farmers of Aiken County are not sticking to the pledges to reduce the acreage 25 percent, and in fact in many instances are not reducing at all. . . . The conditions have been made known to the farmers. It has been shown that there will be at least 1,500,000 bales carried over and the most liberal estimate of the world's consumption is 12,000,000. The inevitable result of persistence in the present course of planting a full crop or reducing 5 or 10 percent and doubling fertilizers will be to make a crop of over 12,000,000 bales this fall, which together with what is held over will cause the price to decline below the cost of production."[5]

In addition to this economic uncertainty, Aiken's rural population (especially its African American population) was greatly underserved by Aiken's political elite. Townspeople rarely made rural education a priority, believing that it offered little in the way of preparation for country folk, whose job was to plant and harvest cotton. Black education was looked at with an even more jaundiced eye, as it was often asserted that educating African Americans would ruin the region's labor system and upset its racial hierarchy.[6] The head of the Aiken County Cotton Growers' Association gave voice to these fears when he spoke of "the dangers of letting the negroes get more education than the white people." He argued, "If whites do not keep pace with the negroes in the education of their children, there will be cases where white girls are stenographers to negro men."[7] That such concerns were taken seriously is borne out by the amount of schooling offered to Aiken's different racial groups. In Aiken white children's schools remained open for thirty-six weeks, compared to only sixteen weeks for African American children. Among Aiken's rural schools white children received an average of twenty-one weeks of education each year, compared to fifteen weeks for their African American counterparts.

Even when school time was available for children of agricultural families, attendance was often a challenge because of the poor condition of Aiken County's roads. Like much of the rural South, Aiken suffered from poor roads, and the situation was especially acute the farther one traveled from Aiken, Augusta, and the Horse Creek Valley mills. Adding to the farmer's plight was the paucity of resources put toward the development of better roads. Between 1901 and 1905 Aiken County allocated an average of $4,250 (roughly 15 percent of the county budget) for road improvement and maintenance.

THE GROWTH OF INDUSTRIAL AUGUSTA

While three-quarters of Aiken County was typical of Lowcountry counties that were primarily rural, poor, and African American, its southwestern corner more closely resembled the Upcountry counties characterized by the growing textile industry. The impetus for this growth came from outside the county (for that matter from outside the state), across the river in Augusta.[8] Much of Aiken County's cotton had for some time made its way to Augusta; it had been a prominent trading center for antebellum cotton farmers seeking to ship cotton downriver to Savannah or by rail to Columbia and Charleston. Unlike these other cities, Augusta had been spared by Sherman's armies during the war and parlayed this good fortune, along with its location on the Savannah, to recast itself as a manufacturing center in the South's nascent postwar textile economy.

One key to this development was the revival of Augusta's banking industry, whose leaders constituted an industrial elite that over time would begin to compete with Aiken's political elite for influence across the region. Within ten years after the war a new cluster of banks was created: the Georgia Railroad and Banking Company, headed by John Pendleton King; the National Bank, headed by William E. Jackson and Charles Estes; the Bank of Augusta, with Howard Hickman as its president; the Commercial Bank, organized by William Sibley and George R. Lombard; and the Augusta Savings Institute, organized by William Young, Patrick Walsh, John P. King, Richard Allen, and Alfred Baker. These financial leaders were also former incorporators, executives, and officials of antebellum banks, industries, and railroads and as such were ideally placed to direct Augusta's postwar economic expansion.

Alongside the reemergence of a stable financial sector was the rapid recovery of Augusta's railroad connections with other southern cities after the Civil War. The Macon and Augusta branch of the Georgia Railroad reopened its services in August 1865. Two trains were running between Augusta and Savannah by February 1866, and later that spring Augusta was reunited with Charleston and Columbia. By the tenth anniversary of Appomattox, Augusta was connected with a plethora of southern cities—west to Birmingham and Montgomery, east to Savannah and Charleston, and north to Norfolk and Baltimore—making it one of the important rail centers of the New South. Across these rail lines came both a variety of agricultural goods, turning Augusta into a commercial market for local farmers, and more important, an increasingly large amount of southern cotton to be processed, refined, baled, consigned, marketed, and transported to other southern cities. Between 1889 and 1900 Augusta averaged 241,000 bales of processed cotton each year, a number that rose to 343,000 in the first decade of the twentieth century.[9]

This boom in cotton and freight receipts put Augusta's banks on firmer financial footing, enabling their presidents to undertake further industrial development and in the process remake the physical layout of the city. "Cotton Row" merchants along the city's riverfront constructed warehouses and wharves to store and transfer cotton, and Augusta's bankers began planning the expansion of the city's nascent textile industry, encouraging the enlargement of existing mills and the development of new ones. Their first step was the expansion of Augusta's canal. As early as 1869, Augusta's outgoing mayor, Joseph Allen, noted that the canal contained "the germ of the future greatness of our city, and needs to be developed to bring a large increase of industrious population, millions of added wealth and profitable labor for our poor."[10] Taking up this challenge, Augusta financier and Allen's successor, Charles Estes, approved a plan in which the city purchased the necessary dredging equipment, awarded the contract to a private company, and imported several hundred Chinese laborers to dig the expanded canal. By 1875 the project was completed at a cost of almost one million dollars (twenty-five million in today's dollars).

The resulting "industrial park" was quickly populated by a plethora of new textile mills, each with intimate ties to Augusta's banks. The Augusta Factory president, William E. Jackson, was also on the board of the National Bank. The John P. King Mill board of directors included not only its namesake, who was also head of the Georgia Banking and Railroad Company, but also National Bank director (and Augusta's mayor) Charles Estes. Sibley Manufacturing Company was led by William Sibley, also one of the directors of the Commercial Bank; on its board of directors were bankers Eugene and James P. Verdery, Patrick Walsh, and Alfred Baker as well as former mayor Joseph Allen. The Enterprise Manufacturing Company featured among its board members Charles Estes and George T. Jackson. Surrounding these large factories were a host of smaller mills and businesses—the Georgia Chemical Works, Lombard Iron Foundry, Augusta Lumber Company, Augusta Ice Factory, and a host of other supplementary industries. As Augusta grew, the men responsible for that growth also took political control of the city. Nearly three-quarters of the city council members between the years 1897 and 1917 made their living at one of three types of occupations at the heart of the city's growth: banking, cotton, or manufacturing and railroads.[11]

Augusta's industrial growth led thousands of people from the corn and cotton fields to Augusta in search of higher-paying jobs. From a population of roughly twelve thousand at the end of the Civil War, by 1910 Augusta's population was just short of fifty thousand, making it the sixteenth largest city in the South. The majority of the white newcomers crowded into two-story brick or wooden houses in Augusta's Factory District, the industrial region directly west of the central business district stretching as far as Lake Olmstead. The great majority of the African American population resided in the region to the south and southeast of Augusta's center, an area known as "the Territory." As with much of the postwar South, Augusta gradually adopted racial segregation laws, and in the process "the Terri" became its own separate community with businesses, churches, and the like catering almost exclusively to African American clientele.

The rise of the "Lowell of the South" was not restricted to the confines of the city limits or the boundaries of Richmond County or the geographical lines dividing Georgia and South Carolina. The genesis of Augusta's industrial expansion into the Palmetto State dated back to the 1840s with the founding of the Graniteville and Vaucluse Mills. Although located across the Savannah, both were Augusta enterprises with a substantial portion of the capital and many of its leaders being Augustans. Begun in 1847 and 1848, respectively, both mills experienced almost continuous growth for two decades, building additions to the plants and acquiring several thousand acres on which to construct wooden frame houses and company stores in the emerging industrial plantation.

At both the Graniteville and Vaucluse Mills prewar facilities were expanded in view of a potential textile boom. "The great success that has attended the manufacture of Cotton in the South for the last two or three years has induced me to recommend the enlargement of Graniteville Mill to at least double its present capacity," wrote Graniteville's second president, H. H. Hickman, in 1872. "I am confident . . . in three or four years to build a new Mill of 20,000 spindles and 600 looms."[12]

From 1874 to 1878 the Graniteville Mill alone paid out dividends amounting to $299,650 ($7,491,275 today), representing almost 50 percent of its capital stock. From 1878 to 1883 the mill earned gross profits totaling $468,977 ($11,724,425) and paid out almost $250,000 ($6,250,000) to stockholders. Such a continual steady return of high profits to Augusta's capitalists meant that they were eager to continue investing in their Horse Creek Valley industrial colony. By the 1890s further capital resulted in the founding of the Langley, Aiken, Warren, and Clearwater Manufacturing Companies. The men who raised the capital, organized the ventures, organized the mill towns, and made the key administrative decisions were, in the main, prominent citizens of Augusta.

The subscribed capital for the Langley Manufacturing Company came from William Langley of New York; William E. Jackson, president of the Augusta Factory; and William Sibley, president of Sibley Mill. At Bath, just six miles from Augusta, the Aiken Manufacturing Company was organized. Among its important promoters and officials was Charles Estes, president of King Mill. James P. Verdery, president and treasurer of Enterprise Mill, along with two Augusta bankers, Linwood Hayne and Charles A. Robbe, combined their fortunes to run the mill at Warrenville. These men soon realized that their mills had to send their goods north to be bleached and, seeing an opportunity, created the Clearwater Bleaching and Manufacturing Company.

The construction and renovation of Horse Creek Valley's textile mills also prompted the construction of mill villages to house the region's growing number of mill hands, a number that reached eighty-three hundred mill village residents by 1907.[13] Alongside rows of plain one and a half–story wood frame cottages, Horse Creek Valley mill companies erected clubhouses with activities designed for worker uplift. Companies invested in health clinics, kindergartens, and baseball teams; in Graniteville the mill village clubhouse included a swimming pool, bowling alley, gymnasium, library, and banquet hall. Graniteville president Hickman justified these improvements by noting that "the mills today that are running successfully are the mills that have satisfied and contented help, and no help can be satisfied and contented that have no means of pleasure and recreation."[14]

In spite of such glowing rhetoric, the contemporary missionary activities of St. Paul's Episcopal Church indicated that poverty and a lack of social services were still serious problems across Horse Creek Valley's mill communities. In 1909 Episcopal deaconess Anna Sands began a missionary program for workers, offering night school, cooking and sewing classes, boys' and girls' clubs, and mothers' meetings, all with an eye toward uplifting Horse Creek Valley's mill populations. Surveying her efforts and the condition of the workers, Sands wrote in 1914, "The life of the average mill hand is at present very hard; it is a life of endless toil, with little visible hope or brightness in it, very, very little to stimulate or to encourage higher standards of living and thinking."[15]

Aiken County residents, like those across South Carolina, worried about the impact of the mills in their county, and these worries were periodically punctuated by riotous behavior in and around the mills. Typical of such complaints was the *Aiken Journal and Review*'s lament following a series of riots in the mill town of Langley in 1905: "Is there any law-abiding people in the county who are not disgusted by the frequent and bloody riots occurring in and around Langley? Is there no remedy for such demonstrations of lawlessness? Beyond doubt there is a serious dereliction of duty somewhere. Where are the owners and officers of the property of that place?"[16] Across the river, in Augusta, the owners of Langley and the other Horse Creek Valley mill towns likely concerned themselves little with their operatives' behavior, so long as those problems remained in Aiken County and so long as it did not interfere with mill operations. By 1906 Horse Creek Valley's operations represented a considerable part of Augusta's cotton business, more than a third of all the productivity and manpower in Augusta's cotton industry.

WEALTHY AUGUSTA AND NORTH AUGUSTA

In stark contrast to the workers in their midst, Augusta's wealthier citizens initially resided nearer the central business district, an eight-block stretch of Broad Street, south of Cotton Row, running west from Fifth (Center) Street to Thirteenth (McKinnie) Street.[17] The areas immediately east and south of Broad Street featured government and religious buildings mixed into moderately upscale residential neighborhoods collectively known as the "Pinched Gut District." As Augusta prospered in the late 1880s, its first suburban district was constructed on the hills just beyond the southwestern edge of the town. Summerville, so called because of the summer residences constructed by wealthy Augustans seeking relief from the ravages of mosquito-bred illnesses, in time also became a fashionable winter resort and golf capital with the construction of several large hotels and the nearby Augusta National Golf Club.

The last of Augusta's suburban neighborhoods to be developed was the land directly to its north, across the Savannah River. Although the Savannah had served as an impediment to earlier expansion, the primary reason for Augustans' reticence to expand in this direction was the town of Hamburg, the most recent settlement built on that site, begun in 1821. In its earlier, more prosperous days Hamburg had itself been a center of commerce and at that time had connected with Augusta across a bridge ending on Fifth Street in Augusta. By the turn of the twentieth century Hamburg had fallen on hard times. Inhabited by African Americans and poor whites, few well-off Augustans would agree to live on the other side of the water if their only access to the city was a bridge that ran through a poor part of town.

The driving force behind the reimagining of Augusta's northern suburb was James Urquhart Jackson, a local stock and bond broker whose father, George T. Jackson, and uncle, William E. Jackson, were both prominent in Augusta's financial community. Recognizing that Augusta's increasing prominence as a textile manufacturing center would result in the need for more housing, Jackson formed the North Augusta Land Company in 1890. Jackson focused his attention on the area west of Hamburg, "some 6,000 acres running from the foot of McKinnie [Thirteenth] Street across the Hamburg bottoms then up a bold ascent, then across a splendid second bottoms, standing high, dry and beautiful, then up a still bolder ascent, two miles from the river, where is to stand ... North Augusta."[18] Originally an antebellum plantation constructed by Robert J. Butler, his daughter Mattie inherited the property in 1888 and sold approximately fifty-six hundred acres of it to the North Augusta Land Company in 1890 for $100,000, keeping the final six acres at the summit for her family.

Once in possession of the land, Jackson hired urban planner Charles Boeckh to map it into a suburb and commissioned "a splendid bridge of modern design, across the broad Savannah, at the foot of McKinnie Street. ... The bridge is being built by Mr. Grant Wilkins, one of the most prominent bridge contractors in the South. It is to be of iron, and will be arranged to accommodate pedestrian, vehicles and electric railway."[19] Constructing the rail line to enter Augusta's Broad Street at the western edge of the business district made it possible for North Augusta residents to avoid both Hamburg's bridge and the growing mill villages to the west of Thirteenth Street in Augusta. With the foundation of North Augusta in place, Jackson gradually added the amenities citizens would desire to tempt them into moving. First, a schoolhouse was built in 1898, followed by two churches, one Baptist and the other Methodist, added just after the turn of the century.

Despite the residential and resort amenities constructed throughout the early 1900s, North Augusta was very much a work in progress. The Boeckh Plan included some 560 lots for houses, yet by 1907 only 223 of them had residents listed in the *Augusta City Directory*. The majority ($n = 123$) of them were white-collar workers in Augusta's businesses who sought a suburban refuge along West and Georgia Avenues. Alongside these families were investors ($n = 12$) attracted to North Augusta because of its clay soil that, when tempered, made the region's distinctive Edgefield Pottery. North Augusta potteries were initially lucrative (ironically) because they produced jugs for the South Carolina dispensary, although they branched out into flowerpots and other objects as the years passed. These companies housed along the town's riverfront were soon joined by a lumber company, a brick mill, and a sawmill, each of which aided the development of housing as Augusta grew. Those who labored in these factories, as well domestics and laborers in Augusta's wealthier homes and hotels ($n = 88$), often took up residence along Bluff Avenue, overlooking their riverside location, thereby reproducing North Augusta's social strata physically across its tiered landscape.

To further raise the town's profile, Jackson organized the North Augusta Hotel Company and built the Hampton Terrace Hotel on the fourth bluff from the river, two blocks below the Butler plantation house. Modeled on the Bon Air Hotel and Partridge Inn in Summerville, the Hampton Terrace aimed to attract privileged guests, who likely would travel with their staff. Accordingly, Jackson designed the hotel to include "accommodations for 500 guests with 300 en suite rooms separated by Redwood double doors and brick surrounding each elevator well. There was a music room, sun parlors . . . [and] amusements to suit every taste: dancing, billiards, tennis, shuffleboard, and ping-pong. In the front of the hotel was a carefully laid-out golf course with nine holes ready for the opening season and a further nine holes to be completed by the following winter. . . . There was excellent fishing and access to a 15,000 acre game preserve owned by Jackson."[20]

THE REGIONAL TOURISM INDUSTRY

When it was founded in 1902, the Hampton Terrace joined an already burgeoning regional tourist industry that had begun twenty years earlier in

Aiken.[21] The town first attracted tourist notice at the end of the nineteenth century as a health resort.[22] Promotional booklets promised that visitors to Aiken would physically benefit from the "tonic qualities of its climate." The dry, salubrious air, scented with " a sweet aroma" from the surrounding long-leaf pine forests, offered a remedy for coastal residents suffering from the effects of malaria or other maladies. "In regard to its wonderful fall and winter climate, Aiken stands unequalled by any other place in the United States, and by few in any part of the world."[23]

In a series of articles in medical and popular journals, physicians praised Aiken's beneficial climate, detailed its healing effects, and described the facilities that were quickly being erected by locals in the hope that visitors would avail themselves of all the town had to offer. A passage from the 1888 edition of the Homeopathic Medical Society of Pennsylvania is typical:

> The yellow pine of the South finds here [in and about Aiken] its congenial habitat, and in every direction the country about Aiken is covered with a dense forest growth of the softly evergreen trees, shading the ground from the rays of the sun and filling the atmosphere with the delicious balsamic odor exhaled from their leaves and trunks. Several varieties of oak are also to be found in the woods about Aiken, and not a few flowering vines and shrubs; but the pine is the characteristic growth, and it is to the soothing and purifying effect exerted upon the mucous membrane of the respiratory passages by the exhalations from this tree that the climate of Aiken owes much of its well-deserved reputation as a health resort.... The other chief factors in projecting the healthfulness of this now celebrated resort are the mildness and general equability of its winter climate, the preponderance of bright sunny days, which enable the invalid to spend much of his time in open air ... and last but by no means least, the remarkable dryness of the air ... no drier air is to be found in the whole United States.[24]

Promotional brochures also commented upon Aiken's sport facilities, describing the stables, polo grounds, racetracks, and golf courses. Spurred by the promise of better health and ample leisure, winter visitors began flocking to Aiken, and as word spread, increasing numbers of the New York social elite spent long stretches of their winter in the South Carolina town. As the number of winter visitors grew, economic growth of the city benefited permanent residents. Entrepreneurial businessmen began to construct facilities and open businesses to cater to the Winter Colony.

By 1892 a *New York Times* reporter describing the town wrote: "Aiken is far enough south for the weather to be pleasantly bracing morning and evening on clear winter days, while the noonday sun is almost hot in January, and it is sufficiently far north for the nights to be cool enough for wood fires and blankets." In the middle of this temperate oasis stood Aiken, "one long broad avenue extending through the place and ending in the grounds of the Highland Park hotel . . . the cornerstone of Aiken . . . supplied with all the conveniences and necessaries that go to make a hotel of the first order."[25] The Highland Park was soon joined by the Park in the Pines and the Hotel Aiken in the center of town, which was "occupied by stores and offices. . . . There are a number of good stores, including several where wagons and coaches are sold and one or two newspapers offices, and some modern brick buildings."[26]

For Winter Colonists who preferred homes, year-round residents were only too happy to rent out either individual rooms or their entire houses. The *State* reported that in the 1900–1901 winter season "among the houses rented . . . were that owned by Mr. W. R. Tramps [who rented] to Col. John Jacob Astor. Price is not stated, but it is supposed to be between $2,000 [$50,000] and 2,500 [$62,500]. The residence of Mr. F. B. Henderson, President of the People's Bank, has been rented to Mr. James Roosevelt, uncle of the Presidential nominee."[27] By 1904 prices for rental houses in Aiken had increased exponentially, with the *State* noting that "the citizens of Aiken caught the spirit and many handsome houses were built by then to be rented to Northerners." With such a demand "the history of real estate deals in Aiken shows no instance of property being sold for less than cost."[28] Looking back on the recently completed 1904 winter season, the newspaper itemized a few of the immense profits made by Aiken's householders:

A New York merchant, finding that he would not be able to visit Aiken this winter, has rented his house for $10,000 for the season.

Another beautiful place near Aiken that may have cost $15,000 to build has rented the last two winters for $9,500.

A lady bought 12 acres of land just outside of Aiken for $1,250. In two years she sold it for $10,000.

An Aiken shoemaker invested his earnings and credit in a $500 farm south of Aiken. In less than three years he sold it for $10,500.

A gentleman from Rhode Island, infatuated with Aiken as a winter home, bought an old place for $3,500. He has been offered $12,500 for his bargain.[29]

As this list suggests, many winter visitors purchased property in the suburbs of Aiken, where by the turn of the century there were "a large number of handsome cottages owned and occupied by wealthy Northern people."[30] Typical of these cottages was the one built by Mr. L. S. Smith of New York, "a beautiful, complete, well-built house, which with the stables included will cost between $12,000 and $16,000. . . . The residence contains twenty rooms, three halls and four bathrooms."[31] Such large cottages required large acreages, and the resulting land boom caused "the townsfolk to gaze in wonder at the real estate operations. . . . Already those prominent in the winter colony own thousands of acres to the south and west of Aiken. In these lands, patches of forest are being cleared, streams are being dammed, and everything points to the inception of the greatest private park and hunting ground scheme in the United States."[32]

These large estates were generally constructed in the "horse district" and included winter stables, steeplechase courses, foxhunting courses, tennis courts, and polo fields. This section of Aiken also featured unpaved roads connecting the Winter Colony residences to the equestrian facilities scattered in the woods just beyond town. By the turn of the century a nationally renowned golf club had also been added, with the annual tournament played there attracting both presidents and "a field of millionaire players."[33]

Local reaction to the influx of northerners around Aiken County was mixed. The town of Aiken was in general "disposed to view with favor the acquisition of land by the rich men of the north because the rich men of the north pay prices that would have been considered fabulous three of four years ago." Others who lived farther outside of Aiken were far more skeptical. "They'll keep buyin' and buyin'," said one farmer, "'till they get all the cotton land around Aiken bought up and then there'll be a game of freeze out between then, and Aiken ain't goin' to be much good in the freeze out game with them folks. They'll have Aiken County to themselves in a few years."[34]

Townspeople hardly cared. Aiken townspeople and property owners also realized that this tourism was their town's only meaningful source of such income. "Aiken's prosperity, in fact Aiken's very existence, is dependent upon the presence of the Northerner," observed the *State*. "Without his regular winter visit Aiken would be dull, very dull. In summer Aiken dozes. But the Aiken landowner or householder slumbers peacefully or otherwise 'takes it easy' for if the preceding winter has been a successful one, his rest is paid for in advance."[35] In the early 1900s each winter season seemed to bring new successes for Aikenites, with record numbers of visitors to their town. By 1905 "the record shows that 3,000 visitors have been here this season," the *Aiken Journal and Review* reported. "This is a large number and they represent the expenditure of a large sum of money among the townspeople."[36]

Although Aiken dominated the local tourist scene, Augusta and North Augusta also built grand hotels to draw tourists away from Aiken and offer them the pleasures of the big city to its southwest. In addition to the Hampton Terrace in North Augusta, Augusta's civic leaders used both personal and city resources to build the Bon Air Hotel in the suburb of Summerville. The Bon Air offered all the latest amenities to its three hundred guests, including a grand ballroom in which they all might congregate. Touting its advantages in comparison with the sleepy town of Aiken, the *Chronicle* crowed, "street cars run to the door from the city; good drives can be found on all sides; Augusta, with its stores, churches and places of amusement, all the charm of the country and convenience of the city are combined. In this particular, the Bon-Air hotel has marked advantages over . . . any winter hotel in the South."[37]

THE AUGUSTA-AIKEN RAILWAY

Tourists made possible and necessary Aiken County's lone area of infrastructure development, as roads were needed to link Aiken with both the main railroad terminal in Augusta and the hotels where they might visit friends and associates. Initially, these connecting roads were railroads and were funded entirely with private money. To link Aiken and Augusta's increasingly networked tourists and mill operations, James U. Jackson also built the Augusta-Aiken Railway, the South's first interurban rail system. As early as 1892, the Augusta Railway Company provided that city with electric streetcar service covering twenty-two miles around the city and providing transportation to roughly two million passengers a year. This system's initial expansion into

South Carolina occurred in 1897, when track was laid to connect downtown Augusta with the newly created community of North Augusta. This short extension gradually became a much more ambitious plan to connect Augusta and Aiken by railroad, completed in 1902.

Once it was completed, the Augusta-Aiken Railway ran the full length of Horse Creek Valley, with its endpoints at the two main towns it served. For a fare of five cents, passengers could take the roughly two-hour trip from end to end or stop at any of the five mill towns along the railway route. Cars left Aiken and Augusta on the hour beginning at 7:00 a.m. in both towns, with the final run leaving from Aiken at 8:00 p.m. and from Augusta at 10:00 p.m.

As the rail line developed, it introduced special cars designed to carry its more exclusive passengers during the Winter Colony season. For those so inclined, it was also possible to purchase a private rail car that would skip all the intermediate stops, making the journey between Augusta and Aiken in less time. As an executive of the Augusta-Aiken rail line and owner of the Hampton Terrace, James U. Jackson created a special transport car, the Hampton Terrace Special, that would run only the first leg of the journey, stopping exclusively at his hotel. "The Hampton Terrace special will make no stops between inter-terminal points," explained the *Augusta Chronicle*. "No passengers will be accepted between these points. It is strictly for the accommodation of the patrons of the hotel.... A special car will be provided for the service, and it is one of the nicest of the rolling stock of the company.... It will be perfect in very appointment.... Special runs are to be timed to meet the arrival of trains from New York" so as to minimize the wait of Jackson's hotel guests.[38]

At its completion, the *Augusta Chronicle* noted, "this railroad between Carolina's famous winter resort city and Augusta, which is becoming every year more popular as a winter resort and passing through North Augusta, a new candidate for popular favor, links together three most attractive localities for northern tourists. The daily passage of the electric cars between Aiken, North Augusta and Augusta will bring the northern guests of these three places into closer touch than has been possible heretofore, and there will be frequent interchange of visits, arrangements of golf matches, fox hunts, and other amusements."[39] For the business leaders of Augusta and its industrial colony, the interurban "would greatly relieve what is now regarded as an arbitrary interstate freight tariff between Horse Creek Valley and Aiken on the one side and Augusta on the other.... [The result] must necessarily bring the industrial sections of the two states very intimately together in a business way."[40]

AUGUSTA, AIKEN, AND A POSSIBLE NEW COUNTY

The opening of the interurban represented a high point in relations between Aiken and Augusta. On the occasion of the interurban's opening in August 1902, the *Augusta Chronicle*'s front page "on behalf of the people of Augusta . . . extends a very cordial welcome to our visitors from Aiken and along the line of the Augusta and Aiken railway. We have been looking forward to this auspicious occasion, and it is believed the opening of this road marks an era in the business interests of Augusta. . . . We grasp hands with Carolina today and say welcome."[41] The *Aiken Journal and Review* responded in kind. "Aiken today sends greeting and best wishes to Augusta! May both live long and prosper, and unlike the buried cities of the plains, become centers of civilization and of all the arts lasting and secure."[42]

This vision of a delightful future of cooperation and mutual benefit was not shared by everyone, and chief among its doubters were members of Aiken's business community, who worried about the impact of increased economic competition with the larger city now only a short rail trip away. "I am not opposed to the road coming to Aiken," opined one shopkeeper, "but I am opposed to its passing down our business street for the reason that a customer will be looking at a pair of shoes in my store and will hear the streetcar coming and will throw them down and jump on, telling me he will see what he can do in Augusta, and we will lose lots of trade. . . . Aiken cannot compete with Augusta."[43] Augusta's business community recognized this new reality, too, and rejoiced that "the establishment of the road has added to the city's tributary territory, by giving thousands of inhabitants of Aiken County cheap rapid transit to and from the city, and making Augusta their market for every necessity and luxury of life."[44] Augusta's burgeoning market life was especially busy on Saturdays, and the *Chronicle* was fond of counting the increasing number of passengers each weekend brought to their city—a number that exceeded five thousand per week by the summer of 1903.

As Augusta's businesses were drawing customers away from Aiken, its chamber of commerce was making a bid to draw tourist trade as well. Reviewing its advertisements spread throughout northern states in April 1904, the

Aiken Journal and Review complained: "The Augusta Chamber of Commerce has recently issued a new booklet setting forth the numerous natural and economic advantages for business and residence purposes of the 'Queen City of the Savannah Valley,' which is represented on a circular map as 'The Hub of the Garden Spot of the World.' Among the twenty specific points of advantage we learn that, instead of stating, as on a former occasion, that the city 'is but seventeen miles from Aiken, the noted health resort of the South,' it modestly claims to be itself the healthiest city in the Union—the author evidently meaning 'Greater Augusta,' and including the Carolina hills across the Savannah. Well, if Augusta don't blow her own trumpet!"[45]

Adding potential further injury to this perceived insult, the *Augusta Chronicle* announced in October 1902 that it was establishing a branch office in Aiken. "In opening this office, it is not the purpose of the Chronicle to antagonize Aiken's county paper or to usurp their realm," wrote the *Chronicle*'s editor. "But the Chronicle, being more general in its scope and purpose [than Aiken's paper] feels that it is also needed, and the nearness of Aiken to Augusta, the many interests which we have in common, and especially the recent connection of the two cities by electric road, naturally suggested this idea, and holds out the promise that the plan will be entirely practicable."[46]

It is in this context of Augusta's gradual overtaking of Aiken's role that James U. Jackson's scheme to create a new county separate from Aiken, with North Augusta as the county seat, needs to be understood. Jackson's proposed Heyward County (so named to curry the favor of then South Carolina governor Duncan Clinch Heyward) with North Augusta as the county seat, was seen as yet another way to enhance the town's reputation as well as its residential and financial base—a county seat would likely lead to lawyers and other local officials taking up residence there. Further, "the people of the proposed territory would be greatly convenienced in reaching their county seat; they come to North Augusta now ten to twenty times where they go to Edgefield and Aiken once. . . . By forming a new county to include North Augusta, the new electric road as far as . . . Clearwater, Bath and Langley towns and mills . . . a small and rich county could be formed whose taxes could soon put fine roads throughout the territory to Augusta."[47] The resulting campaign intensified an already strained relationship between Augusta, North Augusta, and Aiken County as they argued over the distribution of county resources and vied for control in North Augusta's local affairs.

Jackson's chief complaint against Aiken County was financial. "We pay our money now and don't get it back," he argued time and again in making his case for secession. "I have been several times recently by private conveyance through the country between Aiken and Batesburg, Leesville, Monetta and points north of Aiken. Beginning about three miles this side of Batesburg there is a clayed road to Aiken. Similar roads run out from Aiken to within a few miles of the points named. . . . With these roads the town of Aiken drew trade from these other towns. Why is it you do not have these roads south of Aiken? It is because no matter how good roads they built here you would trade at Augusta. Your money has been taken and spent elsewhere."[48] In making this choice for a new county, a citizen going by the name of "Fair Play" suggested that voters "figure for yourselves whether you would rather have good roads to your marketplace, and to attend to your legal and other business connected with a county seat. You . . . know whether or not the roads are clayed around Aiken in every direction. You also know that Aiken cannot and will not spend any money on this for a long time."[49]

By contrast with their current situation, in which "Aiken county which receives the benefit of all such development in that quarter embraces 1,100 square miles of territory. . . . advocates of the formation of a narrower county of about 420 square miles next to Augusta are confident they will have a very rich, small area—far more than in the course of time than it is even at present— from which the county districts will derive large benefit in improved schools, fine roads to Augusta, etc. . . . North Augusta's half million dollar hotel and electric railroad have recently added to the proposed county's wealth [and] advocates of the county argue that all railroads that come to Augusta in the future from that side of the river are obliged to come through Heyward county, adding to the taxable property."[50]

Aiken County officials' initial reaction to charges of neglect was to redress these grievances. "We understand that a good deal of dissatisfaction exists as to the condition of the roads there," wrote the county commissioners, "and it is not so, as we hear reported, that the . . . tax of any one township has been used for work in any other township."[51] Aiken County's representative to the state legislature, T. G. Croft, assured potential Heyward County residents that "the bad condition of the roads in this section have been called to our attention and it is the intention to increase the funds in Aiken county to improve these roads. We are going to give this section fair play."[52]

These kind words might have been enough to mend relationships between town and county had not the Heyward County advocates surreptitiously received a better offer from their neighbors across the Savannah. In a secret letter to Augusta's business community, representatives of "the undersigned committee . . . appointed by the president of the Chamber of Commerce" made clear its mandate "to solicit funds from the business interest of Augusta to promote the establishment of this county. The funds are to be used for legitimate purposes—printing, barbecues, campaign meetings, and as an additional inducement to those already offered by North Augusta for the establishment of a county seat at this point."[53] Such "inducements" "would bring to the new county standard many adherents in those remote sections that suffer from the poor conditions of the roads to Augusta. There is a promise of better roads. But the people there say, very reasonably, 'How do we know we will have any road improvement after the county is established?' We wish that Augusta's bonus could be expended in the direction of assuring these sections that there will be very substantial road improvements; the actual claying of a considerable portion of the main road leading from the opposition country toward Augusta. . . . These are expenses and improvements which the city of Augusta could well afford to meet. . . . A new equipment of road building, costing $4,000 to $5,000 would be of practical and very direct service."[54]

Further asserting that "it would pay the city of Augusta—the business interests—to do this to induce the establishment of this county seat at this point," the committee enumerated the vast financial advantages Heyward County would bring to Augusta:

1. A new court in a suburb of Augusta.
2. Court crowds several times annually—jurors, witnesses, lawyers, judges, country visitors—from a large territory; also expenditure of court money in Augusta.
3. Erection of county buildings to cost over $25,000 in this suburb.
4. Political meetings for the territory at this point.
5. Banking of county funds to the extent of $40,000 to $50,000 annually and expenditure of county money here.
6. Residence of county officers and clerks and expenditure of their salaries.
7. Increase of population by residence of lawyers, county citizens, etc., who will become residents of the county seat.

8. Necessity of constant visiting of country residents for all county and legal business, such as registration, assessment, tax paying, etc.

"This important piece of city building," the letter concluded, "should inspire the cooperation of every patriotic Augustan. No matter which way Augusta grows it is all Augusta—larger Augusta. Additional growth, new enterprises and influences contributing to growth is what is desired and must be obtained at every opportunity."[55]

Intentionally or not, the letter was leaked to the *Augusta Chronicle,* and upon its publication commentators across Aiken County were quick to inform "the people in the new county territory as to what is being done by the people of Augusta to separate them from the their relatives and life-long friends in Aiken county."[56] Some aimed their diatribes against James Jackson and the North Augusta Land Company, asking, "Can one possibly imagine a condition of affairs more dangerous to government by the people than thus placing absolute control of the government of a county in the hands of corporations, especially when every sane man knows in advance that their purpose in establishing the county is to promote their own interests, increase the value of their property and bring dollars into the treasury of the corporations?"[57] "With all good citizens, we welcome capital and good citizenship into our county," added the *Journal and Review,* but the paper cautioned that these good feelings end "when that corporation and its officers turn aside from their legitimate business . . . and undertake to break up the relationship . . . of the people of Aiken County for the promotion of their own selfish ends."[58]

Most of the Aiken commentary was directed at Augustans' perceived violation of the rights of free South Carolinians. One Aiken commentator angrily asserted that "the people of Schultz, Hammond, Silverton, Sleepy Hollow or any other township can tax themselves to improve the roads of their respective townships if they wish to" and suggested that "if this fund is to be used . . . for the convenience of the people of North Augusta and Aiken County, Augusta's Chamber of Commerce might instead focus on . . . McKinnie Street [where] there are five barrooms and about eighteen dives. . . . We believe the ladies of that thriving little town would rather walk upon the worst streets of Aiken County than upon McKinnie street, the thoroughfare by which they must enter Augusta."[59]

Another writer praised the citizenship of the proposed county to be "of the highest order" and warned the Augusta Chamber of Commerce that "those who live in the territory and are opposed to it will work all the harder now that they see clearly that this move is to benefit the people of Georgia instead of South Carolina, and in their efforts they have the sympathy and encouragement of the people of Aiken County, for who can tell where this encroachment will stop?"[60] To rally Aiken county residents, he reminded them of the grave danger such a precedent set. "If the merchants of Augusta are successful in dismantling Aiken County will they stop there? Or will they, realizing their ability to control our county, attempt to dominate our local affairs every time they see an opportunity to enrich themselves? It is but right that we should give warning now so that this interference in our affairs can be stopped at once."[61]

Such charges only further poisoned the pot, with the *Augusta Chronicle* now taking umbrage as it defended what it perceived to be rights to the western part of Aiken County as part of "greater Augusta." "Our Aiken contemporary must not lose sight of the fact that though the Chronicle's publication is on the Georgia side of the river, a large number of its constituents are on the Carolina side. Swing round a circle, with Augusta in the center, and Carolina furnishes as legitimate Chronicle territory as Georgia.... It is not as an interloper, therefore, but as an active participant and fellow worker that Augusta... takes a hand in Carolina affairs.... We have established ferries, built bridges and opened highways... running right to the door of the *Aiken Journal and Review*.... We have not only a sentimental but practical interests over the river, and we have our say in Carolina affairs—the affairs of a large portion of our constituents. The Journal and Review need not ask 'What has Georgia to do with making counties in Carolina?'"[62]

The movement for a new county wound up taking four years to bring to a vote. South Carolina law stipulated that in order to be established, any new county required a two-thirds majority from voters in each county that the new county's residents would hail from. Proponents of Heyward County easily cleared this hurdle in Edgefield, but in Aiken they fell short by thirty-nine votes, with only North Augusta and its immediate environs supporting the new county. Voting results across Aiken County showed that the farmers farthest away from North Augusta gave the new county proposal the least amount of support, an indication that the issue of good roads mattered and that, in making their choice, farmers opted to ally themselves with the county seat closest to them.

Although these results guaranteed the continued political participation of North Augusta in Aiken County, they did little to ease the tensions between Augusta's newest suburb and those residing outside of it. Discussion over the future county resources and control of local affairs continued to plague relations between the two towns and echoed the larger issue of Augusta's increasing encroachment on Aiken's tourist trade and economic hold on the county. The tensions between Augusta and Aiken would find their next (and most dramatic) iteration in 1907, beginning with a striking change in Georgia's liquor policy.

6

LIQUOR IN AUGUSTA AND AIKEN COUNTY, 1900–1906

At first glance Aiken County and Augusta would seem to have been places that would have embraced prohibition at the first available opportunity. Aiken County had a significant rural Baptist population, a constituency that in other South Carolina counties strongly supported dry laws. Further, the presence of millworkers in the Horse Creek Valley and Augusta would seem to parallel upstate mill counties, which all adopted prohibition after the passage of the Brice Act. Despite these factors, neither Aiken County nor Augusta adopted prohibition of their own accord during the local option period. The explanation for this conundrum lies in the types and location of liquor dealers and the resulting spatial arrangement of social disorder associated with liquor.

When citizens of Aiken County considered the liquor question, like everyone else in South Carolina, they did so in the context of the statewide dispensary system. As was the case across the state, Aiken County's citizens grappled with questions of corruption, profit, and social disorder as they debated whether or not to retain their liquor shops once the Brice Act was passed in 1904. Ultimately, the liquor question in Aiken County revolved more around the trouble created by illegal liquor sellers than by the state-run liquor shops, which were typically frequented by very few customers and provided an important source of income from sales to Aiken's tourist hotels.

Unlike South Carolina, Georgia was a local option state that permitted saloons if the local population was so inclined. Augusta, because of its large population, attracted saloonkeepers, and the Augusta city government was more than happy to allow their operation so long as they paid a high license fee, which went toward filling the city coffers. The more critical question for Augustans was the location of these saloons, and over time these liquor shops became segregated into certain neighborhoods, thus ensuring that the most unwanted drinkers would not interact with Augusta's more well-off citizens.

THE AIKEN COUNTY DISPENSARIES TO 1905

Aiken County's dispensary history featured all the same themes that touched the state dispensary system throughout the time of its operation. At the same time, Aiken's unique status as a tourist destination, as well as its location, near Augusta, impacted how the liquor question was ultimately adjudicated. As was the case in every county, the initial dispensary was established in Aiken, the county seat, in 1893. Four years later, as the state system was struggling to compete with the original package stores, Aiken County added two other liquor outlets in what were at the time its only other two railroad towns, both located in the rural eastern half of the county, Salley (population 241 in 1900) and Wagener (population 192 in 1900). The county board of control also permitted Aiken to add a beer dispensary in 1897 and granted dispensary privileges to the town's various tourist hotels as well.

The graft and corruption that bedeviled the South Carolina state system found their way into Aiken County's liquor board as well. Much of the trouble centered around George T. Holley, a political ally of John Gary Evans, author of the initial dispensary bill, who then succeeded Tillman as governor in 1894. Holley first came to the public's attention in 1896, when widespread dispensary shortages were discovered throughout Aiken County, leading to accusations of graft aimed at county dispenser Wade Lamar. Lamar claimed that "he should not be held responsible . . . as the county board, after electing him dispenser contrary to custom, elected his clerk . . . Mr. B. F. Holley and Mr. G. W. Sawyer voting for Mr. G. T. Holley. . . . Mr. Sawyer, so Mr. Lamar alleges, claimed at the time that he had been instructed by Governor Evans to vote for Mr. Holley to the be the clerk for Mr. Lamar."[1] The board never required Holley to report to Lamar, who acted as a free agent as he sold liquor and kept the books. Lamar accused Holley further of "hiring a negro porter under instructions from the Governor and afterward he [Lamar] caught Holley stealing dispensary liquor, but no one knows how much he stole."[2]

Despite these accusations, Holley was never formally charged and continued to serve in the Aiken dispensary system, first as clerk and then as the dispenser in Aiken. His election to the dispenser post also raised eyebrows, as "there had been a systematic fight for a long time against Holley. . . . Informally, two of the [three] members of the board declared to each other that they had voted against Holley. Each was surprised at the other's statement, and the mistake [in electing Holley] is accounted for by the fact that the writing on the ballot was not very plain and that the chairman of the board [who counted the votes] is a very near sighted man and . . . had not read the ballots aright."[3]

In response to such obvious political maneuvering, the Aiken County Democratic Party advocated for direct election of dispensary candidates by popular vote, declaring, "The people of South Carolina know that there is a great deal of complaint with the management of the dispensary, and the sooner the voters are themselves allowed to say who shall manage it the sooner will it be run on a more honest plane . . . of the people, for the people and by the people, not of the dispensary ring, for the dispensary ring, and by the dispensary ring."[4] Pointing out that "a majority of the officers in our county and state are nominated by the votes of the people" and that "the essence of Democracy is that all offices should be filled by an election," the Aiken County Democratic Party requested that its state delegates push for an amendment to the state constitution "allowing any county to elect their dispenser or dispensers and county boards of control in the regular Democratic primaries as other county officers."[5] Although such a constitutional measure was not adopted by the legislature, Aiken County's complaints were one of many that helped bring about the Brice Act, which gave county control over the dispensary in the form of a possible prohibition referendum.

As Aiken County residents, along with the rest of South Carolina, pondered whether to call such a referendum in 1905, G. T. Holley's political shenanigans were quickly shunted aside as citizens weighed the financial impact of dispensary profits on their county as well as the social harm they saw arising from the dispensary. In terms of dispensary finances, Aiken County was middling compared to other South Carolina counties. The dispensaries in Salley and Wagener served towns that were in reality nothing more than train depots, and as such, these liquor shops brought in very little revenue. Aiken's liquor and beer dispensaries brought in quite a bit more, owing both to Aiken's larger population and the extensive season of the Winter Colony, which brought with it a host of servants, horse trainers, and the like who would have frequented the local liquor shop. (Table 6.1 shows the sales figures for Aiken's three dispensary towns, along with their relative ranking across the state.)

Table 6.1. Aiken County dispensary sales, 1900–1905 (dollars)

Year	County	Aiken	Salley	Wagener
1900	47,958 (17/38)	35,519 (19/92)	6,730 (77/92)	5,709 (80/92)
1901	58,901 (15/38)	43,978 (16/104)	8,143 (80/104)	6,780 (83/104)
1902	66,232 (15/39)	52,070 (12/111)	7,323 (88/111)	6,839 (90/111)
1903	70,234 (16/39)	54,875 (15/109)	8,039 (86/109)	7,320 (87/111)
1904	80,651 (14/39)	59,842 (18/108)	11,524 (88/108)	9,285 (91/108)
1905	91,209 (13/38)	66,243 (16/109)	12,614 (87/109)	12,352 (89/109)

Source: South Carolina General Assembly, State Dispensary Auditor, *Annual Report.*

Note: The figures within parentheses represent the rank of that year's sales among those of all dispensaries in the state.

Table 6.2. Contributions by dispensaries to Aiken County schools, 1900–1905

Year	Percentage of school funds from dispensary
1901	7.3
1902	9.5
1903	9.1
1904	11.9
1905	9.4

Source: South Carolina General Assembly, State Comptroller General, *Annual Report.*

The profits deriving from dispensary sales were divided into three parts, one-third each for the dispensary town (based on its sales), the county, and the county school system. This arrangement benefited the town of Aiken the most, as Salley's and Wagener's sales figures amounted to very little profit. Outside of Aiken the greatest benefit to the county came through the payout to the schools. By 1905 dispensary money amounted to not quite 10 percent of the total school intake (table 6.2).

Although the amount of dispensary income going to schools was significant, it was hardly overwhelming for Aiken County. Because of the extensive development of Horse Creek Valley, Aiken County brought in $54,579 for its school budget for the 1905 fiscal year, more money in school taxes each year than all but five other South Carolina counties. Aiken's high population of

African American schoolchildren (whose education was underfunded in Aiken, as it was across the state) kept payouts to Aiken's school system lower than South Carolina's other mill counties; compared with Greenville and Spartanburg, which exhausted almost their entire school budgets in 1905, Aiken used only $35,585 (63 percent of its total intake). The result in Aiken County was a surplus of $18,994, an amount that would have been considerable even had the $5,166 in dispensary funds been removed.

THE LIQUOR PROBLEM IN AIKEN COUNTY

Although profits accrued from dispensary sales were not significant enough to move Aiken County residents to defend their liquor shops, neither did the social harm arising from dispensary sales register much alarm across the county. A close reading of Aiken's newspapers from this period revealed nary a complaint about the dispensary in Aiken or in the county beyond. This is not to say that Aiken County residents saw no harm in drinking alcoholic beverages. Citizens did indeed have concerns about alcohol, but they associated this social harm with illegal alcohol sales stemming from the proliferation of blind tigers. Of particular concern for Aiken citizenry was the perceived low quality of illegal booze and the likelihood that such unregulated liquor could lead to sporadic outbreaks of violence. Other commentators stressed the saloon-like quality of illegal sites of sale, worrying that such places could undermine the civic life and political stability of Aiken County.

Violence in Aiken took two forms in the early twentieth century, both seemingly random and therefore frightening. One type tended to be the work of small numbers of people who were said to roam the countryside with evil intent. By 1905 random attacks in the rural sections of Aiken County had become so ubiquitous that they interfered with county functions. In his 1905 annual advertisement given to the papers, the Aiken County treasurer informed his fellow citizens, "I do not think it would be doing justice to myself or the county to risk my life and their money by traveling through the country in private conveyance as heretofore and so in the future I will only go to such points as can be reached by mail." "It seems a sad commentary on civilization in South Carolina," wrote the *Augusta Chronicle,* "that the treasurer of Aiken County is obliged to advertise that he will not visit points in the county not touched by railroads, for the purpose of collecting taxes on account of the numerous hold-ups. No one can blame the county treasurer when ... at least half a dozen hold-ups have taken place around Aiken and no arrests made."[6]

Although holdups were no doubt a concern, even more frightening was the specter of mob violence, a situation that erupted with increasing frequency, especially in Horse Creek Valley. In one such incident "a bloody riot occurred on the Augusta-Aiken trolley line on Saturday night in which one man lost his life and four others were wounded. Eight or ten men took part in the shooting and about forty shots were fired.... Car No. 108 left Augusta at 9:30 and when it was in front of Dr. Mealing's residence in North Augusta about one mile on the Carolina side, a row started between Maxie Boyd and a negro named Charles Willis. Boyd was drinking and cursed the negro and asked him if he didn't like it. Willis said he didn't and pulled his knife.... The conductor put the negro off the car and this angered him and as he stepped from the car he drew his pistol and commenced firing. The car was soon emptied of its passengers and both white and colored who were armed took part in the shooting."[7]

Despite the implication that riots such as these were at least partially due to alcohol, not all commentators saw it that way. "The race riot at Langley was caused by forcing the white passengers to go into the colored coach for standing room," argued one citizen. "If the railroads will give their passengers a seat in the cars on Saturdays you will never have a riot on them.... Passengers are taken on to as great a number as 135 to ride 25 miles perhaps when the capacity is only 48. You can see the terrible condition we are placed in, just like a cattle car and with no comfort or safety."[8] Others saw violence as resulting from the widespread use of pistols, leading the "Aiken County Law and Order League [to] call on the county commissioners ... requesting that the commissioner authorize the sheriff to appoint two deputies to enforce the law against carrying concealed weapons."[9]

But for other writers the role of moonshine liquor was paramount. This intoxicant, referred to as "tussac" liquor by local writers, was said to be brewed "down in the Edisto River section of Aiken County [where] thick swamps [and] the distiller of 'tussac' liquor has long reigned." A combination of cheap molasses, alcohol, and concentrated lye, tussac was described as "powerful in its effect, unrelenting in its power, unbounded in its capacity for mischief. One drink of tussac will make a man think he is once more than a child of the stone age when cruel might held sway and the weak and helpless were objects of disgust and hatred. Two drinks of tussac will make a man angry with the wife of his bosom, enraged with his children. Three drinks of tussac will make a man a maniac and four drinks will kill him. One quart of tussac will destroy the peace of the community, one gallon will convert a camp meeting into a barbaric orgy, a barrel would overthrow a principality."[10]

To fight this menace, wrote the *Aiken Journal and Review*, "the good people … in this county have organized a local law and order league to fight the growing spirit of lawlessness which they say is destroying their young men, disorganizing their churches, and demoralizing their community." At the root of this lawlessness the Edisto Law and Order League placed the locally brewed liquor, which they pointed out "is made and sold in their community without any regard for law or license." As a result of the widespread use of tussac liquor, "white men [needed] to be hauled away from church because they were too drunk to stay there. Fathers have followed their sons at night to haunts in the woods where drinking gambling and carousing is nearly always in progress. One such resort is said to be within a mile of the Tabernacle Church."[11] Another Law and Order League member "stated that there are blind tigers in his neighborhood and the authorities seemed ignorant of them, and yet several people have been killed lately. Rowdies with Winchesters go around shooting promiscuously and do not seem to fear the law."[12] Shortly after its organization in late 1905, the Edisto Law and Order League issued a proclamation aimed at local tussac producers, "earnestly admonishing all persons engaged in this unlawful activity to discontinue same at once. . . . All persons who do not heed this admonition will be dealt with according to law."[13]

In the Horse Creek Valley section of Aiken County, Law and Order League members were more concerned with the possibility that illegal sites of alcohol sales would also double as sites of political organization. Some of this apprehension reflected the bias of so-called town people across South Carolina who looked askance at the political appeal of candidates who resisted the progressive agenda among mill villagers.[14] Horse Creek Valley had long been a bastion of open labor support, and as such, any political movement supported by mill villagers was looked upon with great wariness and often labeled as illegitimate. "By 1904," according to the *State*, "the Horse Creek Valley had acquired an unsavory reputation for the widespread practice of bribery, according to a local editor, 'political corruption having been allowed to grow and flourish there' for years."[15] Such arguments about the easy corruption of millworkers were easier to maintain when alcohol was said to be a contributing factor. One commentator argued that "he could take fifteen hundred dollars and open four or five blind tigers in the factory district . . . and get elected to any office regardless of his fitness."[16]

The 1904 election season had been a particularly rancorous one in Aiken County, and its result had "left a very bad taste in the mouths of all persons who have any right to any pretension of decency, for it was the most corrupt election held since reconstruction and radical days."[17] Of special concern was the alleged bribery of not only voters but also candidates, among them Cal Courtney, who wrote to his fellow citizens, warning them of such dangers: "In my public and private life I have always endeavored to do what is right and to earn the respect of my neighbors in Aiken County. I was therefore much surprised that certain parties approached me with the request that I withdraw from the race for the house of representatives in favor of other candidates and as an inducement for my withdrawal should offer to pay my expenses and even intimated that . . . cash would be given me if I but named the amount."[18]

Aiken County's citizens identified the evils associated with liquor sales, lawlessness and political corruption, which had brought about prohibition in other counties and eventually led to the demise of the entire state-run system. Yet across Aiken County the dispensary system rarely came under attack. Instead, good government advocates argued that the county could be cleaned up by ensuring that dispensary officials be elected by popular vote, limiting the activities of illegal producers, whose whiskey was understood to be far more dangerous than the dispensary product, and cracking down on illegal liquor dealers, who could exert an inordinate political influence on less-educated voters.

WHO DRANK WHERE?

What Aiken County did not share with other counties that adopted prohibition was the problem of significant social disorder related to drinking in the vicinity of its county dispensaries. Therefore, Aiken citizens could focus on illegal liquor sales as the root of their county's problems, leaving dispensaries untouched. It is of course virtually impossible to ascertain with any certainty exactly who purchased liquor at any South Carolina dispensary. The law requiring individual signatures, which might have been used to glean such information, was apparently rarely followed, and the remaining records of the dispensary housed in the state archives offer no such list of signatories. Despite this lack, several pieces of information, taken together, strongly suggest that Aiken County millworkers, who prompted other counties to pass dry laws, tended to do their carousing across the border, in Augusta. Aiken County, then, was largely free of such disturbances in its three dispensary towns.

Salley's and Wagener's liquor sales totals were minimal, and their location far from the mills likely meant there was little threat of public disorder associated with their dispensaries. Sales figures from the Aiken dispensary also provide clues about who purchased liquor there. The first such clue can be gleaned from the seasonal distribution of liquor sales. Table 6.3 demonstrates that dispensary sales were largely seasonal, with the winter months predominating. This trend reflects the rhythms of the planting and harvest seasons for what was a largely rural population. It also points to the impact of the Winter Colonists. The season for northerners to visit Aiken typically ran from early December through mid-April. Aiken dispensary sales peaked at the beginning of this period and only truly dropped off during the summer months.

County sales records also list the types of liquor carried in each dispensary. In addition to the South Carolina dispensary brands (rye and corn whiskey in various grades from *X* to *XXXX*), dispensaries could also provide their

Table 6.3. Aiken County's average dispensary sales, by month, 1900–1905 (dollars)

	Aiken	*Salley*	*Wagener*
January	5,631	938	677
February	3,666	136	188
March	4,542	224	252
April	4.294	122	183
May	1,364	262	250
June	2,214	213	165
July	2,488	112	162
August	2,532	197	219
September	3,502	634	486
October	3,203	788	519
November	6,631	1,150	1,007
December	4,751	1,080	919

Source: South Carolina General Assembly, State Dispensary Auditor, *Annual Report.*

customers with various out-of-state products spanning the whole range of alcoholic beverages. The supply at any dispensary was based primarily on predicted sales, with dispensers keeping on hand only what they thought their customers would buy. An examination of stock lists from individual dispensaries shows that Aiken's were among the most varied across the state, with only Charleston carrying a wider variety of alcohol (table 6.4). Likely, such variety would have appealed to Aiken's northern visitors. Included in Aiken's supply were cognacs, brandies, whiskeys, wines, champagne, bourbons, scotches, rums, gins, vodkas, and tequilas; other than Aiken, only Charleston and Columbia dispensaries carried such varied stock lists.

South Carolina dispensary law made it possible for Aiken's tourist hotels to offer such variety to the guests in 1894 with an exemption that read, "The State Board of Control shall have the power, upon proper showing and under such rules as they may adopt, to exempt hotels where tourists or health-seekers resort from being considered nuisances or as violating this [the dispensary] act by reason of the manager of these hotels dispensing liquor bought form the dispensary ... but before such exemption shall be granted the State Board of Control shall require the manager of such hotel to give good and sufficient bond in the penal sum of three thousand dollars."[19] Not all hotels across South Carolina could post such a bond, but secure in the constancy of their wealthy northern clientele, Aiken's Highland Park and Park in the Pines Hotels both readily posted bonds.

Table 6.4. Number of liquor items in county dispensaries, 1900–1905

Number of items	Counties
1–25	Abbeville, Berkeley, Chesterfield, Colleton, Edgefield, Fairfield, Hampton, Horry, Oconee, Pickens, Saluda, York
26–50	Bamberg, Barnwell, Beaufort, Cherokee, Chester, Clarendon, Darlington, Dorchester, Kershaw, Laurens, Lee, Lexington, Marion, Newberry, Union
51–75	Anderson, Florence, Greenville, Orangeburg, Spartanburg, Sumter
76–100	Georgetown, Richland
100+	Aiken, Charleston

Source: Monthly reports of county dispensers, South Carolina State Archives.

Of course, just because Aiken's hotels bought dispensary liquor does not mean that Horse Creek Valley millworkers were not also dispensary customers; after all, mill hands could have reached Aiken via the Augusta-Aiken interurban railway. The interurban also ran to Augusta, and thus millworkers had a choice of where to purchase liquor. In making this choice, workers likely would have been swayed by the conditions surrounding these liquor outlets. The first was the dispensary law, which prohibited drinking on the premises. Although it was not always vigorously enforced, the police could patrol those areas, making it a less hospitable environment than that offered by Augusta's saloons, many of which operated largely free from police surveillance unless partiers drifted too close to Augusta's residential sections. Second, carousers in Augusta's saloons could extend their revelry longer than in Aiken. The Augusta-Aiken Railway's last scheduled departure for Horse Creek Valley towns left Augusta at ten thirty on Friday and Saturday nights, whereas Aiken's last departure time was eight thirty.

Finally, there was the cost of liquor at the different outlets. As the dispensary was (at least among legal dealers) a monopoly, it was free to charge whatever prices it felt were appropriate, while Augusta's saloons faced keen competition within the city, which kept prices lower. As the editor of the *Aiken Independent* pointed out, "Aiken County is peculiarly situated, a large part of the county being connected with the city of Augusta by a trolley line, which affords quick transportation to the open bar room where liquors can be bought cheaper that at the dispensaries and to these people it matters not whether there be prohibition or the dispensary as they will continue to purchase liquor in Augusta."[20] The resulting lack of social disorder near Aiken County's dispensaries meant a quiet summer and fall of 1905 across the county. While other counties were working feverishly to prohibit liquor sales, the "dispensary situation" was "not agitating the people in Aiken County, the majority of the people being apparently indifferent."[21]

THE LIQUOR QUESTION IN GEORGIA

Like Aiken County, which saw its options with regards to liquor control limited by actions taken by the state, Augusta's discussions about its liquor problem were shaped by the actions of the Georgia legislature.[22] As was the case in South Carolina, post–Civil War anti-liquor agitation bore its first fruits with local legislation aimed at curbing the liquor trade. By the early 1880s, 78 of Georgia's 145 counties had enacted "three mile laws," so named because they eliminated saloons within three miles of any church or school in the county. In other counties prohibition was established, while still others experimented with other forms of alcohol control. During this time, Georgia prohibition historian Henry Anselm Scomp notes, "the legislatures passed a great number of local acts, affecting several hundred towns, churches, factories and communities. . . . Indeed, no county in the State was left wholly unaffected by the restrictive statutes."[23]

Seeking to bring some order to this patchwork legislation, anti-alcohol advocates across the state joined forces in the early 1880s in search of a statewide county option law that would allow them to dry up larger areas of land more quickly. Although they initially met with failure in the early 1880s, by 1885 dry forces succeeded in electing a local option legislature, with the result being a county option bill enacted a few months later. This law stipulated that "upon application by petition, signed by one-tenth of the voters . . . shall order an election . . . to determine whether or not spirituous liquors shall be sold within limits of such designated places. . . . If a majority of votes shall be against sale, it shall not be lawful for any person within the limit of such county to sell . . . any alcoholic, spirituous, malt or intoxicating liquors."[24] Although the law seemed on first glance to be a straight-out local prohibition measure, section 8 made clear that the legislature intended it only as an antisaloon measure, allowing that "nothing in this act shall be construed to prevent the manufacture, sale or use of domestic wines or ciders, or the sale of wines for sacramental purposes; provided such wines and ciders shall not be sold in bar-rooms."[25]

Following the adoption of local option, counties across Georgia experimented with barroom prohibition. In many rural counties, where saloons were few in number prior to 1885, their removal caused little consternation. In urban areas such as Atlanta the loss of revenue from bar license fees, coupled with the quickly multiplying number of blind tigers, led citizens to readopt liquor sales. Smaller towns, too, faced the seeming ineffectiveness of prohibition. "Our city has been filled with bar-rooms ever since prohibition went into effect, and they are constantly increasing," wrote the editor of the *Athens Daily Banner*. "They are run as openly as if licensed—you can always tell these resorts by the half-tipsy men standing at the doors. They are making prohibition a farce for a man can get all the beer and whisky he wants."[26] Manifestly, prohibition had failed, yet Athenians viewed a return to saloons with equal disdain.

As a way around this dilemma, the Clarke County prohibition club proposed an adaptation of the Gothenburg [Göteborg], Sweden, liquor control system, in which the town itself would open and run a liquor dispensary. Pitched as "a temperance measure, framed by temperance men,"[27] the dispensary idea seemed like a way to rid the town of saloons (either legal or illegal) once and for all. Of course, winning an election for a local dispensary did not establish one, as the state of Georgia's liquor law allowed for no such option. Clarke County prohibitionists sent a delegation to the Georgia legislature, making the claim that the dispensary should be seen as an extension of the local prohibition law, which had already licensed druggists to sell liquor. According to the *Atlanta Constitution,* "The dispensary simply takes the sale out of the hands of physicians and drug stores and puts it in the hands of the city."[28]

Athenians imagined little resistance to their dispensary request, as it was merely a local measure that would not impact the state as a whole. Surprisingly, several state legislators did protest that, because Athens was the site of the state university, easy access to liquor would serve as too great a temptation to the student body. Ultimately, these legislators were swayed by testimony from university chancellor Williams E. Boggs, who testified that in his estimation the dispensary "is a better plan than the blind tigers [that flourished under prohibition] but also that it is a preferable alternative to open barrooms."[29]

The resulting dispensary law bore all the same features of the South Carolina law that would come a year later. Sales to minors and drunkards were prohibited, no drinking was permitted on the premises, and the dispensary was to close at sunset each day and was to remain closed on Elections Days, holidays, and days when the circus or other major event made its way into town. No liquor was to be sold to university students, except with written permission of the university chancellor. Any profits, which were understood to be incidental to the dispensary's operation and not actively sought out, were to be divided equally between the town of Athens and Clarke County.[30]

The dispensary opened on October 6, 1891, with the *Athens Daily Banner* announcing its arrival with the heading: "Presto Change! With the Rising Sun Begins a New Era." The editor further opined: "The Dispensary will be started as an untried experiment, and much depends on its management as to whether it will be a success. If the law is strictly enforced, and there is no reason why it should not be since it is in such reliable hands, then it will be a success. The average Athenian citizen will necessarily feel rather queer today when it dawns upon his mind that for the first time in over six years he can walk up to the counter and buy the ardent legally. The United States license is here, and the whiskeys have been analyzed by Prof. H. C. White and all pronounce to be pure; the spirits have been bottled up and sealed and made ready for sale; and the rules have been adopted by which the dispensary is to be controlled. And this morning with the rising sun, the doors of the dispensary will fly open and the thirsty Athenian can wet his whistle."[31]

The dispensary became big news throughout Georgia and in neighboring states as well, and state and local lawmakers from across the Southeast came to see the new liquor shop. By the end of its first year of operation the *Athens Daily Banner* reported that the experiment "has worked so well that to all appearances the entire community is satisfied with the decision."[32] In neighboring Oglethorpe County the editor of the *Oglethorpe Echo* wrote: "We are inclined to think that this will prove the solution of the whiskey traffic problem. . . . If the sale of whiskey is an evil, the better it is controlled the less the evil. The dispensary puts it under the control of the municipal authority. They can so regulate its sale as to lessen its objectionable features to a great extent. . . . It will also keep revenues at home and in the hands of the government, which can spend it on education and other improvements. . . . We think it has come to stay."[33] Over the next decade twenty-four of Georgia's counties experimented with their own dispensaries, with fifteen of them retaining their county-run liquor stores until the onset of state prohibition some fifteen years later.

By the turn of the century, then, Georgia offered its counties a varied menu of potential options to address the question of liquor sales: open saloons with high license fees, have county-run dispensaries, or enact outright prohibition. Financial records make clear that the choices made by Georgia's counties were influenced by the same economic considerations as those in South Carolina. Each liquor dealer in the state (either saloonkeeper or county dispenser) was required to pay a state tax of two hundred dollars, with the entirety of the state liquor tax being used to help Georgia's public school fund. Over time not only did liquor profits increase, but their percentage of the public school allotment went up as well, rising from 6.8 percent in 1898 to 13.5 percent by 1906.[34] The growing dependence on liquor sales made it increasingly unlikely that

Georgia's state legislators would seek prohibition without worrying about its impact on the state's school system.

Of course, it was still possible for prohibitionists to dry up Georgia on a county-by-county basis should they be able to garner the necessary votes. Of Georgia's 145 counties many consisted entirely of sparsely populated rural areas that were both fruitful ground for dry campaigners and arid ground for potential liquor dealers. Among sellers few could imagine earning enough in sales to offset the costs of both maintaining a business and paying the state and local licenses. Georgia's four largest cities (Atlanta, Savannah, Augusta, and Macon), each with a population exceeding twenty-five thousand by 1900, promised far greater riches for liquor dealers. Although each city could (and did) charge a municipal license fee in addition to the one required by the state, such fees were more easily counterbalanced by the large number of potential customers. By 1906 Georgia's four largest cities accounted for three-quarters of the state's liquor tax. Within each municipality saloon taxes also contributed significantly to the overall civic budget (table 6.5).

It was in Georgia's smaller cities that the prohibition battle was most hotly contested. In these places local populations were not large enough to attract liquor sellers, but a local dispensary, in which the municipality and county split whatever profits came from liquor sales, was often considered a viable option. Unfortunately, dispensary profits were not tracked by the state, and the only county liquor store that was reported on consistently, likely because of its standing as the first dispensary, was the store in Athens, which saw profits rise from $11,000 in 1900 to $55,573 in 1906.[35] Although Athens's population of roughly fourteen thousand gave it a somewhat larger pool from which to draw customers than other Georgia towns, it nevertheless

Table 6.5. Municipal liquor taxes in Georgia's four largest cities, 1905

City	Municipal liquor tax	Number of saloons	Saloon municipal fees	Percentage of liquor fees in total city budget
Atlanta	$1,000	129	$129,512	9.6
Augusta	$400	96	$38,400	9.9
Macon	$500	68	$34,000	11.8
Savannah	$250	217	$54,337	7.3

Source: Georgia General Assembly, State Comptroller General, Annual Report, 38.

Table 6.6. Population and local option status in Georgia counties, 1890–1906

Largest population center	-5,000	5,000–20,000	+20,000
Had saloons throughout local option period	—	—	5
Had dispensaries throughout local option period	7	8	—
Adopted dispensaries, then rejected them	—	9	—
Had prohibition throughout local option period	115	1	—
Total	122	18	5

Sources: U.S. Bureau of the Census, Twelfth Census; Georgia General Assembly, State Comptroller General, Annual Report.

provides a point of comparison for the likely profits those other towns might have seen.

The profitability of Georgia's various saloons and dispensaries, then, often impacted the decisions counties made in local option elections. Most counties with population centers under five thousand consistently opted for prohibition, while those whose largest towns had populations above that number experimented, at least for a time, with a county dispensary (table 6.6). Georgia's largest cities each continued to house saloons throughout the entire local option period.

THE "LIQUOR PROBLEM" IN AUGUSTA

As one of Georgia's largest population centers, Augusta naturally reaped a financial windfall from permitting saloons to operate within its borders. Although this income offered a strong enticement to continue liquor sales, it was counterbalanced by the rapid influx of lower-class whites and African Americans in search of work in Augusta's textile mills and related industry. Thus, middle- and upper-class Augustans had to reckon the value of their liquor profits against the potential social harm and disorder that could result if their city's newest citizens were permitted easy access to saloons.

Several rounds of agitation between the Ministerial Alliance, the Liquor Dealers' Mutual Protective Association, and the "conservative business interests" led to a system, adopted in November 1904, in which the town permitted liquor sales but restricted them in two ways. First, each liquor dealer was required to pay a yearly four hundred–dollar license fee. Second, territorial restrictions limited the operation of liquor stores to only those sections of the city that were removed from churches and schools and were not exclusively residential in nature.[36] This compromise was not reached without considerable political wrangling, and the opinions held by the various segments of Augusta's population about their so-called liquor problem presaged North Augusta's dispensary fight.

Discussions about Augusta's saloons emerged from a growing consensus that "the saloon that is located too near some church or school house or in some residential section of the city where it is not wanted, OR THE DIVE THAT CATERS ONLY TO THE LOWEST ORDER OF HUMANITY, is not only a public nuisance but a public danger."[37] Enumerating the conditions inside Augusta's saloons became fodder for Sunday sermons, as in these words from Baptist minister Osa P. Gilbert: "I have personally inspected a number of these places. There are pictures hanging on the walls of these saloons that are too vile for public display. . . . In the twenty-five or thirty places there are gambling dens in the rear of the saloons."[38]

Nor was it easy to eradicate the saloon evil because the liquor trust reached into all corners of the city's politics. "I refer you to the recent election for Council in the Second Ward," pointed out Minister Gilbert to his parishioners. "Two men were running for council. One was a saloon man. The other was a prominent gentleman of the city and a leading member of one of the leading churches of the city. Who was elected? The saloon man."[39] Once in power, "they voted the saloon upon us. They voted it under the doors of helpless women and children who did not want it. What they did has been done in every section of the city. They have voted them into existence at the very doors of churches, as if the people were accustomed to going out of church into the saloons."[40]

Although many Augustans agreed with church leaders that such businesses posed a threat, they were less in agreement about the threat's true source and therefore what might be the best response to it. Some emphasized the saloon itself as a site of temptation to sin. "The weak and thoughtless enter into these places," wrote Minister Gilbert, "and are entrapped by the damnable vices found there."[41] According to this view, only one remedy was possible in the fight against the saloon, "prohibition, the wiping out of the evil."[42] Others emphasized individual sin and frailty, beginning with the assumption that people would often fall into bad behavior (and drink), whatever their social surroundings. Because the primary social problem, as they saw it, was not the saloon but the drunkard, they argued for "the LEGAL sale of whiskey— because we believe prohibition means the ILLEGAL sale of whiskey. We regard the sale of liquor as a necessary evil, and we simply prefer to have such sale legally carried on under strict police regulations and within proscribed limits than to see blind tigers spring up in out of the way places all over the city."[43]

Discussions adjudicating these disparate points of view did not take place in a vacuum, and a close reading of Augusta's newspapers suggests that two other factors played important roles in the city's decision to adopt high license fees and territorial restrictions on saloons, rather than outright prohibition. The first was money, as some citizens feared that "property values across the city would be depreciated" if saloons were removed, leaving empty shops.[44] Other Augustans worried about the impact of a reduction on Augusta's income from saloons, which at the turn of the century amounted to roughly fifteen to twenty thousand dollars per year.[45] Still others pointed to "the records of the police department and the extra cost of policing the outlying territory in which these saloons are located" as sufficient argument in favor of raising the license fees on liquor shops.[46] Beyond these financial necessities, raising license fees might also guarantee a cleaner saloon business, or so the *Chronicle*'s editor argued: "If there is a so-called saloon in Augusta that can't pay the city $500 a year for the privilege of selling liquor—LESS THAN IT COSTS THE CITY TO POLICE THE TERRITORY IN WHICH IT IS LOCATED—that saloon ought to go out of business. What can you say for a business whose license is worth more than its stock and trade? Doesn't it strike you that there is something wrong with such a business? Does any reasonable man doubt that the liquor business ought to be taken out of the hands of such people as these, and confined to people of GREATER PERSONAL AND FINANCIAL RESPONSIBILITY?"[47]

A second concern of Augustans was ensuring peace and safety throughout the city, but especially in its residential sections. "Every new barroom would immediately result in the loss of peaceful homes to every citizen in that locality," worried one citizen. "The home makers who have spent their best years there, always paying into the city's treasury whatever assessments were made, and helped to maintain a peaceable government, have a right to demand freedom from a bar room in their midst."[48] Another Augustan commented, "It is unfair to the residents of outlying sections of the city that some man should be allowed to open up a barroom under the very noses of their wives and children and almost at the very doors of their schools and churches."[49]

Ultimately, argued the editor of the *Chronicle*, the combination of high license fees and territorial restrictions "simply means $300 per month more for the privilege of selling liquor in Augusta, and decent orderly saloons. . . . It also means fewer saloons—but it does not mean that you or any other man can't buy all the liquor you can pay for. . . . Will anybody contend that forty or fifty saloons can't supply the demands of this city and surrounding territory for liquor? IT IS UP TO THE COUNCIL TO SAY WHETHER OR NOT WE SHALL HAVE A RATIONAL SALOON SYSTEM IN AUGUSTA."[50]

The city council's final vote for this "rational system" sought greater financial benefits of saloon taxes while minimizing their territorial damage for the most well-off of the city's residents. Raising license fees from $200 to $400 a year ($100 less than anti-liquor advocates had demanded) for each of Augusta's ninety-six barrooms guaranteed the city $38,400 in saloon taxes from 1905 to 1907, roughly 10 percent of the city's total revenue for those years.[51] The city's territorial restrictions limited the saloon operation to one of three sections of the city: the business district, which housed sixty-two saloons; the mill villages of the West End, which housed eighteen saloons; and the African American neighborhood southeast of the city, which housed sixteen saloons. The middle- and upper-class white neighborhoods in the Pinched Gut District, Summerville, and North Augusta were all free of liquor shops.[52]

Of course, these territorial limits meant little if "beastly drunk men or boys with money gone could be rolled out over the divide [into saloon-free neighborhoods] and left there in the open to sleep off the debauch."[53] Keeping the streets free of drunkards was tasked to Augusta's police, and their yearly activity reports show that arrests for drunk and disorderly offenses made up roughly three-quarters of all arrests in Augusta for the years 1902–7. The majority of these arrests came not from the central business district, which housed most of Augusta's saloons, but typically from sections with both saloons and residences or areas where saloons from one district were in close proximity to residents from another, such as North Augusta (table 6.7). North Augustans would likely have been accustomed to encountering drunkards emerging from West End saloons near the corner of Thirteenth (McKinnie) and Broad Streets, either as they walked or rode across the Thirteenth Street bridge. Not surprisingly, the numbers of arrests near that corner increased dramatically as North Augusta's population grew. This spatial strategy of liquor regulation allowed Augusta the financial benefits of saloons while also guaranteeing that continued alcohol-fueled disturbances could be contained within certain parts of the city.

Table 6.7. Police patrols by city section, 1902–1907

	Southeast	West End	City Center	Pinched Gut District	Pinched Gut District / City Center	Pinched Gut District / West End	West End / North Augusta
1902	398	250	113	103	215	215	272
1903	294	597	123	87	229	294	403
1904	300	761	105	89	240	241	434
1905	282	939	77	38	173	227	556
1906	286	918	76	60	159	217	463
1907	314	969	76	59	247	197	610

Source: City of Augusta, Georgia, *Mayor's Message.*

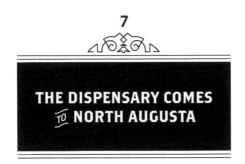

7

THE DISPENSARY COMES _TO_ NORTH AUGUSTA

Before 1907 the South Carolina dispensary system's chief impact on the town was through its purchase of liquor jugs from the town's pottery companies. If North Augustans wanted to drink, they likely traveled either across the bridge to Broad Street or, if given an invitation, to the Hampton Terrace Hotel. Few would have traveled to the nearest county dispensary, some eighteen miles away in Aiken. Although they provided little income for the town, none of North Augusta's local liquor outlets threatened the town's peaceful suburban idyll, though drunkards stumbling onto McKinnie Street and the occasional drunken episode while riding the Augusta-Aiken interurban likely caused consternation for travelers to and from Augusta's central business district. North Augusta had managed to isolate itself from the liquor problem that plagued other southern communities, and therefore its citizens had shown little interest in the issue. All this was about to change.

PROHIBITION IN THE PEACH STATE

The impetus behind North Augusta becoming a focal point in the prohibition debate occurred many miles away, in Atlanta, beginning with the gubernatorial race in 1906.[1] The newly formed Georgia Anti-Saloon League (GASL) worked actively in support of Hoke Smith, a successful attorney and owner of the _Atlanta Journal_. Smith was known to be a temperance supporter, albeit one whose instincts led him more toward local option as the ideal remedy to the liquor problem. Nevertheless, both the GASL and the state Woman's Christian Temperance Union (WCTU) believed that Smith could be persuaded to adopt prohibition if enough pressure were applied. Smith's chief opponent was the editor of the *Atlanta Constitution,* Clark Howell, making this campaign one not only between two men but also two newspapers, each trying to outdo the other in affixing negative labels on its rival.

No label was more damaging to a political candidate in Georgia in 1906 than being soft on black disfranchisement. Part of the reason was political, as neither candidate had enough support by themselves to win an election without help from populist leader Tom Watson, who had made black disfranchisement the price of such support. Part of it was due to the rapidly deteriorating race relations in Georgia after the turn of the century. White progressives sought black elimination from the polls as the only sure way to ensure the success of their agenda (it was widely assumed that black pro-liquor votes would be bought by liquor dealers), while other whites, concerned about the "wave" of black attacks on white women and the resulting rise in lynchings, argued that the only way to secure racial peace was to eliminate black voting rights.

Liquor played an important part in these narratives, with southern progressive Alexander McKelway remarking that because drunkenness was responsible for crimes ascribed to African Americans, "whiskey must be taken out of their hands."[2] Rebecca Latimer Felton, the head of the Georgia WCTU, echoed these sentiments, declaring that white women had become the helpless victims of "drunken raving human beasts," and went so far as to advocate lynching as a deterrent to the crime of rape.[3]

The summer campaign of 1906 was punctuated by a series of alleged rapes of young white women by black men in and around Atlanta. Each new report brought increasingly sensationalized headlines and op-ed pieces proclaiming that newspaper's favored candidate to be the only real choice to avert such horrors in the future. These stories also encouraged white citizens to take the law into their own hands. On August 1, 1906, the *Constitution* reported that a group of thirty white citizens tracked and shot a black man accused of raping a fourteen-year-old white girl. Less than two weeks later, a black man accused of a similar crime was dragged from a swamp near Atlanta and lynched while a crowd of over one thousand spectators looked on. On August 24 Georgia governor Joseph Terrell offered a $250 reward for the capture of an African American accused of assaulting two women. Between September 1 and 21 there were two more attempted rapes in the city. With tensions reaching a peak, on September 22 a mob of ten thousand whites attacked the African American section of Atlanta, pulling passengers from trolley cars and murdering at least fifteen. For five days Atlanta was in a virtual state of siege as state troops and militia attempted to bring order. All the while the Atlanta newspapers continued their war of words and candidates, in the process continually reigniting racial tensions.

Assessing the wreckage after the violence subsided, many Georgians pointed the finger at drunkenness as the major cause of the Atlanta race riot. Predictably, among this group was the Georgia WCTU, which in its annual report accused Atlanta saloons of displaying nude pictures of women, thus precipitating violent behavior among their clientele.[4] To many Georgians prohibition now seemed the best method to usher in a "return to reason in the South."[5] The WCTU declared that 92 percent of all crime in Georgia was the result of the liquor traffic and denounced saloons as the "hot bed of crime, anarchy and bloodshed—hence the enemy of law and order."[6]

At least partly due to the events of September 1906 and the shrill coverage of them in the *Journal* and *Constitution,* the gubernatorial race, which ended in a victory for Smith, also resulted in a legislature sympathetic to a statewide prohibition bill. Unconcerned by Governor Smith's inaugural address, in which he expressed the desire to see local option continued, the WCTU and ASL campaigned aggressively across the state and within the legislature, convinced that if a prohibition bill were laid on the governor's desk, he would have no choice but to sign it. While support for prohibition was strong in Georgia's 125 rural counties, the city councils of Atlanta, Augusta, Columbus, and Savannah adopted resolutions opposing the passage of the prohibition bill. One Atlanta alderman voiced the opinion of many when he said, "We stand for dryness of Sunday and a portion of the night, but we don't want it all the time."[7]

Chief among the anti-prohibitionist's concerns was the loss of revenue from whiskey sales. Antis declared the losses could mount up to $250,000, and they were not far off; in 1906 Georgia collected $243,000 from the liquor tax. Financial concerns were also at the heart of Augusta's anti-liquor campaign. In response to an inquiry made by the Georgia Liquor Dealers' Association concerning the impact of prohibition on Augusta's real estate, W. Lyon Martin, the city council clerk, calculated "it will adversely affect Augusta realty generally from ten percent to twenty percent . . . [and] advanced the opinion that it would be ten years before Augusta realty gets back to its present worth if state prohibition goes into effect in 1908 or 1909."[8] Based on such prognostications, the Augusta Chamber of Commerce went on record as being strongly opposed to prohibition, passing the following resolutions:

> Whereas, the directors of the Chamber of Commerce of Augusta are convinced that the proposed legislation favoring state prohibition will result injuriously to the business and moral welfare of Augusta, take away a considerable portion of its revenue, and reduce the funds now available for the education of the children of the state; and,

> Whereas, it has been proven by the experience of other states that such laws do not prohibit the sale of liquor, but simply result in its sale without the advantage of police regulations; therefore be it

> Resolved by the directors of the Chamber of Commerce of Augusta that this body is opposed to state prohibition;

> Resolved further, that we favor legislation looking to the regulation and control of the jug trade with dry counties;

> Resolved further, that we feel that the counties of the state opposed to the enactment of a state prohibition law should be given the opportunity to present their views before any restrictive legislation be attempted.[9]

Despite the legion of protests form Georgia's urban leaders, the state senate passed the prohibition bill forty-three to seven on July 14, 1907. The House debate proved to be quite a bit more vociferous, as the anti-prohibitionists began a filibuster, which continued for an entire week. On July 25, in an effort to speed the filibuster on its seemingly endless way, the Speaker of the House, John M. Slaton (Fulton County) halted all applause and condemnations from the gallery and warned several times that at the first outburst the galleries would be cleared. Eventually, prohibition legislator Seaborn Wright (Floyd County) had enough and, rising to his feet, interrupted the filibuster by condemning the Speaker for not putting a halt to it.

Wright's speech worked the largely prohibition gallery to such a fever pitch that the Speaker had the galleries cleared. As the sergeant-at-arms attempted to usher out the men and women who were hissing and shouting at the anti-prohibitionists, Representative Hall of Bibb County (Macon) leaped from his seat and accused Wright of being unworthy of his chair and prohibitionists of having created a state of anarchy. Amid the tumult Wright shot back, calling Hall a liar, and the two men came to blows, which understandably added considerably to the bedlam. For twenty minutes the capitol was filled with "the howls and cries of the crowd which thronged the corridors and overran the capitol square."[10] After the Atlanta police forcibly removed the crowds, WCTU president Mary Harris Armor went immediately to the offices of the *Atlanta Constitution*. Once there, she made a defiant public statement condemning the political proceedings and vowing "if we do not get this legislation at once there will be an uprising of the people."[11]

Speaker Slaton kept the galleries clear for the remainder of the prohibition debate, which mercifully ended on July 31 with the passage of the South's first statewide prohibition law. Despite several attempts by the antis to modify the measure through a series of amendments, the bill passed in its original form, prohibiting "the sale or keeping or furnishing in public places or business, or trade, any alcoholic, spirituous, malt or intoxicating liquors, bitters, or other drink that when drunk to excess cause intoxication, except in certain conditions to provide for medicinal purposes. . . . Nothing in this act shall prohibit the sale of alcohol for medicinal, art, scientific or sacramental purposes."[12] When word that the bill had passed reached the crowd assembled outside, the fifteen hundred men and women who had been gathered in prayer vigils for the previous month celebrated the victory with the singing of the doxology amidst a chorus of church bells ringing throughout Atlanta. That night in Valdosta, over two hundred miles away, another celebration of a different nature took place as people poured into the bars of that city, consuming roughly ten thousand dollars' worth of whiskey.[13]

Surveying the new reality in Augusta, the *Chronicle* pointed its finger at the state's least fortunate, arguing:

That this legislation was forced by the race issue can hardly be questioned. The recent riots in Atlanta and the various mob demonstrations throughout the state wherein the vicious negro has been the provoking cause have all had their origin indirectly at least . . . in the whiskey dive. It was believed impossible to stop mob violence as long as the incentive thereto existed, and so the conservative masses, going to the aid of the radical temperance reformers, decided to make a test of total prohibition to learn what effect it would have upon the morals and conduct of the negro. . . . It will, undoubtedly, for a while at least, check the growth of cities and prove a rather expensive experiment for the industrial enterprises. . . . At any rate Georgia has got prohibition and has got it largely because of the negro; and of one thing we may be sure—it will be all to the good for the negro, whatever it may do for his white neighbor.[14]

As for those white neighbors, the *Chronicle* reported that "the city will meet the loss [of revenue] calmly and will offset it by some gains." Among those Augustans who had previously dealt in the liquor trade, "they regret what has been done, as do the majority of Augustans, but are not going to blame the city for it for they know that every business interest in Augusta loyally tried to stay the tide. Augustans have stood by the liquor interests and now, appreciating this, the men who have engaged in the business intend to stand for Augusta and not against it." The *Chronicle* concluded by suggesting that "the outlook for this city is most hopeful. Already the gloom is lifting and Augusta is adjusting herself to the situation. It will all prove for the best eventually."[15] Such faith was soon to be tested.

GEORGIA PROHIBITION AND NORTH AUGUSTA

As the events of July and August unfolded across the Savannah, Aiken County's liquor board began thinking about opening a dispensary in North Augusta. As the proposed liquor shop would open coincidentally with the closing of Augusta's ninety-six saloons, Aiken County leaders were hopeful such a move would keep Horse Creek Valley drinkers away from the county seat and even more hopeful that some (if not all) Augustans might make the short walk across the Thirteenth Street bridge in search of legal liquor. If Augusta's citizens did so, the potential profits to Aiken County would be a windfall compared with the earnings of the county's existing outlets in the county seat of Aiken and its next two largest towns, Salley and Wagener. Together the three towns had a combined population of roughly five thousand in 1900, only one-tenth as large as the number of potential drinkers in Augusta. Summing up the argument, the editor of the *Aiken Journal and Review* did the math for its readers. "From the profits for the last quarter the present dispensaries will make about $32,000 clear this year. If a dispensary is placed in North Augusta and one in Hamburg they would clear twice as much as the present dispensaries do, or $60,000, which would make a total of at least $90,000. The expenses of the county should not be more than $40,000, so there will be a surplus of $50,000."[16]

Although most envisioned these inevitably larger profits continuing to benefit the county schools or be used to improve county roads in need of such services, the editor hinted that perhaps the profits might also be used to help taxpayers more directly: "Some fellow may suggest how to spend this and may be able to influence the Board of Control, but they if they will take our advice they will pay dividends every 1st of January and July, sending to each man known to be an ardent supporter of the dispensary a check as dividend from dispensary profits. The result is easily seen. Every voter would immediately become a dispensaryite and the population would increase, people being anxious to live in a county where instead of paying taxes they receive dividends. Of course some cranky fellows will object to this but we trust the Board will adopt it after January first when prohibition goes into effect in Georgia. We are in favor of dividends and we don't want anybody to show us how or why we can't get them. We believe we ought to have them."[17] Aiken county residents, sitting at a comfortable distance from North Augusta, could afford to engage in sophistry about better schools, new roads, lowering taxes, or the possibility of dividends resulting from dispensary profits. For many citizens of North Augusta the establishment of a dispensary in their town seemed only to promise the threat of "their beautiful little suburban home of women and children being overrun by a booze shop for the accommodation and edification of drunken whites from Augusta and Aiken and Edgefield negroes."[18]

When considering North Augustans' reaction to the proposed liquor shop, it should be noted that prior to the dispensary matter, North Augusta was not a hotbed of prohibition. Not only had its residents shown a willingness to tolerate saloons in Augusta, but within their own town the Hampton Terrace Hotel served liquor to its guests. Instead, those citizens in North Augusta who opposed the dispensary did so in the interest of public safety, much as Aiken's residents sought to do and as Augusta's citizenry had done three years earlier. Letters and petitions to the Aiken County board make clear that North Augustans' interest was in protecting their town, which they understood to be "a town morally far above the ordinary.... The percentage of decent, law-abiding, home loving, town loving citizens is very large, out of all usual proportions in a town of its size. Not a single . . . arrest had been made within the past three months."[19] Another citizen described North Augusta as "quiet and orderly, made up of people who love their homes and to a great extent own their homes . . . where wives and children would be safe on the streets and where we could enjoy perfect quiet and peace."[20]

This peaceful residential town stood in stark contrast to Augusta's "famous McKinnie Street, a well-known center of meanness, immorality and at some times indecency."[21] Concerned primarily for "the personal safety of the inhabitants of North Augusta, especially the women and children,"[22] citizens explained that "at the present time many North Augustans do not enjoy the walk to Augusta on account of the many loafers who hang around the bridge."[23] If a dispensary was established in North Augusta, "the vile McKinnie street gang, the rakings and scrapings, the scurvy of the neighborhood, the refuse of society and the carrion of society would be immediately transferred to North Augusta to trample our town where ladies promenade and children play . . . convert[ing] our town into a boisterous, noisy, ill-smelling, hellhole whose pure air would be filled with vile oaths, curses and a smell of a mixture of mean liquor, onions and peanuts."[24]

Beyond the impact near the bridge itself, dispensary "customers" spread their social ills when they boarded the interurban trolley also patronized by the good people of North Augusta. One citizen painted a graphic picture of the results in a letter to the Aiken County board: "A week or two ago I boarded a car . . . my attention was attracted to a pile on the floor and a smear of filth down the side of the car. Some sot had drank liquor and it was so mean that it wouldn't stay down."[25] Under such conditions, he asked, "would any man of North Augusta like to see his daughter drive across the bridge . . . ? Would any of the pleasure seekers of Augusta drive over to North Augusta . . . to enjoy the beautiful scenery and the pleasure of the country and picnics in the woods, if they had to pass through the crowds of loafers who now hang around the saloons in Augusta?"[26] Surveying the grave damage a dispensary would visit upon North Augusta, one citizen argued that if a liquor shop opened there, he would propose to change the town's name to "just plain Hell, and the Pure Food Law wouldn't accuse me of misbranding."[27] Appended to these testimonials, North Augustans attached a threat to "pledge our influence and support to a prohibition campaign started against dispensaries in Aiken county, and to vote against the sale of liquor in our county at the ballot box, and whenever the opportunity presents itself, *unless this dispensary is removed.*"[28]

Although the majority of North Augusta's residents shared these concerns, support for prohibition was hardly uniform. Evidence of these disparate opinions comes from the signatories to the petitions sent to the Aiken county board. Two such petitions were sent, one each supporting (*n* = 31) and opposing (*n* = 95) the proposed dispensary. Signatories' names were listed in the *Aiken Journal and Review*, and though information on each person was not available, listings in the *Augusta City Directory* (which included North Augusta) confirms that anti-dispensary advocates had reason to emphasize the protection of home and family (table 7.1).[29]

North Augustans' pleas about the character of their community are a little harder to assess, but one way to get a sense of how community oriented citizens were is through their affiliations. Rosters of North Augusta's Baptist and Methodist churches and Augusta's Presbyterian church, which list church officers, local Elks and Masons club member lists, and newspaper records of town council members demonstrate that anti-dispensary advocates were often involved in civic institutions, while those supporting the dispensary were notable in their absence from the positions.[30] In addition to being less tied to family and community, pro-dispensary signatories were more likely to be those with investments in Jackson's North Augusta Land Company or the pottery manufacturers or else temporary laborers who worked in the factories at the foot of the hill (see table 7.1).[31]

Table 7.1. Position on dispensary by marital status, civic involvement, and social class, North Augusta, 1907

	Pro-Dispensary	*Anti-Dispensary*
Marital status	Married 16 (22%)	Married 57 (78%)
	Single 12 (46%)	Single 14 (54%)
Involvement in one or more civic institutions	Yes 9 (14%)	Yes 53 (86%)
	No 19 (46%)	No 22 (54%)
Social class	Investors 8 (67%)	Investors 4 (33%)
	White-collar workers 4 (8%)	White-collar workers 45 (92%)
	Laborers 14 (67%)	Laborers 7 (33%)

Source: City of Augusta, *Augusta City Directory.*

THE BATTLE OVER THE NORTH AUGUSTA DISPENSARY

South Carolina dispensary law both stipulated that the task of adjudicating these disparate dispensary opinions rested with the county dispensary board and gave local citizens the right to petition the board with the presumption that it would take their opinions into their deliberations. Not surprisingly, as the Aiken County Board of Control debated the merits of a dispensary in North Augusta, it received petitions from both pro- and anti-dispensary advocates. Sizing up the determination on both sides, the *Aiken Journal and Review* editor opined, "All in all, the fight over the dispensary at North Augusta may develop into more than a mere 'tempest in a teapot.'"[32]

To give both sides a chance to state their case, each was invited to speak before the meeting of the County dispensary board on December 15, 1907. The antis went first, with Dr. Mealing, Reverends Carpenter and Woodward, and several citizens emphasizing that theirs was a community centered around home, morality, peace, and quiet, all of which would be shattered by a dispensary, which would invite in "the disturbance and liscientiousness [*sic*]" of Augusta's black and poor white populations. The final speaker, J. B. Davenport, summed up these sentiments: "Over there we have an ideal home town, quiet and orderly, made up of people who love their homes and in a great extent of people who own their homes. I, for one, and many others probably, went to North Augusta to find a place where our wives and children would be safe on the streets and where we could enjoy after work hours in perfect quiet and peace, but this dispensary that is threatened will overthrow all of our features that are desirable, and make our streets a place unfit for ladies and children. . . . We don't want it; we don't need it; if we did, we would ask for it."[33]

Tellingly, the principal speakers for the pro-dispensary side, the Honorable T. G. Croft, an Aiken attorney and one of the county's current representatives in the General Assembly, and Leon J. Williams, a former member of the South Carolina State Dispensary Board, were not residents of North Augusta. Likely Croft and other members of the Aiken County leadership relished this opportunity to repay North Augusta's seeming betrayal over the Heyward County matter. Yet with the majority of North Augustan opinion seemingly stacked against the dispensary, county leaders needed a viable reason to ignore this popular mandate. Croft supplied it by playing on the nakedly racist and classist biases of North Augusta's citizens.

The key for Croft was North Augustans' attitudes toward the liquor license held by the Hampton Terrace Hotel, where James U. Jackson entertained wealthy northern industrialists seeking a healthier climate. North Augustans had no objection to this exception to the dispensary law; rich visitors to their town both enhanced its prestige and brought in revenue, and rich drinkers were looked at in a very different light from the rabble of Augusta. "Everyone knows that the rich man is never seen lying drunk in the gutters, or standing on the street corners using vile language, or often getting into shooting scrapes and doing harm to the innocent passerby. If he did he wouldn't be rich," opined one citizen, while an Augusta man noted, "The reason why women of Augusta are now afraid to step out of the house after dark is not because they fear rich people from the hotels will insult them . . . but because they are afraid of the drunkards going home from the saloons."[34]

Croft baited his trap by making the seemingly innocuous point that most of North Augusta was in fact for the dispensary rather than against it, as the anti-dispensaryites had claimed. "Mr. Croft showed that the property represented by the antis amounted to only about $80,170 while the property represented by the other side was more than $300,000. The antis denied this and Mr. Croft began to itemize. He claimed that the interests represented by Mr. James U. Jackson are all with the dispensary side, and that item alone would far exceed the property of the antis. Several antis cried out that Mr. Jackson was with them. 'Then,' said Mr. Croft, 'how can he say that the citizens of North Augusta and surrounding county should be denied privileges he reserves only for his tourist visitors. There he is, ask him.'"[35]

The room quieted as everyone looked toward Jackson. To this point he had studiously avoided discussing his opinions on the dispensary, realizing that any opinion rendered could compromise the license of the Hampton Terrace. Now placed on the spot, he again avoided the question, replying that "he would not be there if he had not received a summons from the Board. He requested the gentlemen not to demand any efforts on his part on one side or the other as his position is an embarrassing one. He said that a hotel privilege is as necessary at the Hampton Terrace as at the Park in the Pines hotel (in Aiken) and he earnestly hoped that the county board would allow matters so far as the hotel privilege is concerned to remain as they are, as he felt sure that no anti-dispensaryite in North Augusta objected to the present arrangement."[36]

It is not clear whether Croft knew in advance how Jackson would respond—he likely could have guessed. Either way, he correctly surmised that few North Augustans would demand the abolition of all liquor sales, including those at the prestigious hotel. He was right. "Almost the entire delegation of antis here spoke up and assured the gentlemen of the county board that there is no objection to the hotel arrangement there but they do not want a dispensary in the town," reported the *Aiken Journal and Review*.[37]

This action closed the meeting, and after some deliberation the board decided to keep the Hampton Terrace liquor license intact and also to grant the dispensary to North Augusta. Summing up the thinking of the board, the *Aiken Journal and Review* referred to the apparent inconsistency in the anti-dispensary position, noting that "in some way the board seemed to take this as indicating a grave inconsistency, a fault to be remedied only by a dispensary at North Augusta."[38]

THE STATE LEGISLATURE DEBATE

This decision was not the end of the matter, as true to their word, the anti-dispensaryites took their case to the state legislature. In doing so, North Augusta's citizens drew upon a wealth of support from around the state—by now most every newspaper editor had denounced Aiken County's blatant attempt "to get money by putting a dispensary under the nose of thirsty Georgians" as "nothing short of an outrage."[39] Noting that "the people of the town of North Augusta did not want it but it was forced upon them,"[40] commentators portrayed the dispensary as "a shame and disgrace to the state of South Carolina. It is nothing more than an open bar-room for the people of Augusta. We hope to see our lawmakers close up the North Augusta liquor shop by making it unlawful to establish a dispensary . . . where the majority of citizens in that town declare against the dispensary."[41] Even editors whose sympathies lay with the dispensary system found the Aiken County board's decision hard to defend: "We believe the dispensary system is to be preferred to prohibition . . . but we see no excuse for the establishment of the North Augusta dispensary. It is a money making proposition pure and simple and is on the same level of the blind tigers that are operated in Augusta in defiance of the Georgia law. The Aiken county board have the legal right to operate a dispensary at North Augusta but have committed a moral wrong against the people of Georgia. If the people of Augusta want liquor bad enough to go all the way to Aiken to get it no objection will be raised, but it is not right or decent to open a liquor shop right under their noses."[42]

Faced with "the strong sentiment that prevails throughout the state against the action of the Aiken county dispensary board in establishing a dispensary in the town of North Augusta against the wishes of the community in order to hold a booze nozzle to the city of Augusta for revenue only . . . the house of representatives this morning pass[ed], without a dissenting voice, a resolution introduced by Mr. Lane of Georgetown, condemning the actions of the Aiken Board as undemocratic and subversive of good government."[43]

With the House prepared to countermand the county board's decision, it looked as if North Augustans would soon be rid of the dispensary—that is, until Representative T. G. Croft returned to the House (he had been absent while the resolution had been debated) to chastise his colleagues for mishandling the matter. Croft began by reminding his fellow legislators that "under the law it is in the discretion of the county board to place a dispensary in any town where, in their judgment, it is to the best interest of the people. Such being the law, what has Aiken County done? How has she violated it?"[44] He then recapitulated the discussions that had taken place before the county board a month earlier, highlighting the obviously conflicted state of North Augustans' opinion on liquor sales as the context that made plausible the county board's decision.

Then, noting that the majority of those opposed to the dispensary also worked in Augusta, Croft appealed to the sovereignty of the state government: "Shortly after the establishment of this dispensary, it seemed to set the moral city of Augusta wild. The city council passed a resolution to send a delegation to this assembly to lobby against our law. They did not rest there. They wanted to charge a toll over the bridge unless we abolished the dispensary. And, finding that impossible, some of its leading men suggested to condemn the bridge and cut it down. Who are these people in Georgia passing resolutions to control the policy of Aiken County? The same people that for near 150 years has debauched our people with its red light saloons and drained our state of millions of dollars. Now that a few Georgians may spend their money with us under a clean system for the sale of liquor they seek to change our law." Croft concluded: "I trust that this body will not condemn our county until we violate a law. If the law is wrong, change it. But do not cast reflections on a county for attending to its own business."[45]

Swayed by this plea for county autonomy, the House reversed itself, "deeming it unwise to put it in the power of a town in a wet county to negate the action of the county itself by allowing the town to vote out its dispensary."[46] Undaunted, North Augustans protested further, asking for a countywide referendum on all of its dispensaries. Wearying of the North Augusta dispensary debate, representatives seized on this opportunity to "pass the bill and let those people over there fight the thing out for themselves."[47]

THE DISPENSARY CAMPAIGN

Aiken County's referendum on its dispensary system was scheduled for April 15, before which the dispensaries, including the one in North Augusta, were to remain open. Fearful of the "large percentage of imbibing done just outside the dispensary in plain view of trolley car passengers, pedestrians or other passers-by," the North Augusta town council passed "an ordinance which prohibits drinking on any street of the town and provides a maximum fine of $100 or imprisonment at hard labor for thirty days."[48]

Across the river Augusta police chief Norris announced "the establishment of a new beat . . . comprising the territory between the foot of the North Augusta Bridge on Thirteenth [McKinnie] Street out to Broad Street." In placing extra police in that section, Chief Norris acknowledged that "in view of the fact that the dispensary is operating . . . Thirteenth Street from the bridge to Broad Street will be tempting territory for the illegal sale of whiskey,"[49] both from illegal dispensary competitors and from those wishing to make a profit from recently bought dispensary goods.

With these firm (and hopefully temporary) bulwarks in place against local drunkards, North Augustans turned their attention to convincing their fellow countrymen of the folly of the dispensary system. In planning their anti-dispensary appeal, North Augustans understood that they could not rely on the harm done to North Augusta by the dispensary. Few others in the county would visit there often, if at all, so they would not perceive the harm as relevant to them. Recognizing this hurdle, North Augustans instead enlisted the noted prohibitionist Will Upshaw, who, according to the *Augusta Chronicle,* was "one of the most remarkable and brilliant men who has ever addressed this section." Upshaw's prohibitionist arguments rested primarily on the harm that would come to the sons of all citizens if the dispensary remained as a source of temptation: "He asked if it was necessary or desirable that men should educate their young children with the proceeds of the debauchery of young and old men. If you build macadam roads in Aiken county from the proceeds of the dispensary you will do it with the ones of your young men and the young men of Augusta."[50]

In addition to shielding the young from temptation, Upshaw also appealed to Aiken County residents on behalf of those across its western border. "The eyes of America are upon Georgia at present. If she is able to enforce it, the prohibition cause throughout the country will be greatly benefitted. . . . Help us to enforce it by doing away with the dispensary in Aiken county and North Augusta."[51] Upshaw traveled across Aiken County giving addresses reminding voters of their duty both to their own children and their brethren across the Savannah River.

His voice was soon joined by a chorus of pastors from around the county. As the election neared, dry forces armed their children: "Yesterday 1,000 badges were given out to the children, mostly of Aiken, and they are now being worn. On the badges is printed: 'close the dispensary and save our boys.'" As the election neared, "members of the Women's [*sic*] Christian Temperance Union made arrangements to serve lemonade, sandwiches and light lunches at all the polls throughout Aiken County."[52]

While ardent anti-liquor activists proudly carried the prohibitionist mantle, others who had supported the antis began to rethink their position, as the imagined social chaos associated with the dispensary did not materialize. "I joined the petition against the dispensary," wrote *Augusta Chronicle* editor and North Augusta resident Thomas Murphy. "I feared disorder at the foot of the hill on which I live. They put the dispensary there anyhow. It is the best regulation of legal sale of whiskey that could be imagined."[53]

Others across the county had cause to reconsider their decision when an item appeared in the newspapers a month before the scheduled vote telling of the county's recent gains: "The county [liquor] board advocated a reduction of two mills from the tax levy of the county. This reduction was suggested because of the profits derived from the county dispensary. It is estimated that the county dispensary will clear a net profit for the county schools and towns of 85,000 or more the present year."[54] Closer to North Augusta, local businessmen also let their preferences be known, albeit subtly. "Rumors have been circulated in North Augusta . . . that Mr. J. B. White of Augusta had said if the li-

Table 7.2. Votes to retain the dispensary versus prohibition by precinct, Aiken County, April 1908

Precinct	Dispensary	Prohibition	Percentage for prohibition
North Augusta	54	103	65
Dispensary towns	226	211	48
Mill districts	273	244	47
Remainder of county	470	309	39
Total	1,023	867	46

Source: Aiken Journal and Review, April 22, 1908, 1.

quor establishment stayed there he would invest extensively in North Augusta property, near the bridge, erect a department store and make other liberal improvements. If the dispensary was voted out, though, it is said he would not spend a dollar across the bridge."[55]

Across the river Augustans looked on with more than just passing interest in the results. "Many in Augusta contemplate the legal destruction of the North Augusta dispensary with satisfaction and are pleased that to Augustans and Georgians is due the credit of eradicating the liquor shop," wrote the *Chronicle.* "They want it broken up in order that Georgia may give the state prohibition law a fair, square, unhampered trial which is ... not possible with liquor on sale in great volume two hundred yards from the city limits. Georgians ... therefore pitched in to help, and are teaching the Aiken county Carolinians a lesson in good manners and good morals. Had Aiken County not stuck it [the dispensary] under Augusta's nose ... the Georgians would not have interfered now to despoil Aiken County of her liquor for revenue only establishments. A Dispensary at Aiken would have been tolerated, as would probably the dispensaries at Salley and Wagener. But when they put a liquor establishment in the shadow of Augusta homes it became necessary to discipline our friends over the river."[56] The election results gave a narrow majority to the dispensary, with the biggest disparity for the liquor shop coming from the county's rural landowners. Not coincidentally, this was the same group that stood to gain the most if property taxes were lowered as a result of dispensary sales (table 7.2).

Surveying these results, the *Columbia Record* noted:

We are not surprised at the result of the election in Aiken County against prohibition. Though the majority in favor of the dispensary was small, it was sufficient to make sure what everyone had reason to expect. We are confident however, that had the election been held prior to the establishment of the North Augusta dispensary the result would have been altogether different. That from the start the dispensary has been a money making concern and a great reducer of taxes. On account of the nearness of the dry Georgia city, the profits that accrue from it are probably in excess of all the other dispensaries in Aiken county put together. Naturally, therefore, the people of Aiken were not disposed to give up such a money-making business as the whiskey traffic, especially since most of its patrons come from another state. In speaking this we want it understood that we are not alluding to that portion of the people in Aiken county which reside in North Augusta; for in the election recently held the vote there was two to one against the dispensary. . . . The responsibility of forcing a dispensary on a community that didn't want it rests therefore upon the rest of the citizens of the county who saw in the North Augusta dispensary too good a thing to give up. For the sake of decreasing their taxes they were mean and selfish enough to subject a whole community to bear the burden of a great nuisance.[57]

8

THE TOWN *AND* COUNTY
THE DISPENSARY
BUILT

In early January 1908, just a few months before the *Columbia Record* was writing its obituary of North Augusta's anti-dispensary movement, Columbia's other daily newspaper, the *State,* surveyed the plight of its neighbors across the Savannah River: "Not a bar open in our sister State. Not a tiger stirring. Not a single demijohn is left in Georgia cellars, not a little brown jug that is not empty, not a quart bottle nor a pint bottle. Not a julep. Not a highball. Not a drink. Folks who were want to cast slurs about South Carolina booze are evading the customs officials and slipping over the line to get a morning gulp and are mighty glad to get even the stuff that South Carolinians have been drinking. Extra coaches are required to transport our cracker friends from over the line and back again. Augusta, along with all the other Cracker towns, has gone dry—bad dry—and that part of South Carolina on the opposite side of the river has gone wet—bad wet."[1]

The *State* was not the only paper to notice Augustans' increased desire to take a stroll across the Thirteenth Street bridge. Throughout 1908 and 1909 reporters journeyed to North Augusta to see for themselves "the aproned salesmen kept busy all day shoving the stuff through the apertures in the wire screen to the eager purchasers lining the narrow space between the partition and the brick wall."[2] These "hundreds of excursionists who ... visited the dispensary and purchased souvenirs in the shape of bottles of all sizes filled with rye and corn liquor [brought] hand satchels valises and suitcases to aid in carrying away their supplies of liquors to their homes."[3] Noting the occasional dispensary closings for restocking, one writer opined ironically "the people of the little South Carolina town have tried to close the liquor shop and failed on several occasions; but the people of Augusta have been more successful. The little shop was closed, the third time since its opening . . . because the stock had again been exhausted."[4]

Soon, reports began to appear about fantastic sums of money being made by the little shop in North Augusta: "The North Augusta dispensary sold eleven hundred dollars' worth of liquor on Saturday," wrote one correspondent,[5] while the *Augusta Chronicle* tallied the monthly take: "During January $16,971.40 worth of liquor was sold by the North Augusta dispensary, most of it destined for this side of the river. Not quite enough to float a battleship in, not nearly as much as was sold monthly by the Augusta bars, but considerably more than was needed for strictly medical purposes."[6] As the extraordinary sales piled up, so did "rumors to the effect that the authorities in North Augusta are seriously considering the stopping, in the near future, of all tax levys [*sic*], as the income from the dispensary source seems sufficient to defray all her municipal expenses. Dispensary money is building new streets and avenues and putting the old ones in fine condition."[7]

For any readers inclined to dismiss such fantastic tales as journalistic hyperbole designed to sell newspapers, the annual report of South Carolina's dispensary auditor removed all doubts about North Augusta's profitability. Tabulations of all ninety-eight of South Carolina's dispensaries' sales figures for 1908 showed North Augusta's $163,112 ($4,182,191.60) as the highest total, exceeding all of Charleston's and Columbia's dispensaries as well as sales in all but five of South Carolina's counties (table 8.1). Although sales fell off somewhat in 1909 as Augustans began locating other (legal and illegal) sources of liquor, the little oasis across the bridge still took in $94,560, higher than half of South Carolina's twenty-one dispensary counties.

BUILDING NORTH AUGUSTA

Aiken County law stipulated that dispensary profits be divided equally between the county, the county schools, and the host towns based on the profits those towns generated. For North Augusta, in the first two years when the dispensary was placed in the town, it yielded $21,280 ($489,440), and the Augusta Chamber of Commerce proudly reported that "almost the whole amount is being expended on civic improvements, making the suburb one of the most attractive in the South."[8]

Undoubtedly, the chief concern of the town council were the town streets,

Table 8.1. Dispensary sales by county, 1908 (dollars)

County	Sales over 100,000	County	Sales under 100,000
Charleston	606,145	Chester	88,741
Richland	506,076	Williamsburg	87,437
Aiken*	315,833	Lee	82,641
Orangeburg	220,218	Bamberg	82,368
Sumter	186,565	Colleton	78,024
Barnwell	175,486	Lexington	71,692
North Augusta	**163,112**	Fairfield	70,229
Abbeville	153,377	Dorchester	67,884
Florence	148,192	Berkeley	67,556
Laurens	138,093	Hampton	60,131
Beaufort	128,535	Clarendon	41,698
Georgetown	116,454	Chesterfield	22,226
Kershaw	114,001	Calhoun	19,583

Source: South Carolina General Assembly, State Dispensary Auditor, *Annual Report,* 231.

* North Augusta's home county

which, like many across the South, amounted to no more than dirt roads. In North Augusta they were often impassable, "owing to the flow of water off the terrace during heavy rains." Accordingly, "Mayor [B. C.] Wall stated that they are going to spend every cent they can get from the dispensary and use it to install a system of underground drainage, and in this way the washing away of the streets will be insured against."[9] Describing the final result in early 1909, the *Augusta Chronicle* reported: "The streets . . . are slightly elevated in the center, allowing the water to flow into drains on each side. In many cases there are terra cotta pipes in the drains presenting a very neat and pleasing appearance. Three quarters of an hour after a rain or even less time, the streets are in perfect walking conditions, firm as asphalt and no water standing on any parts."[10] Once the hazards of rainstorms had been addressed, the town streets were "graded and surfaced with clay and gravel; sidewalks were made . . . and the streets kept in perfect condition by a street machine owned by the village [which] . . . is used to level off the bumps in the streets and to fill any holes that may wash or wear in them."[11] Surveying the town at the end of 1909, the *Chronicle* reported that in terms of quality and safety, the streets were "unequaled for a town the size of North Augusta."[12]

To further ease pedestrians in their sojourns both around town and to and from Augusta, "forty new Tungsten lights will be placed on the streets. There will be a light at the intersections of the streets and they are so powerful that it is expected that there will be plenty of light to extend halfway up each block. A light will be placed just over the North Augusta bridge, and there will be several along the roadway from the bridge to the foot of the hill, and the darkness which has been prevalent and which is a source of annoyance both to pedestrians and to those traveling in vehicles will be stopped.[13] Streetlights were followed in short order by "parks—especially a fine one at the school house reservation . . . fire equipment, beautifying the cemetery, putting up drinking fountains for dumb beasts,"[14] and "an auxiliary water basin at the lower end of Georgia Avenue . . . sufficiently high to insure great pressure, and of sufficient size to meet immediate demand."[15]

Equally impressive as North Augusta's civic improvements were the additions made to the town's schools, the results of which were enumerated in the 1912 yearly report of the state education superintendent:

In the year 1907–1908 . . . the high school department consisted of a single three year course, and the pupils of that department were taught by two teachers, one at a salary of $1,200 and the other at a salary of $360. The common school department had in it four teachers at a salary of $360 each. In 1911–1912 the high school department had in it a four year course taught by four teachers, one at a salary of $1,200, and three at a salary of $450, each. In the common school were six teachers at a combined salary of $2,500. In the meantime the school district . . . has erected a second school building at a cost of $12,000. This building is equipped with steam heating and a gymnasium is yet to be added. This increase in school facilities is not due to rapid increase in attendance upon the school, as is shown by the fact that in 1907–1908 the high school attendance was sixty-two and the common school attendance 184, while in 1911–1912 the high school attendance was fifty-five and the common school attendance 169. . . . The principal and trustees of the high school are now planning to install with the next month a course in domestic science for the girls. Too a night school . . . will be established if there develops a sufficient demand for it. . . . The growth and development of the North Augusta High School during the past four years will compare favorably with any high school in the state.[16]

Surveying all this progress, the *Augusta Chronicle* editor took the opportunity to chide his state's liquor policy: "The county of Aiken forced the dispensary on the town of North Augusta. The anti-dispensaryites took charge of affairs, and by good management, and by leave of the liquor shop, they have drained, seweraged, fire-fighted and beautified their little town in the finest kind of manner. More they have declared taxation off for the latter half of their fiscal year.... It is easily understood why property—improved and unimproved—has so rapidly enhanced in value and is in such demand there. Prohibition in Georgia—well again and again there comes proof that it is an ill wind that blows no good."[17]

SOUTH CAROLINA POLITICS AND AIKEN'S DISPENSARIES

While North Augusta benefited primarily from the Georgia prohibition law, events across South Carolina were about to do the same for the rest of Aiken County. South Carolina prohibitionists, inspired by Georgia's example, welcomed the Anti-Saloon League to the Palmetto State in March 1908.[18] Formed at a Greenville meeting of South Carolina church leaders, the league sought the complete eradication of the liquor traffic by three means: "agitation, legislation and law enforcement." League president Rev. Charles E. Burts explained: "By agitation I mean the building up of a vigorous righteous public sentiment by means of the printed page and the spoken word. By legislation I mean securing of such anti-whiskey laws as the public opinion will support: and by enforcement I mean to utilize and uphold such Legislative enactments as may already have been secured as a preparation for further advance.... We have put a superintendent into the field and he will as rapidly as possible go over the state and organize the churches and we fully expect the influence of the League to be felt in the next summer's campaign."[19]

The man charged with orchestrating this campaign was Rev. J. L. Harley of Greenville. At the time of his appointment Harley was pastor at St. Paul's Church in that city, the most recent such position he had occupied over a decade and a half in pulpits across the state. A lifelong South Carolina resident, he received his license to preach following two years of schooling at Wofford College, followed by further study under the tutelage of his soon-to-be father in law, another Methodist preacher. Described as a "strong rugged manly soul [who] has convictions and dares maintain them at all hazard," Harley was selected to champion prohibition because "regardless of fear or favor of men, he may be relied upon for yeoman service. His preaching is eminently practical and looks to immediate results. He binds the hearts of those among whom he labors to him because of his evident earnestness and sincerity of interest in their spiritual welfare."[20] What Harley was not was an experienced ASL man, nor was he familiar with the rough-and-tumble of politics and the organizing and tactical necessities of waging a statewide campaign.

Harley's limitations might have been mediated if the Anti-Saloon League leadership featured men skilled in politics. Instead, the SCASL surrounded Harley with a group largely made up of preachers and Greenville's business elite who were also strikingly biased in favor of the Upcountry dry counties. Of the twenty-three members of the SCASL's original leadership, only three were neither preachers nor Upcountry residents.

The SCASL's first foray into prohibition politics was its effort to secure a statewide prohibition law during the 1909 legislative session. Following the lead of southern drys elsewhere, SCASL leaders worked with legislators to draft a bill creating statewide prohibition through legislative enactment.[21] Their argument was rooted in concerns widely held across the prohibition counties from which the majority of the SCASL came, namely that "the local option law . . . nullifies prohibition in certain counties; where there is a dispensary the adjoining prohibition county or counties could be hurt thereby."[22] Comparing this harm to the spread of a disease, Representative C. C. Featherstone (Laurens County) noted, "We might as well let the people in each county say whether or not they will vaccinate to keep down smallpox and expect the disease not to spread as to undertake to confine to county lines the evil results of the sale of whiskey."[23] Adding statistical weight to the dry position, Harley testified in both the House and Senate: "If the subject were put to a vote in this State the people would vote for prohibition by a 40,000 majority. In the 21 dispensary counties of 600,000 people one-fourth are white and three-fourths colored; in the 21 prohibition counties the conditions are reversed. . . . Under such conditions, the legal sale of liquor is wrong [and] it is time for the one-fourth whites in the dispensary counties to come to the aid of the prohibitionist majority."[24]

Despite assurances from legislators in already dry counties that "the people are now ready to rise up and crush out the whole liquor business,"[25] it soon became evident that their colleagues from dispensary counties were solidly against the proposed law. Their miscalculation came in part from assuming that previous legislative efforts to eliminate the statewide dispensary would translate to sentiment for statewide prohibition. Yet even legislators from dry counties were reticent to take this next step. "My county voted out the dispensary," admitted one representative, "but it was largely due to the disclosures of rottenness in the State dispensary made by Mr. Lyon [former state attorney general] and Mr. [Niels] Christensen and the other members of the committee. We were unilaterally opposed to the continuance of the State dispensary."[26]

As they contemplated statewide prohibition, chief among legislators' concerns was protecting the rights of their constituents to weigh in on the liquor question. Support for local option was especially strong in dispensary counties, where no liquor votes had taken place in almost two decades, little agitation had been made to change people's minds about the advisability of selling liquor, and the general sentiment was in favor of allowing those places that thought it profitable to continue to do so if they had no negative impact on their neighbors. Troubles along these lines became apparent even before the prohibition bill was introduced. When Harley invited Senator Niels Christensen, a noted teetotaler and therefore presumed supporter, to speak at a prohibition rally, Christensen declined, replying:

> The prohibition leaders point with pride and satisfaction to the good effects of prohibition in the twenty-one dry counties in this State out of a total of forty-two. These results are the results of local option prohibition.... The people of these now dry counties made up their minds gradually and without coercion.... Counties in the southern and eastern portions of the State are being educated up to prohibition; and under local option will, I believe, in the next few years, vote liquor out. But if it is attempted to force them through a State-wide law, the growth of prohibition sentiment will be checked and juries and local officials will not attempt to enforce a measure that may be considered obnoxious.... I was re-nominated to the Senate and I am not pledged or in any way committed to my constituency as between local option and State-wide prohibition. Personally I have always been a teetotaler and wish to do what I can to bring the day when liquor shall be no longer used.... But I believe that we can establish an enforced prohibition sooner through local option than through State-wide prohibition.[27]

Once the bill was introduced, other legislators from dispensary counties added their voices to the chorus protecting the rights of their citizens to decide the matter for themselves. "The regulation of the liquor traffic has to be reached by degrees: that there should be no dictation in the matter," argued Georgetown County senator Lagrande Walker. "If the matter were submitted to a vote of the entire state, this would be manifestly unfair, as the counties now dry would have a 'say so' and this would be in reality dictation. If you wish to do this, do so by education."[28]

In addition to protecting local option, a second consideration for legislators were the potential profits arising from liquor sales. This of course had always been an important issue in dispensary discussions; politicians since Tillman had argued that "prohibition would mean the illicit sale of whiskey and the people would be enriched—those who dealt in whiskey—and the county would not get the benefit as is now the case."[29] The devolution of liquor sales to the counties after the state dispensary's demise only accentuated this objection, as all dispensary profits now went into county coffers. Seeking to remind his colleagues of the enormous impact on county finances, a representative from Aiken declared his county "would have to pay no taxes this year—unless the dispensary should be removed, for out of the profits of the North Augusta dispensary the revenue has been large enough to run the fiscal affairs of Aiken County. On the other hand, it is declared that the schools of Edgefield, where there is prohibition, must suspend this month because of an insufficiency of funds to run them."[30]

Nor was it only the counties with successful dispensaries that were considering the financial repercussions of statewide prohibition. With North Carolina's adoption of a statewide dry law only a few months earlier, a representative from a county near the North Carolina border noted, "If we had a dispensary in our town we could sell enough liquor in nearby North Carolina cities to remove all taxes from our county, and there would not be so very much more sold at home than now comes in by the express company."[31]

Acknowledging the near-certain failure of the prohibition bill, dry forces instead accepted a compromise measure proposed by Senator Christensen. The state would go dry for two weeks in August 1909, after which every county that currently had dispensary sales would hold a referendum. Those that voted to keep their dispensaries would reopen these establishments, and those that voted against sale would keep their dispensaries closed.[32] Each decision would remain in place for four years, at which time any county might revisit the liquor question. After voting to accept this compromise, C. C. Featherstone opined: "I must confess I had hoped for better things. My preference all along has been for a State-wide referendum act. This in my judgment would have been better by a great deal than the plan adopted by the general assembly. Our trouble all along has been that there are in the general assembly a good many men who, at heart, are prohibitionists, and some of them from dry counties, who felt that they were virtually instructed to stand by local option. There are others throughout the state who are just as good prohibitionists as any of us but who might be local option prohibitionists. . . . The thing for us to do is to make the best of what we have. I am satisfied that at least two thirds of the wet counties can be voted dry next summer, if the proper effort is made.[33]

As they sought to make the best of what they had, Harley and other ASL leaders threw themselves into campaigning across the half of South Carolina's counties that permitted dispensary sales. The themes taken up by prohibitionist speakers were already familiar to many across South Carolina and the South and reflect the degree to which the Palmetto State's citizens shared anti-liquor sentiments with their counterparts elsewhere.

Chief among the prohibitionists' concerns was the harm done to family by the liquor trade. "Liquor in its nature is dangerous to the morals, good order, health and safety of the people," argued Rev. George Cromer. "If there were no boys what would become of the liquor traffic? Your answer to that makes the fight not against selling liquor, but a fight for the boys, because unless they can get your boys they have got to go out of business."[34] For "those who oppose prohibition because it abridges personal rights and liberty," noted Rev. Charles E. Burts, they "must concede that the defenseless wives and mothers and innocent children of the country also have rights that should not be abridged."[35]

Not only would boys be free from the temptation of liquor if dispensaries were eliminated, but the neighborhoods in which families resided would also be safer. Such arguments were typically made with reference to police statistics, such as those Cromer pointed to from Newberry: "There were 171 arrests made for drunkenness in that city in three months while the dispensary was in operation as against 57 in the same length of time since the prohibition law has been in effect."[36]

Prohibitionists pointed to such statistics as evidence against the dispensary advocates' contention that "if we have State-wide prohibition, conditions will be worse. . . . We are told that the law cannot be enforced in the lower counties, and that we must wait until the people are educated up to a higher standard of citizenship and morality."[37] "It is true that a law could not prohibit absolutely," lectured Reverend Cromer, "but we can make it mighty unpleasant for the men who violate the law"—if only local officials were willing to take on the task. Pointing to the difference in permissiveness of local officials, Cromer exclaimed, "In Greenville a blind tiger is put on the chain gang, in Charleston he is put on the grand jury."[38]

The typical dry address concluded with an invocation to fight the liquor trust, first laying out the magnitude of the problem, as in one reported in the *Newberry Herald and News* in July 1909: "The liquor people are thoroughly organized in every county in South Carolina. They have men running for office, and I would swear it that they have a candidate for Governor in this State. . . . A secret warfare is being waged against good citizenship; against the interest of the people; against the morals of the people; against the ministry; against the Church of God."[39] Despite the forces arrayed against them, these prohibitionists asserted: "We are Democrats, and we claim that the white people are in authority—that we can, must and will rule. Let the weak-kneed backboneless officials who whine and fawn at the feet of their constituency get out of the way and give place to men. Let every true man join in this fight for reform and better government, and let us leave a heritage to our children that will cheer us in our old age, rejoice and comfort us when we come to the end of the way, and which our descendants will be proud when we are gone."[40]

Of course, not everyone was convinced, and many were insulted by what they saw as high-handed remarks by Harley. Surveying the conditions in Charleston, the editor of the *News and Observer* fired back at the prohibitionists: "In Charleston are men who regard the sale of intoxicants as not less legitimate than the sale of coffee. Many of these men are citizens who in their morals and in their virtues are the equals of Mr. Harley and his friends and in respect to their unwillingness to set themselves up in Pharisatical [*sic*] judgment of the conscience of the people in Barnwell and Spartanburg they are better Christians than is the Rev. Mr. Harley. Because, forsooth, he must believe that the sale of whiskey is evil and neither the civilized world nor the

Christian Church agree with him in this belief. Who made him a judge in Israel? Where are his saintly credentials that any of us should receive his dogma and that of his friends as the law of God and righteousness?"[41]

Other citizens saw deeper conspiracies at work as they examined the northern roots of the Anti-Saloon League: "The people do not want instructions from Chicago as to what they want; nor do they want Chicago money to influence them.... Preachers do not know anything more about right or wrong than do ordinary citizens. Their place is in the pulpit to explain the Bible; and not to dictate even when backed up by the Chicago Anti-Saloon League with its millions of dollars.... No reasonable man would oppose temperance. At the same time, no man can call himself a Democrat and subscribe to the dictates of the Anti-Saloon League. No man is a Democrat who is opposed to local option."[42] Although scathing in his attack on the SCASL, this citizen's remarks proved to be a harbinger of good news for the prohibitionists. As "most reasonable men" went to the polls in August 1909, they chose to support temperance, giving dry majorities in sixteen of the twenty-two counties.

As had been the case in the 1905 county option referenda, dispensary profits were a primary consideration for voters. As the state law had mandated that only counties with existing dispensaries hold referenda on their continued operation, the Upcountry counties heavily populated with millworkers were absent from this round of elections.[43] Where the twenty-two remaining dispensary counties differed was in the amount of profit their liquor shops contributed to county funds. Comparing the profits of counties that retained their dispensaries with those that opted for prohibition shows the impact of liquor sales (table 8.2).

AIKEN COUNTY'S WINDFALL

For the counties in which dispensaries remained, profits increased even further as each found themselves isolated outposts bordered on all sides by prohibition counties. For the Aiken County liquor board the 1909 elections brought prohibition to three of the four counties that shared its borders (Barnwell, Lexington, and Orangeburg). These new developments, combined with the Georgia prohibition law, meant that Aiken County's liquor shops offered the only legal supply of liquor for over fifty miles—the next closest dispensary was in Columbia, two counties away.

Table 8.2. Dispensary profits and prohibition adoption, 1909 (percentage)

County and percentage of dispensary profits going to county

Charleston 30.0	Williamsburg 16.0
Bamberg 28.5	Kershaw 15.6
Aiken 25.9	Lee 15.6
Georgetown 24.7	Dorchester 12.8
Sumter 23.7	Colleton 10.5
Beaufort 22.6	Fairfield 8.1
Richland 19.5	Berkeley 7.8
Abbeville 19.4	Hampton 5.6
Orangeburg 19.3	Lexington 5.0
Florence 18.2	Clarendon 4.7
Barnwell 17.4	Calhoun 4.0

Sources: South Carolina General Assembly, State Comptroller General, *Annual Report,* 1908; South Carolina General Assembly, *Acts and Resolutions.*

Note: Counties that retained their dispensaries appear in boldface type.

Among Aiken County's dispensaries the one that stood to gain the most from the political developments of 1909 was located in Salley. Located in the northeast corner of Aiken County, Salley was less than twenty-five miles from both the Orangeburg and Barnwell County lines, making it the most likely destination for citizens in those newly dry counties interested in purchasing dispensary liquor. Although certainly not all (or even most) of those two counties' ninety thousand inhabitants lived along the border nearest Salley, both county seats with a total of nearly ten thousand between them did, leading many in the area's lone dispensary town to dream of civic improvements and tax relief similar to those achieved in North Augusta. Such glorious predictions soon made their way in the press across the entire state, the *Charleston News and Courier* telling its readers:

> The little town of Salley, just inside Aiken County, bids fair to be a rival of North Augusta in the sales of the dispensary. The sales have been gradually growing each week, since the thirsty friends of the dispensary system over in the neighboring counties of Barnwell and Orangeburg have been unable to purchase from their own dispensaries. Salley is located conveniently for an oasis in the dry sands of prohibition territory surrounding that section.

A few days ago the sales were about $600 ($15,000) one Saturday. Before long Salley will be enabled to cut out its own taxes as North Augusta was able to do long ago. Those who stocked up before the closing of the dispensaries have not exhausted their supplies yet, so it can be readily seen that Salley will soon have paved streets, water system, sewerage and what not![44]

Between 1909 and 1913 Aiken remained the lone legal liquor provider to its neighboring counties and the city of Augusta. This monopoly, combined with the continued robust liquor sales to Aiken hotels catering to Winter Colonists, meant a steady stream of money across the county. Precise sales records for each of Aiken County's dispensaries were not kept after 1908, and the original dispensary reports have long since disappeared. The countywide figures that we do have show a gradual increase in both dispensary sales (from $267,947 in 1909 to $282,038 in 1913) and profits ($66,854 in 1909 and $74,635 in 1913).

When they voted to retain their liquor shops in April 1908, Aiken County residents also established parameters for the disbursal of their profits. The county law divided them in thirds, to be disbursed evenly to the towns from which the sales came, the county, and the county school system. The funds for the schools were to be further divided among the sixty-seven school districts, though how the funds were to be shared was left to the county superintendent of schools. All disbursements were to be overseen by the county treasurer.

This arrangement greatly benefited the towns that sold the most liquor, as they received one-third of all of the profits created by their liquor shops. North Augusta made major civic improvements with its dispensary profits. So, too, did Salley and Aiken. In the county seat several leading citizens "have been appointed a committee to fully investigate the water question . . . and make a report upon the possible sources for a future supply." Two plans were ultimately put forth: "the installation of a different system" or supplementing "the present supply with some good spring water carefully filtered. It is estimated that it will cost something like $100,000 to bring into the city a new supply of water while a supplementary supply can be gotten for around $15,000."[45]

Ultimately, the town, flush with dispensary money, opted to "have this corps of engineers . . . making estimates upon the cost of laying water pipes" and "erecting a power plant to pump the water into the city." [46] By the beginning of 1910, the *Augusta Chronicle* informed its readers that "an unexcelled waterworks and sewerage system has been constructed by the [Aiken] city government. The water supply is derived from a series of artesian wells. Upon analysis, this water has been found to be pure, and to the eye, it is clear as crystal. These facilities, together with the splendid electric light system and trolley car service, render Aiken a most desirable and delightful place of residence."[47]

Aiken, North Augusta, and Salley had a relatively easy time making such improvements as their share of the dispensary money was substantial relative to their populations. Across Aiken County and its various school districts, decisions about how, or if, to spend dispensary profits fell into familiar patterns that pitted town against county, Aiken against Augusta, and tourists against locals.

AIKEN COUNTY'S SCHOOL FUND

Outside of the towns the institutions that stood to benefit the most were Aiken County's schools, but the benefits were minimal, as dispensary money only served to enhance an already considerable surplus. This surplus was the result of two factors. The first were the taxes paid to the county by the Horse Creek Valley mills. Textile mills were one of the major sources of tax dollars across South Carolina, and the taxes paid by Aiken's mills provided the county with an income exceeded by few others across the state. The second factor was Aiken's proportion of African American schoolchildren. Although Aiken's African American population paled in relation to Lowcountry counties, when compared to South Carolina's other mill counties, Aiken had a greater proportion of African American schoolchildren. As was the case across South Carolina, funds for African American schooling were paltry in Aiken, averaging a total of only $2.29 per student in 1908. Aiken's mill taxes, combined with low spending on a majority of its school population, meant that Aiken used fewer of its school funds than all but one other South Carolina county. When dispensary sales increased, the county surplus ballooned to a total $42,909 by the end of 1909.

Although some citizens were likely inclined to spend none of this new pot of riches, the condition of Aiken's schools left plenty of room for improvement. A 1909 survey of twenty-four of the sixty-seven districts done by North Augusta High School principal J. F. Thomason pointed to some of the areas of greatest need: "Thirteen districts report very good buildings. Eleven districts report bad buildings. Twelve districts say at least $1,300 is needed for repairs. Fourteen need new buildings at an estimated cost of $11,700. . . . Only five out of twenty-four report anything like an adequate supply of blackboards. . . . Only two schools report having good maps. Seven report that their school is badly heated. Seventeen report that their schools and grounds are unattractive. . . . Eleven schools need more teachers."[48] To get better materials to more schools, county education leaders sought to combine schools, thus conserving resources, a plan that drew little support within the county. County superintendent Cecil Seigler explained: "One of the growing needs of our county as I see it is the consolidation of some of our small one teacher schools. The greatest thing to retard this is the objection the people have to letting their children be hauled to school. They will admit the advantages of consolidation [better buildings and teachers], yet they won't consent to transportation."[49]

In an effort to gin up support for consolidation in particular and school improvement in general, Superintendent Seigler organized a countywide campaign in which he and others in Aiken's education leadership toured the county, explaining the gravity of the situation to their fellow citizens. "There are 171 schools in the county, only 103 buildings are owned by the county, 68 are rented or borrowed," Professor W. L. Booker chastised Aiken's citizenry. "Poor school buildings show a lack of interest. . . . In this county the average salary per teacher is $254 a year; in the State it is $289. Aiken County stands 23rd in point of efficiency in schools." Alluding to the large amount of unspent dispensary money, Booker continued: "Money lying idle in the treasury cannot make good schools. Forty percent of the children are not enrolled in the schools and only 57 percent of those enrolled attend school regularly."[50]

Further hammering home the need to spend money on the schools and push young people to attend them, the *Horse Creek Valley News* calculated that "the amount of taxes paid by the average mill worker . . . would not keep one child in school a month." Challenging its readers, the editor asked: "Is the privilege of denying a child the right to learn to read and write worth having? Is that a kind of 'personal liberty' that any considerable number of people in South Carolina are willing to preserve?"[51] The county school campaign succeeded in increasing Aiken County's pursuit of new schools, longer school years, and better teachers—at least for the county's white students. The spending increases paid dividends in every area that concerned Aiken County educators, as Aiken constructed twenty-one new school buildings by 1913 and that year was above the state averages in per capita expenditures for white schoolchildren, length of the school year, and teacher salary (table 8.3).

Table 8.3. State spending and school improvements by race in Aiken County and South Carolina, 1909 and 1913

Year	Aiken County	South Carolina
Per capita spending		
1909	White $12.35, Black $2.29	White $10.34, Black $1.70
1913	White $21.09, Black $2.27	White $14.94, Black $2.38
Days in school term		
1909	White 110, black 70	White 124, black 78
1913	White 131, black 83	White 126, black 67
Average teacher salary		
1909	White $218, black $92	White $236, black $88
1913	White $377, black $119	White $368, black $114

Source: South Carolina General Assembly, State Comptroller General, *Annual Report.*

The continued limits on spending for African American schooling meant that in addition to the gains made in Aiken County's education system, the county schools still ran a surplus of better than forty thousand dollars every year between 1909 and 1913.[52] This surplus would prove a tempting target for other county initiatives.

AIKEN COUNTY ROADS

The most substantial initiative undertaken by Aiken County was the development of its roads. In 1909 virtually all the roads outside of Aiken and North Augusta were made of nothing more than dirt, meaning that any rain made them practically impassable. Although most people across the county agreed the condition of the roads (especially those they had to travel) was poor, few were willing to authorize a road tax to pay for improvements. As Aiken was a large county with roughly 1,280 miles of unpaved roads, few citizens trusted the county leaders enough to imagine that if road taxes were paid the resulting improvements would be made to roads they actually traveled. As profits from the dispensary grew throughout 1908, some in the county cast an eye toward the county's school surplus as a possible way to improve their roads without having to raise taxes.

As was the case with the development of the interurban railroad, the needs of the Winter Colonists and the planning of Augusta's businessmen took the lead in reimagining the county roadways. In May 1908 the *Augusta Chronicle* reported that "there is a plan afoot to build a fifty-foot macadam or gravel boulevard from Aiken and the Park in the Pines hotel directly to the Hampton Terrace hotel and North Augusta and to Augusta and the Bon-Air hotel. A number of citizens realize that the tourist visitors who come to this section every winter will soon take up more and more the automobile fad and Aiken and Augusta must provide facilities for the proper enjoyment of the horseless carriage."[53]

The proposed road was the brainchild of North Augusta business leader J. Carey Lamar and had the backing of Augusta's business elite as well as the political leaders of both Aiken and Augusta. The public kickoff meeting was well attended by all members of the Augusta Chamber of Commerce and the Cotton Exchange, each of them speaking in golden tones about the benefits of the venture. "The boulevard will strengthen the bonds of friendship between South Carolina and Georgia . . . despite the River that divided Augusta and Aiken . . . the citizens of Augusta and Aiken were one people, of one mind and ideas of progress," proclaimed Aiken mayor Sally, with Mayor Dunbar of Georgia responding in kind: "South Carolina can always count on a response from Augusta. Augusta heartily welcomed the guests and would delight in assisting them in their project."[54] The *Chronicle* concluded, "It is probably unnecessary to attempt to stress the importance and value, not only to Aiken and Aiken County but to Augusta as well, of a boulevard such as is proposed."[55]

The meeting concluded with the appointment of an Aiken-Augusta Boulevard Association, which was charged with hiring experts in road construction, surveying and marking off the land, and raising the necessary funds to undertake the project. To many the plan seemed foolproof—except for the financing. Such a large venture required nine thousand dollars to complete. By early October the association had raised four thousand dollars. For the remainder the Boulevard Association proposed asking the Aiken County legislative delegation to draft a bill permitting the association to borrow five thousand dollars from the Aiken County school surplus. The proposed private-public partnership would rely on the county dispensary system's continued solvency, as the funds borrowed from the county schools would be repaid from future dispensary profits in Aiken and North Augusta, the two towns that stood to benefit from the proposed boulevard. Petitions were quickly drafted and signed supporting such a measure, and in February 1909 "it was announced that $5,000 had been provided for the Augusta-Aiken Boulevard. The funds will be borrowed from the Aiken County school fund, and was brought about after a conference between a delegation of citizens from North Augusta and Aiken and the Aiken County delegation."[56]

Once news of the proposed "loan" made its way through Aiken County, the backlash was considerable. Rural dwellers not living near the proposed boulevard objected to their school funds being taken to build a road that was obviously not intended for their benefit. Numerous aspects of the deal were brought up in public discussions, many of which were summarized by a Beech Island farmer:

Why does the Association not go, as other promoters do, into the open market for this loan? Even as farmers do, as hundreds of chattel mortgages recorded at the Court Houses show. Why should this twenty miles of highway between the twin towns of Aiken and North Augusta have preference of the 2,000 miles of public highways in Aiken County? Do not the two railroads, a trolley line and numerous dirt roads already unite these towns? Is the majority of the delegation aware of the fact that the public highways of Aiken, owing to long neglect, are in deplorable condition making it difficult and even dangerous for country people to go to market and to church? Why was the surplus not apportioned according to law among the 67 school districts of the county? How does it happen that most of the schools have already closed? Have the 15,000 persons of school age in the county completed their education? Are there any illiterates in the county? Can no provision be made for agricultural, industrial, business or manual training? Are no better and higher qualified teachers required? Has an appalling apathy settled over our school system? Has faith and hope that our children might share in the vast stores of the world's knowledge been obscured? If the dispensary is voted out, how is this loan to be repaid?[57]

The author concluded by noting ominously: "I have just seen a copy of the Act passed by the majority of the delegation. It is entitled an Act to transfer certain school funds of Aiken County to the ordinary county fund and the sum of $5,000 to be expended in building the Aiken-North Augusta Boulevard. The word loan nowhere occurs in the Act."[58]

Farmers around the county quickly rallied in protest of the loan, drafting an injunction that argued among other points that "the public roads of the county are everywhere in bad condition, and inasmuch as there are already two railroads and a trolley line between these points; and the public schools scattered over more than 1,000 square miles of the open country stand greatly in need of furnishings, libraries and lecturers for their development."[59]

In response to these accusations J. Carey Lamar reminded readers that "the people living in the territory through which this road is to be built voluntarily contributed $5,000 from their private funds." Further, there was precedent for such a loan as "only two years ago they passed a bill making a special appropriation of $4,000 to build a road from Ellenton to Silverton to Augusta in which case the citizens of the community being benefitted thereby did not aid the proposition by raising one dollar of private funds." Finally, the school system was flush with cash: "On January 1, 1909, there was in round numbers a surplus in the school fund amounting to $32,000." Lamar concluded his plea to the delegation by noting, "As the citizens have already raised the $5,000 and stand ready to go to work, we hope the delegation will make this loan from the school fund, especially as neither the county nor schools could be injured in the slightest and in the near future, the larger towns benefitting most could pay the loan back out of dispensary income."[60]

Ultimately, the delegation stuck by its decision and in the process established a pattern of road building that would combine private money with dispensary funds that connected the towns across Aiken County. The next year saw the "establishment of an automobile line to Wagener and Salley from Aiken . . . proposed by a party of Aiken gentlemen. . . . This line . . . offers every convenience to the traveling public that is now offered by the railroad and trolley road."[61] As was the case with the Aiken-Augusta Boulevard, the construction began by raising some five thousand dollars in capital stock and then going to the county to borrow from the school fund with the promise to repay the amount loaned with profits from the Aiken, Salley, and Wagener dispensaries.

While private funds made possible the construction of boulevards serving Aiken County's larger towns, those in rural areas continued to find themselves isolated by substandard roads. One frustrated citizen complained about the state of roads near her farm to the *Augusta Chronicle* in 1912:

> I wish you could ride up the Martintown Road for six or eight miles, starting at the reservoir in North Augusta and see what we have in the way of a public road. This road is one of the most important in the state. It borders the Savannah River and some of the finest plantations and farms in the county are scattered on it. It is our only road to Augusta—our only market, for we have no small towns . . . nor any half-way communication, so we are obliged to travel over these well-nigh impossible roads for about six months a year. A loaded wagon can scarcely pull through the mud, and women and children are afraid to drive over them so they stay away from church and school and from Augusta waiting for the warm weather and a good road—if it is ever good. I have been living in this community for 50 years and the road is no better than when I first saw it and the protests are still as strong and the indifference of county officials as great as 50 years since.[62]

Complaints about Aiken's rural roads often implied that "all the good roads in Aiken County lead to Aiken, the insinuation being that there is a definite policy . . . of spending little or nothing" if the county seat did not stand to benefit.[63] Whether or not this situation was intentional, the editor of the *Augusta Chronicle* echoed the thoughts of many Aiken County residents when he wrote, "In this supposedly enlightened age, in this supposedly progressive county . . . there is no excuse for it, and the situation is one that seriously reflects on whoever is responsible for the roads in that part of Aiken County."[64]

"Our trouble," wrote another Aiken man, "is we have a political system. These county officers are driven in self-defense to please everybody. . . . Consequently we have a hasty temporary patchwork road system." Instead of politicians trying to win support by addressing poorly the complaints of various citizens in a quick and dirty way as they arose, citizens sought "an unpaid commission of good business men to handle the road question and put our roads into the hands of a man who is an engineer, who knows how to drain and mix sand clay, understands drainage and how to keep a road up after it is built, and last but not least, a man who holds an appointive and not an elected office." He concluded by placing the blame squarely at the feet of his fellow Aiken County residents: "Every spring our public spirited, enterprising citizens wake up, hold a few road meetings, bombard, lambast, discuss and fret over the infernally bad roads, contribute a little money and quit right there. And right there is where we all suffer"[65] Taking this cue, Aiken county citizens, led by the county good roads association, called on the county leadership to create "a county road commission, to be composed of three responsible citizens . . . to take over the building and maintenance of roads and bridges in Aiken County."[66]

The commission quickly adopted similar spending habits to the private associations that had begun Aiken's road development. Its first purchase was "$5,000 of road-working machinery, including an eight-horsepower gasoline traction engine. . . . The machine has practically rebuilt the old Martintown Road."[67] By the end of November 1912 the *State* reported that "the Aiken highway commission having spent the last cent of its appropriation of $20,000 . . . asked that they be allowed to have access to the surplus funds in the county treasury."[68] Again, some citizens protested, and again the legislative delegation of Aiken ignored these protests and acquiesced to the request for temporary use of the county surplus with the stipulation it be repaid by dispensary profits. By 1914 Aiken County's use of dispensary funds had allowed the county to surface 27 percent of its roads, more than all but three other South Carolina counties (table 8.4).

AIKEN COUNTY TAXES

While Aiken County school leaders worked on improving education and the county road commission worked on improving transportation, most county government leaders sought to use dispensary funds to lower county tax rates. Many had speculated that such a reduction would be possible as a result of the dispensary, and their thoughts were confirmed in early 1908, when the county dispensary board requested the county delegation lower the tax levy by two mills (roughly $22,000). This recommendation was made "based on the growing profits of the dispensary. . . . It is estimated by the board that the profits will amount to at least $50,000 at the end of twelve months. . . . At this figure, the third which goes to the county will amount to $16,666. . . . From these figures the board believed that the delegation could reduce the levy one mill on the general county tax, leaving two mills, which would bring in $22,000. To

Table 8.4. Miles of surfaced roads outside incorporated cities, South Carolina, 1914

Total no. of surfaced roads	No. of counties	Percentage of roads surfaced	No. of counties
400+	1	41+	1
350–399	1	36–40	0
300–349	0	31–35	2
250–299	0	26–30	3
200–249	3	21–25	2
150–199	2	16–20	3
100–149	5	11–15	3
50–99	9	6–10	8
0–49	22	0–5	21

Source: U.S. Department of Agriculture, *Public Road Mileage and Revenues in the Southern States, 1914,* LXI, table 48.

Note: Aiken's surfaced roads totaled 350 miles, 27.4 percent of the total road mileage in the county.

this would be added the commutation tax and the amount from fines and licenses, which amounted to $8,000. . . . Adding the estimated profits from the dispensary would make a total of $46,666 to meet expenses, which last year only amounted to $36,376."[69] When this proposal was made in January 1908, it occurred in the middle of North Augusta's campaign against the liquor shop in that town. With opinions at a fever pitch around the liquor question, few of Aiken's political leaders were willing to "commit the people to the system without their consent, in that if it were done the argument would be made 'Oh! We will have to sell whiskey this year to meet county expenses.'"[70]

This objection was removed with the dispensary's electoral victory in 1908, and by the next year dispensary profits, combined with county taxes, left the county coffers with $29,582 and the county school fund with $42,909. When asked to account for the county's fine financial performance, "Comptroller-General Jones replied . . . 'Oh, that's a political question.'" But the *State* showed the figures to its readers: "In Aiken the net collection on the 3 mill ordinary county tax was $26,509. The net collection from the dispensary fund was $25,602."[71] By 1910 it was impossible to deny the positive impact of the dispensary in the dramatic amount its profits added to the county's bottom line after the North Augusta dispensary was created. That year dispensary profits accounted for nearly 46 percent of the county's total intake, compared with a mere 13.7 percent in 1907, the year before North Augusta's dispensary came into being.

The most immediate impact of the extra dispensary money was to raise Aiken County's surplus, this in spite of the fact that the county was now also paying more to improve schools and loaning money to improve its roadways. By 1913 Aiken was one of only two South Carolina counties to have a surplus of over $100,000. This extra savings meant Aiken County leaders could make good on keeping county taxes low, which they did by reducing the millage rate, one of only ten counties to do so between 1905 and 1913. Further, Aiken lowered its yearly tax rate without raising auxiliary taxes to cover roadwork and other needs. The result was that Aiken's 1913 rate of eleven mills was the lowest in the state, and Aiken was the only county in the state that had not raised its total millage between 1905 and 1913 (table 8.5).

By the end of 1913 the *State* reported that "the balance in Aiken's general county fund is $41,890 and the balance in the school fund is $54,003. These two items make a total of $95,893. This is indeed a fine statement and perhaps Aiken county is in better condition than any other county in the State." Alongside this savings was the county's enviable tax levy, which the newspaper reported was "as low as any county in the state," as well as its considerable expenditures for road improvement: "This county has spent $72,244 on the roads of the county during the past year." This enumeration led the *State* to praise "a fine set of businessmen for county officers, as the splendid showing of the county finances are in a large measure due to them."[72]

Table 8.5. Total millage paid and increase in millage, 1905–1913

Total millage in 1913	Counties	Millage increase, 1905–13	Counties
18	Barnwell	7	Lancaster
	Greenville		Lexington
	Kershaw		
	Lancaster		
	Lexington		
	Pickens		

Table 8.5. (*continued*)

Total millage in 1913	Counties	Millage increase, 1905–13	Counties
17	Chesterfield Colleton Dorchester Edgefield Oconee Union York	6	Barnwell Chester
16	Cherokee Chester Greenwood Hampton Horry Laurens Lee Saluda Spartanburg	5	Orangeburg York
15	Abbeville Anderson Bamberg Beaufort Fairfield Marion Marlboro Orangeburg Sumter	4	Abbeville Anderson Dorchester Edgefield Greenville Lee Sumter
14	Berkeley Calhoun Darlington Georgetown	3	Bamberg Beaufort Colleton Fairfield Greenwood Hampton Kershaw Oconee Pickens

Table 8.5. *(continued)*

Total millage in 1913	Counties	Millage increase, 1905–13	Counties
13	Clarendon Newberry Williamsburg	2	Berkeley Charleston Chesterfield Clarendon Georgetown Horry Laurens Marion Newberry Spartanburg Union
12	Charleston Florence	1	Darlington Florence Marlboro Richland Saluda Williamsburg
11	Aiken Richland	0	Aiken

Source: South Carolina General Assembly, State Comptroller General, *Annual Report.*

9

AUGUSTA'S SALOONS REVIVED, 1908–1913

While South Carolina's dispensary counties spent the years between 1908 and 1913 using liquor sales to expand their infrastructures as well as their treasuries' financial health, across the river in Georgia the story was quite the opposite. As statewide prohibition took hold at the beginning of 1908, both the state government and Georgia's largest cities lost a significant part of their tax base, forcing state and municipal governments to look for new sources of revenue. Georgians also began noticing that their statewide prohibition law did not prohibit liquor consumption, as Georgia law could not prevent interstate liquor shipments to private citizens. As a result, the state legislature modified their prohibition law to permit the sale of near beer and to allow importations of liquor by members of social clubs to be stored in personal lockers on club premises. Both of these allowances came with the proviso that each establishment engaging in such activities pay a state and municipal tax, thus securing greater income.

In Augusta the municipal government took quick advantage of the new financial opportunity afforded by the law. By 1913 the number of near beer saloons and social clubs serving liquor equaled the number of saloons that existed before prohibition began. Added to Augusta's liquor profits were the increasing number of blind tigers, whose proprietors and patrons were occasionally rounded up, brought into court, and made to pay fines before being released to continue their illegal business. As Augusta became more financially healthy, sales in the city drew customers away from the dispensary across the river, reducing the profits in North Augusta and Aiken County.

GEORGIA'S BUDGET PROBLEM

The adoption of prohibition in Georgia, though held by some to be long over-due, actually arrived at a most inconvenient time, at least as far as the state treasury was concerned. In the quarter-century prior to 1907, the Georgia state government had taken on quite a number of responsibilities for its citizens. In so doing, it had also increased the state's need for the revenue provided by taxes on liquor.

In 1883 the state taxed its citizens at a rate of 2.5 mills. At that time Georgia's citizens received little from the state except the benefit of the courts in which to enforce contracts and the police protection afforded by criminal laws. Soon afterward a new era was ushered in that asked more of the state in several key areas of people's lives. The most prominent among them was education. The state university was expanded by the establishment in 1885 of the School of Technology, the Georgia Normal and Industrial School four years later, and the State College of Agriculture in 1906. State departments were also created to oversee and enhance the state's agriculture, horticulture, and health. Numerous constitutional amendments created several classes of pensioners, chief among them Confederate veterans.

As the Georgia Bar Association noted at its annual meeting in 1913, the list of state accomplishments since the turn of the century was impressive: "Great highways are being built; every needy soldier receives some assistance from the state; instruction in the public schools has constantly increased in quantity and in grade; secondary education is afforded at the state's expense in every congressional district ... the public health is protected by the agencies of the State Board of Health; the scourge of diptheria is guarded against by the keeping of anti-toxin in the reach of every citizen."[1]

Although a realization of the value of these agencies created some public sentiment in favor of an enlarged state government, alongside it there was "the popular impression ... that extravagant appropriations have been made to the institutions of the state and that the treasury has been, thereby, brought to the verge of bankruptcy."[2] In fact, it was not reckless spending on the part of the legislature but, rather, the loss of liquor revenues that had created the shortfall. According to bar association: "In 1907, the liquor tax amounted to $334,282.75. In 1908, on account of the prohibition law, the total sum received from the liquor tax ... amounted to $48,738.03. ... The total loss of revenue ... will have been, before the end of 1913, the sum of $1,914,240.87."[3]

Despite this loss, the public backlash against government spending meant few legislators were comfortable raising taxes, nor did they wish to cut funding to increasingly popular state services. At least initially it was possible for the state to do nothing to address the lost revenue, as costs were paid by drawing down the state budget surplus. Between 1908 and 1910 this resource lost half of its value, going from $820,740 in 1908 to only $486,157 two years later.

Georgia cities were also feeling the pinch. Business leaders argued that prohibition meant a loss of business, as "Georgia is simply sending her good money across the border at a rate, it is said, of a million dollars or more every month. Chattanooga is building new skyscrapers and Jacksonville is similarly thriving on Georgia money."[4] With money leaving the state, less would be available to invest or pay for other civic improvements. In Atlanta "the finance committee of the city council is faced by a lack of revenue due to the prohibition law, and in making out the appropriation sheet will have to cut out many proposed improvements for the city. There will be a great deal of the street paving given up; there will be no extension made at the Grady hospital; no raise in the teacher's salaries; no night school at the Tech; no extra police."[5] Across the state, in Columbus, one citizen reminded voters:

> From the time the question of state prohibition was put before the people of Georgia, the question of revenue derived from the sale of liquor played a most conspicuous part. We were told in distinct terms just what the loss to the state would be, should that policy become law. The prohibitionists replied that so great was the evil of the liquor traffic they would be willing to pay this trifling cost many times over. The sincerity of that claim is now put to the test in Columbus. The withdrawal of the revenue from the saloons will make a deficit in the current expenses of our city. . . . How shall we pay? We can deduct the amount from the salaries of our policeman and firemen. . . . We can raise all our revenue by other forms of taxation. . . . We might close our schools two months earlier, turn the children loose, throw our self-sacrificing teachers out of employment and take their salaries to pay the bill for our righteous fervor.[6]

By 1909 three of Georgia's four largest cities had virtually no year-end budget surplus, and Augusta was running a deficit of $102,324.[7] Nor was financial aid likely to come from the state, as "the next administration will face a deficit of at least $800,000 and maybe a million. About one third of it is due to the enactment of the state prohibition law."[8] Surveying this financial pitfall, the *Houston Post* wryly suggested that "Augusta might solve her revenue problem by stationing a toll collector at the bridge and charging every man who comes from North Augusta 10 cents."[9] The *Chronicle* editor was more sanguine. "Reform is all right in its way," he lamented. "But it is expensive."[10]

PROHIBITION DOES NOT PROHIBIT

Equally frustrating for Georgia's dry advocates was the slowly emerging reality that despite statewide prohibition, according to the *Augusta Chronicle,* "there is no denying—the North Augusta dispensary itself is a proof of it—that people who have been accustomed to drink in Georgia will continue to and where enforcement of the law prevents their getting it at home they will send away for it."[11] Although the paper's editor claimed he had "never disagreed with the prohibitionists as to the evils growing out of the abuse of intoxicants," the utter failure of prohibition to prohibit had led him to question the prohibitionists' preferred method of liquor control. "The truth is there will be traffic in intoxicating liquors just so long as there is a demand for it; there will be people to sell it just so long as there are people to buy it. . . . As a matter of fact—as much as we regret to say it—it [prohibition] has simply changed the manner of selling. It has . . . run a great many dealers out of the business, but many others have come forward to take their places. And those who have come into the business as a result of prohibition are not to be compared with those who went out of it."[12]

Among these unsavory characters now taking a more central place in the liquor business were the upcountry moonshiners. By early 1909 the *Macon Telegraph* reported that stills had grown exponentially in the state during the first year of Georgia's prohibition experiment: "Three hundred and ninety-seven illicit stills were destroyed in . . . Florida, Alabama and Georgia . . . and about two thousand gallons of whiskey seized" by federal agents. Eighty percent of the stills destroyed were in Georgia.[13] During that year across Georgia's northern border "about two hundred illicit whiskey distilleries have been cut to pieces in the 'dark corner' of Greenville county this year. The increase in the whiskey business in the mountains is causing alarm in government circles and the officers here attribute it to the prohibition wave."[14]

Liquor also poured into Georgia from sellers who had relocated across state lines and set up delivery services for thirsty Georgians. The result was "a bunghole on both sides of the state, one at Chattanooga and the other at Jacksonville. Georgia is simply sending her good money across the border at a rate, it is said, of a million dollars or more every month." The wealth of Chattanooga's and Jacksonville's liquor houses fed "a commercial boom in those cities," while "the express office in Atlanta, specially fitted up for the liquor trade, presents a picture of a New York 'bread line' every time the bottle train comes in." Georgia, then, was caught "between the devil and the deep blue sea and getting a plenty of both. Chattanooga is building new hotels and skyscrapers, and Jacksonville is similarly thriving on Georgia money." This building boom was so popular among the citizens of those cities that it was said to guarantee that "Chattanooga and Jacksonville will remain Georgia's booze markets until the state in desperation decides to regulate instead of prohibiting the sale."[15] By 1911 the *Macon Telegraph* reported that "Jacksonville, Florida, is the largest shipping point for liquor in the South and Chattanooga ships 786,000 gallons. . . . The mail order houses have been exceeding the speed limit in this business."[16]

Such large amounts of liquor being brought into Georgia's cities led to the conclusion that "in some respects prohibition in Georgia is a success and doubtless many rural communities will be benefitted by it, but the cities suffer in more ways than one. It hurts business. It is a great loss of revenue. It breeds blind tigers, falsehood, deception, mean liquor and other evils."[17] By late 1908 conditions had deteriorated to the point that the *Atlanta Constitution* and the *Savannah News* debated which city consumed the greater amount of liquor. Savannah eventually acquiesced, ceding the title of wettest city to Atlanta, but only because Savannah "has fewer thirsty souls." In accepting the mantle of most liquor-infested Georgia city, the *Constitution* acknowledged that "Atlanta has recently received a shipment of twenty-seven carloads of beer and whiskey." Yet it reminded readers across the state, "We are all in the same boat—Atlanta, Savannah, and judging from recent news dispatches, Augusta, Macon, and other communities in the state, not to forget those counties where moonshining flourishes and where still capacities have been doubled and trebled since the prohibition law became operative."[18] Surveying the situation from just beyond the state line, the *Chattanooga News* noted that even "the Georgia prohibitionists are freely admitting that statutory prohibition is a failure; that the law is not nor can it be, enforced."[19]

As they grappled with the failure of their preferred solution to the liquor problem, Georgians noted that with no federal law prohibiting such shipments from wet to dry states, liquor dealers were free to relocate just outside of Georgia's borders to continue their trade. Admitting that "there is about as much drunkenness in Atlanta as there was under the license system," Georgia prohibitionists concluded that "until temperance people find a way to protect dry territory from outside shipments of liquor there is no use to talk prohibition as a state-wide law."[20]

Sadly for dry advocates, such a statute appeared to be unlikely. "The forlorn hope of a national law which will prohibit interstate shipment of liquors into dry territory will . . . scarcely be followed much further," predicted the *Columbus Enquirer.* "Conservative prohibitionists are putting little hope in such an enactment, and even if Congress should pass it, which is considered doubtful, it is thought the courts would declare it unconstitutional."[21] The *Macon Telegraph* echoed these thoughts, concluding "that if there be no protection for dry territory short of an amendment to the Federal Constitution, such protection is likely to be sighed for in vain."[22] In the absence of such a law the *Columbus Enquirer* wrote, "The next campaign will be on in two years from now, when, it is predicted by businessmen and politicians alike the [prohibition] issue will be squarely presented with the chances under the current conditions, that Georgia will again legalize the sale of liquor in some form or other."[23] To the dismay of the prohibitionists, it did not take that long.

MODIFIED PROHIBITION—SOCIAL CLUBS

Faced with increasing deficits and with no precipitous drop in the amount of liquor consumed by their citizenry, Georgia legislators began debating whether to let "present conditions continue or shall sane sensible laws having the moral support of the people be enacted and afterwards enforced?"[24] Their focus first turned to the interstate liquor traffic and to the places people used to store their liquor once they had received it. Although many men kept liquor at home, quite a number of others took out lockers in social clubs where they were members, thus sparing their private space of a not-always-welcome item and creating a social space where they might consume in the company of friends and colleagues.

The Georgia legislature had no jurisdiction over the shipments themselves

and fairly little over the social clubs, which were legally considered private organizations. Nor did the prohibition law outlaw such gatherings specifically,
though the general wording that prohibited the consumption of liquor "in any
public spaces" could certainly be read to apply to locker clubs. No sooner had
the statewide dry law been passed in July 1907 than this potential loophole
began receiving attention. The first to notice it (or at least act to close it) was
Senator J. P. Knight of Berrien County, who introduced a bill to prevent the
sale of whiskey and other liquors in private clubs and make it a misdemeanor
for any club member to keep a bottle in his locker. Most Georgians scoffed at
this provision, portraying it as overkill as "we already have a bill—or rather
a law now—that prevents the very thing Mr. Knight aims at. Why should he
specifically point out the club when the bill makes it a misdemeanor to have
whiskey . . . of any kind in your office? So generic is the term 'other places' that
it even prevents a man from carrying a flask with him when he goes fishing,
even though he denominates the contents 'snake bite.'"[25]

Senator Knight proved prescient; his bill failed to make it out of committee, and the legislature turned its attention, instead, to the state's yearly revenue. Many across the state were surprised when the father of the prohibition bill, Seaborn Wright of Rome, "injected into the tax bill a $300 license
on 'locker' or clubs keeping whiskey for their own use." While prohibitionists
were aghast, presuming that "every club can pay $300 and keep all the whis-
key they want,"[26] Wright argued that this license fee was merely a tax measure designed to offset some of the state's lost liquor revenue and also to discourage potential clubs with few upstanding members from engaging in the
liquor trade.

Wright's bill passed the House but touched off a significant debate in the
state senate, where prohibitionists successfully pushed through an amendment that changed the three hundred–dollar yearly tax to a ten thousand–
dollar yearly tax "on clubs where intoxicants are kept in lockers." Not all senators approved of the amendment. Some claimed it was too prohibitory, such as
Senator G. A. Wise, who warned that "if the prohibitionists kept putting prohibition into the general tax act they would wake up such a sentiment against
the general law that it would soon be repealed."[27] Others objected that "such
a tax would interfere with the state's revenue" because few were likely to pay
such a fee.[28] Among the supporters of the higher tax was Senator T. J. Alexander of DeKalb County, who warned that if such a drastic step were not taken,

the streets in his hometown would become "regular hells on earth" as liquor dealers took up residence.[29]

Reconciling the considerable distance between the House and senate tax rates proved to be the hardest and therefore final order of business at what became one of the longest legislative sessions in Georgia's history. The *Augusta Chronicle* colorfully described the all-night proceedings: "It was getting close on to the gray dawn of another day, and it had been Sunday morning by more than three hours and a half when the general assembly finally got together on the locker club tax. . . . Finally, a third conference committee reported a compromise putting the tax of $500 on all such clubs. The members of the Senate were nearly asleep; they wanted to quit and go home, and by a vote of 17 to 14 they adopted the conference committee's report which had already been adopted by the house."[30]

As word spread of the new revenue law, "Governor [Hoke] Smith . . . received numerous requests from over the state urging him to veto the $500 locker tax . . . on the idea that it is a license upon the maintenance of lockers for the keeping of intoxicants."[31] Smith's hands were tied. Because the locker tax was a revenue measure and part of the larger state tax bill, it could not be struck down without rejecting the entirety of the revenue bill, which would necessitate calling the legislature back into session.

Georgia was now a prohibition state that paradoxically also taxed the sale of liquors in social clubs. "To many this was unintelligible," wrote the *Aiken Journal and Review,* "but the action of the Georgia legislature in its closing hours in placing a tax or license of five hundred dollars upon clubs having lockers . . . shows that the legislators were of the opinion that clubs will so increase . . . and lockers . . . so multiply that the state should receive some revenue from the liquor business." The *Journal and Review* then went a step farther, accusing the legislature of class bias: "Of course the clubs are not supposed to sell liquors . . . but this is only a supposition and it would take a large constabulary force to catch up with such sale . . . and no such force is provided for. . . . Should the poorer classes organize clubs . . . they might possibly be disturbed, but not the well-to-do. The wealthy clubmen of Georgia know no difference under the new laws. . . . Prohibition was good enough for the poorer classes who had not the sense enough to control their appetites and needed guardians, but the gentlemen of Georgia must not be disturbed."[32]

As the state prohibition law provided for no enforcement mechanism, the decision of how or whether to license locker clubs fell to the counties and municipalities. Most rural areas of the state quickly passed laws prohibiting locker clubs in their jurisdictions, although much of it was for show only, as such social clubs tended to be urban institutions. Among Georgia's larger towns and cities setting the local license fee was a matter of some calibration. If a fee was set too high, it would discourage any locker clubs from forming, which was the intent in smaller towns such as Albany, Dublin, and Marietta, which set their license fees at ten thousand, five thousand, and five thousand dollars, respectively. Georgia's larger cities were more welcoming to the locker club idea. In the urban areas license fees were typically set between three hundred and five hundred dollars per year, low enough to encourage clubs to take advantage of the opportunity but high enough to ensure a considerable civic profit.[33]

MODIFIED PROHIBITION—NEAR BEER

Further licensing profits seemed possible if states were willing to countenance the selling of near beer, a beverage that potentially met state guidelines for alcoholic content. Invoking a distinction between whiskey, "a drunkard's drink," and beer, "an invigorating, non-intoxicating tonic, containing only $3\frac{1}{2}$ percent alcohol—that never has and never will produce a drunkard,"[34] Georgia governor Hoke Smith opined that "the Legislature . . . may be asked to materially modify the Georgia law" to permit "light drinks such as wines and beer, to be used only at the table as food."[35]

A year later the Georgia legislature took up the issue in earnest. Aware that any modification to the prohibition law would anger dry advocates, who had fought hard for its passage, the legislature worked in the gray area where the law seemed most amenable to alteration. In this instance the question was the precise meaning of the word *intoxicating.* Following the lead of Governor Smith, former house member J. Randolph Anderson of Savannah suggested the legislature place a tax "on near beer not to contain more than 3 percent of alcohol and permit the breweries of the state to manufacture it." Such a measure would surely help the legislature, which "seemed to be looking around for money for the agricultural schools," and "would stop seven-eighths of the shipments of the 4-percent beers that are coming into Georgia."[36]

Not wanting to confront the prohibition law head-on, Georgia legislators, as they had done a year earlier with locker clubs, chose to license near beer dealers in the context of the revenue law. This time it took an extra session, as near beer was understood to be malt liquor, the taxing of which by Georgia law could only be appropriated for the state's schools and not for penitentiary construction, which was what the state budget most sorely needed. Once this hurdle was cleared, Georgia's near beer dealers were free to operate in any city jurisdiction that licensed them, provided they paid a two hundred–dollar fee to the state. The focus now shifted to Georgia's localities as they determined how, or whether, to integrate the two new types of liquor dealers into their civic life.

THE DISPENSARY VERSUS AUGUSTA'S BLIND TIGERS

In backing away from more stringent prohibition legislation, Georgia's legislators again placed the liquor question in the hands of their counties and municipalities. As Augusta was one of Georgia's largest cities, many outside the city expected it would quickly readopt liquor sales. Within Augusta most citizens initially seemed hopeful about giving the dry law a true test. The *Chronicle* used its front page of the first edition of 1908 to issue a warning to those who might seek to evade the liquor law: "This much may be understood from the start, the liquor law is to be enforced in Augusta. Those who doubt it will find they are in error and are apt to suffer greatly. . . . Those who have deferred beginning another occupation with the expectation of selling whiskey illegitimately may as well begin at once to look out for something else, unless they are prepared to stand the consequences."[37]

Ironically, it was the presence of North Augusta's dispensary that gave Augustans such confidence that prohibition would be successful in their city. After all, wrote the *Chronicle,* "the lawful operation of a liquor establishment just across the river in South Carolina makes the blind tiger in Augusta unnecessary. . . . We do not expect to see in this generation a return to what has been called the 'standing bar room.' The people are anxious to give the new law a fair and square test, and will be guided by the results of that test."[38]

This hopeful beginning was challenged almost as soon as the words were written, as rumors spread of blind tigers in and around Augusta. The police were sent to investigate, and after several months charges were brought—"against policemen for drinking 'blind tiger' whiskey.'"[39] By the end of the year further investigation "on the initiative of private citizens—citizens who have right to expect that the law would be enforced by those who are sworn to enforce it instead of having to do this unpleasant duty themselves—uncovered between $12,000 and $15,000 worth of whiskey... in a half dozen blind tigers, NEARLY EVERY ONE OF THEM DOING BUSINESS ON BROAD STREET."[40] "It does seem discouraging," remarked the *Chronicle*, "to think that the police are involved in a sensation or scandal... at the same time the *Chronicle* would like to commend Chairman Philpot for his evident determination to break up the numerous blind tigers now doing business in Augusta."[41]

The guilty officers were eventually tried and removed from the police force. As the remaining officers and new hires tried to repair the department's damaged reputation, Police Chief Norris reached out to citizens, assuring them that he and his men "are doing all in their power to assist in the work of stamping out the blind tigers.... Our greatest trouble... is the fact that we cannot get reliable men to assist us in the work. The man we can hire to go in a place and secure evidence for us is, in most cases, unreliable and the jury will not believe him upon oath."[42]

The police chief was not alone in this observation. Church leaders began pushing their memberships to take a more active role in law enforcement. The leader of Augusta's First Baptist Church, Sparks Melton, chided his members, saying, "It is the duty of every citizen to be a guardian of the peace... and all should have the courage to join in and not permit the sale of liquor." Evangelical minister Rev. J. M. Bass challenged his flock in much the same vein. "There are many people in Augusta who would not assist officers of the law in raiding the blind tigers, because they are guilty themselves," he noted. "Why does this blind tiger keeper sell you liquor when he knows that it is against the law? It is because he knows that if he is caught you will lie to keep him from being convicted."[43] Further chastising dry advocates was Rev. Richard Wilkinson, who challenged Christian men to heed the call to serve in Augusta's juries. "In the blind tiger cases," Wilkinson thundered, "Christian men who will not prostitute themselves and violate their sacred oaths" were needed in the juror's box.[44]

The gauntlet having been thrown down, some in Augusta's prohibition community warmed to the challenge. The Augusta WCTU issued a resolution decrying the "men who have not sustained the [prohibition] law.... They have winked at its violation; they have trodden it under foot; they have flagrantly and publicly set it aside. Therefore, we the women of the WCTU of Augusta do most pridefully declare our determination to destroy this hydra-headed evil that is trading the downfall of men, breaking the hearts of women and throwing a deadly night over the young!"[45] In Augusta's Broadway Methodist Church later the same month, the congregation "put ourselves on record as deeply incensed over the violation of the prohibition law in our community . . . and we call upon our city authorities to exert every effort in their power to crush out the numerous blind tigers."[46] The local branch of the Anti-Saloon League also met and vowed action against the blind tigers. "What we want to do," explained one ASL speaker, "is to remove the temptation of drink . . . from the working man so that he can carry home his week's wages and lay it at the feet of his wife and little children."[47]

For all the sound and fury only a few Augustans went beyond speeches and resolutions to take action against the blind tigers. Their actions resulted in "the biggest raid against the blind tigers since prohibition," in which "many thousands of dollars worth of whiskey was seized by officers. . . . The raids of these places were upon complaints made by . . . ministers, physicians and business men."[48] After the raid little more was done by the good people of Augusta, and the blind tigers continued to ply their trade.

In time the blind tigers took in so much money that their impact was felt across the river. "Business at the North Augusta dispensary has fallen off 50 percent," reported one correspondent, "and the difference between $16,000 a month and $8,000 a month detracts from the good thing they thought they had over there."[49] To the smoke of declining profits was soon added the fire of an Aiken County official's accusation in July 1909 that "there was a man stationed on the North Augusta bridge to turn back prospective visitors to the North Augusta dispensary."[50] Once alerted to this development, the South Carolina government "complain[ed] bitterly that . . . citizens along the state line stayed in Georgia for their nourishment instead of patronizing their own great moral institution."[51]

Defending Augusta's civic officials, the *Chronicle* remarked on the absurdity of such a claim. "As a matter of fact, Augusta has looked upon the North Augusta dispensary as a sort of safety valve. If there was ever a place where there ought not to be blind tigers it is Augusta. There is absolutely no necessity for them here. How can they thrive here is a marvel. That any man would wish to buy blind tiger liquor when there is the legal sale of the very best of the leading manufacturers two hundred yards across the bridge is out of the question."[52] Claims by dispensary proponents of a vast conspiracy to steal money intended for their liquor shops were likely off the mark, given that Augusta initially assessed only a fifty-dollar fine for liquor violations. "Such fines," the editor of the *Chronicle* pointed out, "even were they applied regularly once a month would scarcely amount in the course of a year to as much as the license tax heretofore paid."[53]

Despite these denials, charges by South Carolina officials persisted, and the fight for liquor revenue between Aiken and Augusta became news all across the South. Many commentators saw Augusta's civic leaders as the villains in the story—for example, the editor of the *Macon Telegraph,* who wrote: "Augusta officials have taken the position, tacitly of course, that it is probably better to keep the money at home [by periodically raids and fines] rather than to permit it to go to the Aiken county dispensary, and as a result, blind tigers are flourishing in Augusta. . . . So until South Carolina goes dry by state enactment it is very likely that Augusta will continue to be the home of the blind tiger in large quantities."[54] Other commentators were more circumspect, believing that having South Carolina try to assume the mantle of morality was at best disingenuous. The *Roanoke (Va.) Times,* for example, wrote "in the fight between the blind tiger of the prohibition state and the trained wild cat of the dispensary state, the tiger seems to have the best of it. The Aiken dispensary is $7,000 shy . . . and Carolina, weeping, turns away, calculating bitterly on her chaste fingers . . . that this means at least $84,000 a year she used to get from the foul but welcome scads of Georgia for her hallowed booze, which she doesn't get now and will get no more."[55]

Although the motives of Augusta's city leaders were far from clear (as all their official pronouncements promised vigorous prosecution of all illegal liquor), the question of the city's liquor problem was one that by early 1909 no Augustan could ignore. "The better class of saloons that formerly existed in Augusta have been driven out of business," wrote the *Chronicle,* "but the number of places where whiskey is sold has not been decreased. On the contrary, there are probably two blind tigers in Augusta today where there was one saloon thirteen months ago. All of which is quite as well known to the city authorities as it is known to us. . . . The question that seems to confront us, then, is Augusta to settle down to the definite policy of accepting the blind tiger as one of the necessary evils and license it, so to speak, by a system of occasional fines—or is she to adopt a strong uncompromising policy of enforcement of law?"[56]

AUGUSTA'S LOCKER CLUBS

When the Georgia state legislature passed the revenue bill permitting a tax on locker clubs, the Augusta City Council was quick to answer this question in favor of continued liquor licensing. Among all of Georgia's cities only Savannah ($300 per year) set the club license fee lower than Augusta ($500 per year). Even this relatively low amount, combined with the shipping expenses from Chattanooga or Jacksonville, meant that only high-end social clubs could afford such a dispensation. In Augusta there were five such clubs—the Commercial Club, the Elks, the Augusta Country Club, the Bon Air Social Club, and the Schuetzen—and the description of each made clear that only Augusta's elite were welcome. The Augusta Country Club, for example, boasted that its "new club house . . . situated on the original grounds of 199 acres . . . contains large reception rooms, dining rooms, billiard room and café. Ample locker rooms are provided. . . . The club has laid out a fine gravel road nearly four miles in length that . . . commands some of the finest views in the vicinity of Augusta."[57] In town many of the same "active and associated membership that has always been a great factor in the public life" took respite at the "Commercial Club's home on Broad Street, the center of the business life in the city. . . . In addition to its billiards, card, reading and lounging room, the club has a magnificent dining room where 100 guests can be served at one time . . . a site that has entertained in its spacious quarters most of the distinguished visitors to Augusta."[58]

Although the social club provision left members technically in compliance with the letter of Georgia's dry law, few were deceived. "The Georgia prohibition legislation is after all, not so revolutionary," remarked one writer. "When the Prohibition Bill with its drastic provisions was passed the people generally believed that so far as the law was concerned Georgia was to be absolutely 'dry.' . . . But the action of the prohibition legislature placing a tax or license of five hundred dollars upon clubs having lockers . . . shows that legislators were of the opinion that . . . a man may keep his liquors and that the State should receive some revenue from this liquor business. . . . We must express contempt for a legislature that could enact a prohibition law one day and nullify it the next and of men who would enact such class legislation reserving to themselves rights which they deprive poorer citizens of the State."[59]

Frustrated about the obvious loophole in their hard-won dry law, Augusta prohibitionists challenged this exception, publicly advocating for more stringent restrictions (if not a statewide ban) on locker clubs. As the drys waged their anti-locker campaign, they maintained a careful distinction between "the older and established social clubs [that] are cautious about their membership and withdraw membership where a member overindulges" and "locker clubs, or more accurately the liquor clubs . . . bulging brazen bars run exclusively for the patronage of any man and all men of whatever town or state or name who will pay the one dollar [and whose] turpitude is so great that they have justly called down upon themselves the wrath of all men."[60] "Warfare against the liquor problem," argued one prohibitionist, "would have due regard for these conditions and wipe out the objectionable clubs,"[61] while an Augusta resident pleaded: "Let's close up the clubs and see if we are ready for real prohibition. It can be done. Let the city sell just what alcohol and whiskey is needed for arts and sciences."[62]

Despite the drys' best efforts, the Augusta City Council continued to honor the distinction between Augusta's high-end locker clubs and those of lesser standing that sought equal footing with the social betters. The high-end clubs would continue to receive permits to operate. As they were composed of only the best citizens of Augusta and complied "strictly with the spirit and letter of the law,"[63] only the most ardent prohibitionists raised any concerns about their continued existence. Augusta drys were more successful when it came to preventing less-affluent social clubs from enjoying the benefits of the civic elite. Over the next several years, while the already existing clubs continuously had their licenses renewed, no others were permitted this dispensation. For Augusta's less-affluent citizens there was soon an alternative liquor option, the near beer saloon.

THE IMPACT OF NEAR BEER SALOONS

Augusta's locker clubs created only a slight stir in the prohibition debate, but they also did little to help Augusta's shrinking revenue stream. Of far more potential impact in both areas was the choice of whether to license near beer saloons. Following the Georgia's legislature's allowance of near beer in February 1908, Augusta's city council set their licenses at three hundred dollars per year and pledged to take up where the citizens had left off in cracking down on those blind tigers that refused to pay the fee. This move quickly drew the wrath of many Augustans, who correctly saw it as an almost complete abdication of the city's promise only a year earlier to give prohibition a fair and square trial. As one citizen wryly observed:

> Our liquor legislation is now, as Caesar said Gaul was, in three parts. First there is the prohibition act, which prohibits everything about liquor except getting drunk. Then there is the locker law, which allows liquor if you pay the state its price. The bargain by which the prohibition members in 1907 sold out this privilege to "tony" town and city clubs, while rigidly cutting off the farmers of the country and workmen of the towns from their little nips, has never been ventilated, nor will we now lift the lid. The third branch of our liquor legislation is this near beer act. If you pay the price you can sell near beer, and in consideration of your coming down with the dust liberally— the schedule being from $200 to $500—the powers that be will not give themselves nervous prostration by enquiring too closely how near you get. . . . Five hundred dollar clubs and two hundred dollar saloons make one think that if you raise sufficiently the limit almost anybody can get a permit to drink almost anything. There is a thirst for drink and a thirst for revenue and it does seem as if we are shaping up to a bargain, whereby if you slake the latter you will be allowed to quench the former.[64]

Over the next three years Augusta continued to raise the near beer license fee and at the same time saw greater numbers of saloons. The end of the year report in 1910 boasted that "last year there were 103 near beer saloons in the city. The license paid by each was $300 . . . the total revenue from that source was $30,900."[65] A year later "the finance committee, without a dissenting vote, determined to recommend to council that the license tax for near-beer saloons be fixed at $500 for the ensuing year." After this law was passed and the mayor pledged "a strict application of the prohibition law in Augusta as far as lies within the power of the city authorities to enforce it," the *Chronicle* "most heartily commend[ed] Mayor Barrett . . . the finance committee . . . and the council. The mayor and council are entitled to the unstinted support in carrying out this splendid policy of every man and woman in Augusta who really desires to see a better order of things next year."[66] Over the course of the next five years both the number of near beer saloons and the price of main- taining them increased, so that by 1915 Augusta's near beer revenue reached $83,250—roughly 8 percent of Augusta's total revenue.[67]

Despite their contribution to Augusta's revenue, many Augustans showed far less tolerance for near beer saloons than they did for locker clubs. Much of the campaign, as it had been with the blind tigers, was directed by the Protestant ministers of Augusta, who challenged the city council to reverse course, observing "that the enactment of the thousand dollar license has done very little in the abatement of this terrible nuisance is only too apparent . . . and we sincerely hope that our people have learned from this experience that the evil we face needs to be handled in a far more serious and heroic way."[68]

As ministers rallied their flock within Augusta, across Georgia and United States the city was rapidly becoming known as a place in which "the state laws against liquor selling are set at naught." Some trouble started when a child labor agent came to investigate conditions in Augusta's mills and included in his report several conversations with boys that painted Augusta as a wide-open town. One fourteen-year-old respondent told the agent that, if asked, "I can get drinks . . . in almost any saloon in town, because they know I won't put the cops wise. The cops don't care anyhow." A sixteen-year-old added: "Atlanta don't come near Augusta in sport. There is more right here in one night than you can find in a week down in Atlanta."[69] As Augustans digested these revelations, they found themselves under fire from the neighboring town of Warrenton, whose citizens complained they "are constantly flooded with literature sent out by the barkeepers of Augusta advertising their liquor, and liquor is shipped regularly into the town as in the days of local option from the bar rooms of Augusta."[70] Warrenton's citizens asked Augusta's mayor to clean up the problem, threatening to appeal to the state legislature if it was not addressed.

"What a picture of the present-day traffic in liquor," summarized Rev. John P. Erwin, "when a professional beer taster has said that the Augusta breweries are turning out the finest brew they have ever known and the people endorse and the officials protect this traffic and your lawmakers and office keepers cry out that there is not enough sentiment against the thing to put it out." The results of such willful blindness were everywhere, as the reverend itemized: "It is said Augusta men don't go to church. . . . Too many of them go off on Sundays in this town on a drunk. . . . That famous barbeque where nearly every man was drunk and your recorder, Picquet, took a double-header and landed under the table. . . . God save Augustans from saying in their hearts 'we want liquor.' The time has come when the people must rise and say 'this thing shall stop.'"[71]

Faced with both internal and external pressure to rein in the saloons, Augusta's city council passed a series of resolutions designed to curb the menace, among them many of the same rules that governed Augusta's saloons before prohibition, such as no sales to women and minors, the establishment of closing hours at no later than midnight, and the requirement that all saloon windows be open to the street. It was also hoped that raising the license fee to one thousand dollars would remove the worst offenders from the liquor trade.

While the complaints of prohibitionists and the notes of casual observers led most to question the effectiveness of such measures, far more impactful was the reorganization of the spatial distribution of Augusta's liquor shops. Before prohibition Augusta's saloons had been confined to three areas of the city: the central business district, the West End mill villages, and the territory, where the majority of African American resided. As near beer saloons made their appearance in Augusta, zoning restrictions were quickly put in place to limit their reach. The result was a virtual re-creation of Augusta's saloon map from the period before prohibition, with fifty-four of the city's near beer joints in the central business district and fourteen each in the West End and the territory. Outside of these areas no near beer saloon licenses were granted.

As Augusta's saloon profits grew, they reduced the need for Augustans to take the walk to patronize "the little oasis across the bridge." This increased competition, coupled with the occasional flood that temporarily made the Savannah River unpassable, meant "a most marked decrease for Aiken County liquor profits."[72] The result was a return to what had been the situation prior to statewide prohibition in Georgia, except, of course, Augusta was still a nominally dry city in a nominally dry state.

PART III

FROM LOCAL OPTION
TO PROHIBITION

The border war over liquor between Aiken County and Augusta was a story
that played out across the South in the years between 1907 and 1913. As
four other southern states adopted prohibition between 1907 and 1909, their
neighbors also licensed liquor shops near newly dry population centers in the
hope of gaining revenue. Within states the search for more revenue led counties located near dry neighbors to make similar choices. The result was six
years of constantly shifting liquor laws and highly contentious elections—all
in a quest for profit.

What put a halt to this pattern of behavior was the passage at the federal
level of the Webb-Kenyon Act in March 1913. This law prohibited the interstate shipment of liquor into dry states, thus making it possible for drys to argue that prohibition could be effective if only the proper laws were written and
enforced. Determined to give prohibition a fair trial, southern states gradually
tightened restrictions on the importation of alcohol, first limiting it to only
personal-use exemptions and eventually crafting Bone-Dry laws that prohibited all but medicinal and sacramental uses for liquor.

10

THE SOUTH STEPS BACK FROM PROHIBITION, 1909–1913

A few months before the North Augusta dispensary's opening in January 1908, South Carolina's legislature had eliminated the statewide dispensary system allowing counties such as Aiken to proceed on their own accord. Although disgusted with the corruption rife within the state system, most Palmetto State citizens reasoned that county-run dispensaries might do better, and as of 1909, twenty-one of the state's then forty-one counties continued operating their dispensaries. That year the newly formed South Carolina Anti-Saloon League (SCASL) had organized a prohibition campaign that succeeded in drying up all but six counties.

Although the results of the 1909 referenda could be reckoned as a prohibition victory, it was at best an imperfect one. The biggest issue still confronting prohibitionists after 1909 was the continued operation of dispensaries in six counties. These liquor shops served as a source for illegal blind tigers to buy their whiskey and transport it into neighboring counties, making prohibition in those counties more difficult to enforce. Equally disconcerting were the enormous liquor profits in those six dispensary counties, which contributed significantly to county treasuries in the years following 1909.

Such good fortune served as a hopeful beacon to counties across the state and the entire region. In South Carolina, as the county's next opportunity to vote on the liquor question arrived in 1913, voters wrestled with the liquor question with one eye toward the moral claims of prohibitionists and the other on what neighboring counties were doing. With dispensary money the primary motivation for either retaining or reinstating their liquor shops, voters knew that the best profits were attainable when the counties around them had adopted prohibition. In this instance they might hope to do what Aiken had done with the North Augusta dispensary: namely, to tap into the desperation of drinkers in dry counties who would make their way across county lines. This was of course a risky gamble. If counties nearby also adopted liquor shops, then profits across each would dwindle, and all any county would be left with was a business that added little to the county treasury while creating more drunkards for local law officials to handle.

Across the region southern state legislators grappled with the same sets of concerns. As five southern states had declared themselves dry in the years between 1907 and 1909, their neighboring counties also followed North Augusta's lead and set up liquor shops just across state lines. Without any means of preventing interstate liquor sales, Alabama, Mississippi, North Carolina, and Tennessee followed Georgia's lead in using their revenue laws to permit licensing of presumably illegal liquor dealers, making a bid to keep profits at home and thereby make the best of a bad situation. South Carolina, too, continued to wrestle with the allure of liquor profits against a widespread prohibitionist sentiment.

THE 1910 GUBERNATORIAL CAMPAIGN

As "prohibitionists . . . congratulated themselves upon the results of their labor" following the 1909 referenda,[1] they agreed to pursue enactment of a statewide law at the approaching legislative session. Noting that "the existence of dispensaries in territory contiguous to prohibition territory is a constant menace to the enforcement of the law,"[2] dry leaders cautioned that a statewide bill was effective "provided the Legislature furnishes at the same time the means for strict enforcement of said law." Without such a system a statewide bill would prohibit liquor in name only, and dry leaders were unanimously "opposed to nominal prohibition."[3] With renewed vigor, and led by C. C. Featherstone's candidacy in the 1910 gubernatorial race, prohibitionists looked forward to a successful conclusion of their campaign.

Such hopes were quickly dashed. The 1910 election proved to be a virtual replaying of the SCASL's experience the year before. While easily mobilizing voters in dry counties behind one of three prohibition candidates, Reverend Harley and the SCASL found the going more challenging in dispensary counties and those that still imagined they might, too, readopt their liquor shops.

As hopes dimmed for the election of a majority dry legislature, Harley's attacks became more strident and personal, leading to an inevitable backlash.

After one particularly vitriolic campaign stop in Union, the local option senatorial candidate for that county nearly came to blows with Harley, shouting after him, "You are a scoundrel to come here and poke your nose into matters that are no concern of yours!"[4] Newspaper editors also fired back at charges they were under the thumb of the whiskey trust. "It is alright for Mr. Harley to do all that he can to further the cause he is salaried for, it is alright for him to get people to contribute money," wrote the editor of the *Manning Times*, "but it is not right for him to be making charges he cannot sustain."[5] The editor of the *Newberry Herald and News* was even more vociferousness toward Harley:

> If there is any man in South Carolina who by his public expressions has done the cause of prohibition more harm than Rev. J. L. Harley, secretary of the Anti-Saloon League, the name of that other man is unknown to us.... In a communication published in the *Newberry Observer,* Rev. Mr. Harley discusses the present political situation in this State as it relates to prohibition, essaying to answer the arguments advanced for local option.... In the course of his article he says "Just here is where the local option principle as applied to the liquor business is a farce. The scheming politicians and the subsidized liquor papers will harp on local self-government. . . ." The politicians, whether scheming or not, can take care of themselves as well as of Mr. Harley should they choose. But as one having pride in the independence and integrity of journalism in South Carolina, and as one not unfriendly to the cause of prohibition, the *Record* desires to say that Mr. Harley owes it not only to the Press of the State, but to the anti-saloon league which he represents to name if he can any paper subsidized by liquor interests. Put up or shut up Brother Harley![6]

The results of the first gubernatorial primary revealed that little had changed from the previous year, with the eighteen strongly prohibition counties throwing their weight behind one of the three prohibition candidates and the six strongly dispensary counties doing likewise with either of the two local optionists. As had been the case in 1909, the race was most contentious in the

Table 10.1. Support for local option candidates, first Democratic primary election, 1910

Vote given to local option candidates (%)	Dispensary counties	1908–9 prohibition counties	1905 prohibition counties
66+	6	5	—
50–66	—	13	5
33–49	—	1	12

Source: Columbia (S.C.) State, August 31, 1910, 1.

remaining eighteen counties. Results from these counties made clear that the dry gains of the previous years were far from permanent (table 10.1).

The first primary results also made clear the composition of the legislature, and it, too, did not bode well for the dry forces. "The State now has county local option," observed the editor of the *Yorkville Enquirer*. "The majority of the senate stands committed to the maintenance of this condition and it is exceedingly doubtful as to whether the house is any stronger for state-wide prohibition than it has been."[7] The *Sumter Item* added: "The first primary proved conclusively that South Carolina is opposed to a Statewide law. The people proved it in two ways—a large majority of them voted for local option candidates for Governor and also elected a local option legislature. Mr. Featherstone, if elected Governor, will owe his election to the suffrage of thousands of local optionists and knowing, as he now does, that a majority of the people are opposed to any attempt being made to force prohibition upon those counties that have voted to retain the county dispensaries, he will scarcely be so unwise as to persist in the effort to carry out the State-wide program."[8]

Should he persist, argued the *State,* "Mr. Featherstone as Governor could do little to obtain a State-wide prohibition law except to approve a State-wide prohibition bill—and it is practically certain that he would have no such opportunity."[9] This being the case, the results of the second primary between Featherstone and Coleman Blease, an avowed local option supporter, held little meaning about the outcome of prohibition. "Whatever may have been the hopes of the prohibitionists that question is now eliminated," wrote dry campaigner L. D. Childs. "The result of last Tuesday's primary shows that the election of Mr. Featherstone could not be claimed as a victory for prohibition."[10]

THE DRYS' DESPAIR, 1910–1913

The years following the 1910 gubernatorial election confirmed these apprais-
als. The seemingly remote chance that a Featherstone victory might provide
a rallying point for dry activists disappeared as Blease's electoral victory in
1910 and again in 1912 ensured a governor who had time and again stated that
he enjoyed a drink of liquor occasionally himself and who believed that prohibition was a threat to law and order "in the form of free niggers backed by
white men."[11] Once elected, Blease made clear his intentions regarding a possible statewide law in his first inaugural, cheekily opining that, rather than
encouraging the "evil, habitual drinking of coca-cola, pepsi-cola and such like
mixtures," he believed it would be better for the people if they had "nice respectable places where they could go and buy a good, cold pure glass of beer,
than to drink such injurious concoctions."[12] Blease pressed further, advocating that the dispensary law be expanded to allow counties to decide if they
wanted county dispensaries, privately owned liquor stores, or prohibition.[13]

As governor, Blease made some effort to enforce existing liquor laws, although his attempts were often halfhearted and met with great skepticism
by South Carolinians, who were familiar with the governor's preference of liquor policy. By the end of 1913 Blease, fed up with the continuous insinuations
of his failure to uphold the law, angrily wrote the *State,* "You will please be
kind enough to furnish me with the names and locations of these barrooms of
which you speak and the names of the party or parties in control thereof along
with an affidavit and the names of your witnesses that beer and whiskey are
being sold in such places, and I promise you that within a few short hours . . .
warrants will be sworn out and these places will have been searched and re-
lieved of their stocks . . . and every man connected therewith will be arrested
and either locked up in your county jail or placed under sufficient bond to appear for trial."[14] That little came of this attempt surprised no one familiar with
Blease's posturing on the liquor issue; prohibitionists had long since given up
hope of support for their cause from this governor.

At the county level the years following the 1909 referenda made clear
that those elections had accomplished far less than was originally thought.
While the Upcountry mill counties continued their long-standing opposition
to the dispensary, in the six dispensary counties prohibition had made little
headway mainly because liquor sales continued to be an important source of

county revenue. By 1912 four of the six dispensary counties saw the percentage of their operating budgets rise to higher levels than at any previous time (table 10.2).

Even more alarming for prohibitionists, among the counties that had been won for the dry cause in 1909, few remained solidly in the prohibition column. At the beginning of 1913, when counties could reopen the liquor question after a four-year trial, pro-dispensary petitioners began making the rounds across the state. Such attempts were expected by the Anti-Saloon League, which had recently coaxed the legislature into raising the bar for when another election could be called, now requiring one-third of all registered voters rather than the original one-quarter. What the SCASL had not prepared for was the strong undercurrent of dispensary support across so many counties. Ultimately, petitioners in twelve counties succeeded in gathering enough votes to hold new elections on the liquor question during 1912 and 1913; eleven of these contests would be held in currently dry counties, nine of them having gone dry in 1909.

The resulting elections were held in an environment that featured renewed calls by progressives to address the key issues of the day, among them "the public health, the school system, good roads and respect for law are some of the questions which should receive the earnest attention of men."[15] Suggested improvements in these areas often meant greater government spending. As taxpayers balked at the price tag of the progressive agenda, many around South Carolina began reviving the dispensary idea for its financial advantages. Through liquor sales it seemed possible both to create a better society and to leave its citizens' taxes unchanged.

Table 10.2. Percentage of county revenue resulting from liquor profits, 1909–1912

County	1909	1910	1911	1912
Aiken	22.1	23.9	22.7	29.2
Beaufort	30.6	31.0	30.8	30.1
Charleston	25.0	31.4	30.4	24.2
Florence	18.7	20.6	27.8	47.1
Georgetown	19.7	19.2	20.0	25.9
Richland	21.1	26.8	30.8	38.4

Sources: South Carolina General Assembly, State Comptroller General, Annual Report; South Carolina General Assembly, State Dispensary Auditor, Annual Report.

TAXES AND SOUTH CAROLINA'S SCHOOLS

The year 1913 opened with ominous news for South Carolina taxpayers, with the *State* reporting a "higher tax levy may be necessary" because of the "difference in revenues and expenditures." The paper declared, "The state must borrow money." It turned out the new estimated tax of 6.25 mills, "one-half mill more than last year[,] is rendered necessary to carry out the plans for building the new State Hospital for the Insane." The comptroller general further explained that "if a half a mill is levied for this particular purpose every year . . . it will take about six years to pay for the buildings," which had been approved with a bond issue the previous year.[16]

Already reeling from this news, South Carolinians were soon asked to consider a new initiative to aid the state's poorest schools. The 1913 proposal was the latest in reformers' attempts to shore up the weakest parts of the state's school system, an effort that had begun in 1909 with the passage of the Term Extension Act, giving state matching grants to school districts that could not finance a hundred-day term relying on the three-mill school tax alone. By 1912 the Term Extension Act had doubled state aid for public school appropriations from the $60,000 allotted for high schools only to $120,000, which was spread across the poorest districts in the state.[17]

Now voters were being asked to consider another one-mill levy, "the proceeds of which 50 percent shall be retained in the county in which collected to be known as the county board fund . . . 50 percent of which shall be deposited with the state Treasurer and disbursed by him on the warrant of the chairman and secretary of the board of education . . . for high schools . . . the extension of public schools . . . for consolidated grade schools . . . and for rural libraries."[18] Making the case for this new appropriation, the state secretary of education, J. E. Swearingen, detailed the precarious financial situation of many of the state's public schools. "Many of the most progressive schools in the state are in need of state aid . . . to be paid form the one-mill state school tax. . . . Some $30,000 is needed to meet the demands of the schools. . . . If the money to settle these claims cannot be secured the schools must close and some 25,000 white children will suffer."[19] W. K. Tate, state supervisor of rural schools, also noted the monetary shortfall, reminding legislators that "the appropriation of last year lacked $12,000 of meeting the demands and many country communities which have qualified will be disappointed and seriously handicapped if the amount is cut." Tate also sought to ease voters' concerns, noting that "participation in the benefits of this act requires first that a district help itself" by levying its own school tax.[20]

Objections soon arose to the tax, largely along two lines. The first was rooted in the method of apportionment of school funds, which was required by law to be based on enrollment. As African American schools always had far less spent per student than white schools, this apportionment, in the words of one frustrated Richland County farmer, "merely piles up balances in districts with heavy negro enrollment and starves districts with a large white enroll-ment." This farmer wondered why "when we are mostly white people in our district we can't have a very long term. But our relatives live in another dis-trict. The blacks are in the majority there. They have more money than they can spend."[21]

The more common complaint against the new school tax, as it was with all proposed and existing levies, was that taxes were already too high and, as one taxpayer put it, "we are not getting the value received."[22] "If you do not know your taxes are high it is because you haven't paid yours yet," complained the *Newberry Observer.* "People are paying a lot of money for city, county, and state taxes. Are they getting the value . . . ?"[23] Others asserted that the tax "is generally unnecessary. The educational fund from state taxes already levied is, in our estimation, sufficient, if properly and economically used, to furnish all the educational facilities our people at present need and can utilize. Conse-quently, an additional tax would probably lead only to more lavishness and ex-travagance in the use of public funds or to a perverted use of the same, both of which would in every way be hurtful to the State." Beyond merely representing wasteful public spending, "excessive taxes confuse and cripple our productive industries, which is farming in this state, by withdrawing the capital required to run and develop them and by creating and promoting competing lines of non-productive industries."[24] Despite such protests, the rural grade school tax was passed and in the process added another fifteen thousand dollars to the state's educational budget (from taxpayers' bank accounts) for the 1913–14 academic year.

TAXES AND GOOD ROADS

Alongside industrialization and education in what Francis Butler Simkins called "the Trinity of Southern Progress" stood the development of good roads.

By 1913 this goal had grown considerably more urgent across South Carolina as motor travel had become more popular and counties and municipalities sought increasing connection to the outside world. They had a long way to go. Automobile travel in South Carolina inevitably entailed navigating the many creeks, streams, and rivers that lacked bridges or ferries. As John Hammond Moore explains in his study of the state's highways, "A sudden shower could turn a shallow, placid expanse of water into a swift torrent and wreck the best laid plans for any outing." Avoiding such trouble spots often meant taking circuitous routes to arrive safely at one's destination. "Until well into the 1920s," Moore writes "anyone living in eastern South Carolina, say Florence, drove to Charleston via Camden and Columbia where bridges spanned the Wateree and Congaree Rivers."[25]

In the Upcountry conditions were not all that much better, as a reporter for the *State* found when he set out from Columbia to the North Carolina mountains in July 1912. "Within ten miles of Columbia," Moore writes, "he was hopelessly mired in Lexington County mud and had to be rescued by horses. He finally got to Laurens at 6:15 P.M., having set out eight hours earlier. The next day he drove to Greenville in two hours along a road flanked by random 5-foot stone and plank pillars covered with ad and mileage signs. The trip from Greenville to Hendersonville, plagued by minor delays, took another five hours. In summary, this intrepid reporter offered these words of advice: put on chains at the first provocation . . . a slight shower and red clay can cause big trouble, have a pail handy . . . an auto consumes a surprising amount of water, and carry an axe . . . a few braches work wonders when stuck in mud."[26]

Despite the obvious need to improve roadways, good roads advocates often had difficulty making their case. Some of the difficulty was in demonstrating that roads, once made, would continue to be passable. Virtually all of South Carolina's roads at this time were made of a mixture of sand and clay. This mixture was preferred to either substance on its own because each had "the tendency to overcome the bad qualities of the other. The sand renders the clay less sticky and clay overcomes the liquid character of the sand."[27] Although it might seem that any mixture of the two would work for road construction, the required mixture was actually a very precise one—and one that road builders got wrong. Further, simply mixing sand and clay in the right amounts did not ensure a workable road because each lump of clay had to be reduced to a paste by the addition of water, a process called "puddling." It was at this stage, wrote road expert William L. Spoon in 1910, "that the stoutest-hearted road builder often loses hope and courage and feels that he has made an utter failure, when he should know and the public should know that this is the opportune time to effect the contact mixture."[28]

The public did not always understand the necessity or difficulty of the puddling process and the time needed to turn the potential road into something passable rather than a pile of watery mush, leaving many to question the outlaying of funds for a road that seemed as if it would be impassable. In one remarkable instance E. J. Watson, a South Carolina road construction engineer, reported that he became the first man in the state to be "indicted in the criminal court, tried and convicted," for building a sand-clay road. Writing in the April 1911 issue of *Southern Good Roads,* Watson recalled a sand-clay road that he had built in Marion County. When rain transformed the road into an impassable bog, he was taken to court and charged with destroying a public highway. Watson summarized the judge's decision: "The judgment of the court was that I must put the road back like it was before and it was so ordered. In the opinion of the court, it was best to choose the lesser of two evils. The old road was bad and the new one was worse."[29] Watson further reported that, despite the order, he did nothing, and when the road dried after the rain, it was in fine condition.

Another concern preventing spending on public roads was their financing. Few counties had the budget surpluses that allowed Aiken County to lend out money, nor did most have the guaranteed dispensary profits to pay off such debts. Thus, most counties were forced to issue bonds, which were generally unpopular and widely opposed. As the *Manning Times* explained: "Our people do not vote blindly for or against such a proposition. They count the cost and take into consideration the benefits. They know that in most instances bond issues under our present plan become permanent debts; that they are never paid and the interest on them is a never ending load for them and their descendants to carry."[30]

The combination of seemingly unfinished roads and permanent debt was enough to counter the drive for further construction, with many in the state figuring the cost was too high, as in this enumeration of conditions in Lee County: "A total of $67,708.33 for the past six years. All this money has been spent on our country roads with no bridges of importance being constructed nor any stability to the roads that have been built. Drawing from these figures, we can safely say that at least $100,000 has been spent on the public roads in Lee County since its establishment in 1902. . . . [Yet] there is nothing permanent about the roads we get."[31]

BLIND TIGERS

Aside from wrangling over the relative merits of civic construction and tax relief, the issue occupying most South Carolinians' attention in 1913 was the question of illegal liquor and its relationship to county dispensary policy. Almost everyone agreed that the problem of illegal liquor had become more acute since the 1909 referenda, though there was considerable disagreement about its true nature. Most, if not all, South Carolinians acknowledged that the trouble was most manifest in the seeming inability to stop blind tigers, a problem so pervasive that they caused even Governor Blease no little frustration. "I have had more trouble and worry in the last two or three months with complaints as to blind tigers than one poor fellow can stand," Blease lamented. "I have had my constabulary force full, my detectives at work, and recently counties have been calling on me to send them special men, and I have been tightening the screws."[32]

Readers familiar with Blease's gift for hyperbole and his own personal preference for legalization of liquor might be tempted to dismiss such a statement, except for the consistent flood of letters from county officials asking for state constabulary aid. A typical example came from the Lexington sheriff: "The biggest stumbling block to order and good work which we have met in this section is the blind tigers and bootleggers that infest the vicinity. Most of our troubles arise from corn whiskey. We have two officers, whose salaries are paid in our office, but this jurisdiction only extends for a radius of one mile. . . . Any assistance you might be able to extend in suppressing these nuisances would be greatly appreciated."[33] Blease was even pressed to act by the federal government, lest blind tigers cause "plans to enlarge the naval detention barracks at Port Royal . . . [to] be abandoned. Secretary [of the Navy Josephus] Daniels holds it as useless to attempt to reform work in behalf of the men, when, after leaving the reservation they 'fall into the lowest kind of environments.'"[34]

Aside from the sheer volume of supposed illegal activity, what scared many South Carolinians was the seeming intractability of the illegal trade. Some commentators pinned this persistence on the operators of the illegal shops. "Years ago," explained the *Beaufort Gazette,* "white men were engaged in this illicit traffic. They were forced out of business. . . . Today we have to deal with negro shopkeepers satisfied with small gains from the precious trade. They are treacherous and persistent and difficult to handle."[35] The blind tigers' persistence was aided by the steady need of their clients, as one commentator noted: "When the topers cease to guzzle, the whiskey distillery, the bar-room, the blind tiger will go out of business. Law or no law, they will not do it before."[36]

Adding to this sense of the inevitability of illegal liquor was that drinking occurred not only in "disreputable and notorious blind tigers" but also in "mutual organizations, equipped with all club and home conveniences and with scores of members."[37] Such respectable club drinkers posed an even greater problem because they compromised other members' willingness to join the fight against illegal liquor. "Let us suppose . . . you approach one of our representative citizens and ask him to co-operate in a movement for civic righteousness," opined a Charleston clergyman. "As likely as not he will tell you . . . 'I cannot take part in the movement to enforce the law because my hands are tied.' When you ask him why his hands are tied, you get this extraordinary answer, 'because I belong to a club that is a blind tiger.' That is, he goes to a club which sells liquor to its members, contrary to law, and which is to all intents and purposes a blind tiger. 'I am therefore one of the law breakers. How can I help to enforce a law against a man lower down when I am a member of an organization that breaks the law?'"[38]

Of course, not everyone threw up their hands in surrender before the blind tigers. Sheriffs and police officers all over the state seized illegal liquor, in some instances so much of it that they had to take extraordinary measures to seize and store it. In Jasper County "State Detective E. F. Hammond and Constable Paul Hutson . . . trailed a negro by the name of Warry Orr . . . all night through the swamps" before arresting him and his liquor in the early morning hours.[39] In Calhoun County "Sheriff Hill seized seven hundred pints of contraband stuff. . . . This liquor is now under lock and key in the cells of the local 'calaboose.' Negros peer in every once in a while and deplore the incarceration of anything which could give so much joy to a thirsty public."[40]

Citizens, too, joined in the fight against blind tigers. In Colleton County "the prohibitionists have exerted themselves to a remarkable degree and have aroused the county to realize the present laws are not being enforced," while in Allendale "a mass meeting of representative citizens held resulted in 20 or more of the best citizens volunteering to give the blind tigers a warning and accordingly today visited half a dozen places suspected of violating the law."[41]

Despite such attempts, many people likely would have agreed with the editor of the *State* when he wrote, "The liquor traffic conditions . . . are not so satisfactory as they were a year ago and there is an unmistakable tendency on the part of the people to consent quietly to a steadily increasing habit of law-breaking."[42] In Sumter the situation deteriorated so much, according to the *State*, that the mayor in frustration "says that the city government has had to face the situation and to suppress the blind tiger all by itself, and that the citizenry has not helped, and he thinks the prohibitionists and other good citizens should help; that it is almost impossible for officers, known and in uniform, to gather evidence."[43] In response the *Watchman and Southron* chided the mayor, asking, "Is there a man in this county so foolish as to believe that because he stood and voted for prohibition . . . it is his duty as a private citizen to go out and drag in the blind tiger or haul the social clubs into court?"[44]

Even if such work was done by citizens, little help was forthcoming from authorities. In Spartanburg the *Journal* noted that "a blind tiger may be as guilty as he can be and it is certain that he will continue to work. There are lawyers who, by appeal or otherwise, will have the sentence held up and the blind tiger will give bond and resume business in twenty four [*sic*] hours."[45] With the tigers so completely ensconced, "the respectable politician, despairing of success by legitimate methods . . . is likely to enter into the market for the corruptible vote. If two or three men of this class be candidates, it is likely that corruption and bribery will be on a large scale."[46]

By 1913 such political chicanery at the highest levels of the state government was again in the South Carolina headlines. Its source was the state dispensary system. Although legally dead since 1907, it lived on through a special commission appointed by Governor Ansel to close out dispensary business. During much of its existence the commission had recovered large amounts of money lost by the state to graft. Many lawsuits were launched, and an Atlanta law firm—Anderson, Felder, Roundtree and Wilson—was employed by the state to handle these cases and settle once and for all the dispensary's accounts.

The commission's work began making news again when Blease was elected governor, as many of his friends were facing court action when he assumed office in late January 1911. Anxious to protect his political allies, Blease first called upon the legislature to appoint a committee to investigate the dispensary commission, which he claimed was swindling the state in a far worse manner than the dispensary had ever done. Eventually, Blease appointed his own team of investigators whose sole aim, it seemed, was to discredit Thomas Felder, the chief attorney handling cases for the dispensary commission. A former member of the state dispensary board and one of Blease's friends testified that Felder had tried to bribe him on behalf of the liquor companies, and in response Felder sent open letters to South Carolina's newspapers denying the charges and attacking Blease as a "plunderbund," a "mental and moral pervert,"[47] and a "miserable miscreant, not even fit to be governor of a nigger colony."[48] Although he had no proof of any wrongdoing, Felder implied that someone of Blease's low moral standing was likely involved in corrupt activities.

Charges and countercharges flew back and forth between Blease and Felder throughout 1912, with Blease demanding Felder testify and show evidence against him and Felder claiming he was afraid to enter South Carolina because Blease had offered a two thousand–dollar reward to anyone who would "get Tom Felder two feet this side of the Savannah River."[49] In order to hear Felder, the commission moved to Augusta. The governor aired his opinion of this choice with his customary vitriol: "This guttersnipe, stinking, filthy commission which has been trying to find something on me are going to crawl on their bellies to Augusta to take the testimony of a scoundrel who is afraid to come to South Carolina."[50]

When Felder testified before the committee, he again renewed his charges against Blease, declaring that he had hired a detective, Williams Burns, who had obtained a dictograph recording of the governor selling pardons to dispensary grafters. Upon further questioning the source of the recording claimed to be drunk at the time it was made and would not substantiate the charge. With no way to firmly implicate Blease, the governor used the remainder of the 1912 campaign to clear his name from the "damnable conspiracy" engaged in by "this cowardly character, thief debaucher and pimp [who] has attempted to injure the chief magistrate of the state with the assistance of this committee."[51]

Although Blease was never acquitted, his character and those of other dispensary agents again cast a pall over the whole enterprise of liquor sales, both legal and illegal. By the time of the 1913 dispensary referenda, the county liquor stores were rarely viewed as a buttress against illegal liquor sellers. Instead, dispensaries were often seen as "a convenience to blind tigers in that the source of supply will be right at home."[52] In Beaufort, one of the state's six dispensary counties, the blind tigers had become "so bold and flagrantly lawless . . . that the citizenship of that county has become greatly alarmed. A dispensary constable was recently foully murdered while making an effort to apprehend tigers. . . . Mr. [Niels] Christensen [Beaufort County representative] says these blind tigers after obtaining a supply from the dispensary 'go into the country districts where there is no police protection, and sell day and night to men, women, and children.'"[53]

Illegal sales were seen as even more disruptive in prohibition counties, where such activity went against the presumed prevailing voter sentiment. Thus, dry counties nearest to dispensary counties were among those said to be most under siege, with many in these counties asserting that "the wet counties are selling the liquor to our people and getting the revenue while we are getting the drunks and court expenses."[54]

ELECTION RESULTS OF 1913

It was the complex of sentiments toward liquor revenue, government tax policy, and blind tigers that voters had to consider as they went to the polls to decide the liquor question anew in August 1913. The elections themselves were in the main closely contested, and results in several counties remained unclear even after the polls closed. Of the twelve counties that held referenda in 1913, five had results that were challenged. Requests for recounts were made in both Union and Orangeburg Counties, where dry campaigners alleged voter fraud. In Williamsburg County "dispensary adherents presented affidavits to the effect that at Muddy Creek and Hebron polls voters were not required to present registration certificates and . . . demanded that the vote at these precincts be thrown out. . . . The prohibition forces also filed affidavits to the effect that at the Kingstree poll voters were not sworn, and demanded that the vote at Kingstree not be counted."[55] Similar charges were made in Lexington County, where prohibitionists lost by fifty-six votes. In addition to challenging "irregularities and specific instances where men had been allowed to vote without their registration certificates,"[56] the dry campaign hired an attorney to investigate whether all those who had initially been registered to vote had the legal standing to do so. The biggest electoral brouhaha occurred in Sumter

County, where the election was initially called for the dispensary by four votes, this after the county election commissioners—at a daylong review of each ballot box attended by "attorneys for prohibition on the one side and attorneys for the dispensary on the other side . . . and a crowd seemingly equally divided . . . each person an interested spectator and participator"—judged ten prohibition ballots and four dispensary ballots invalid.[57] Ultimately, all five sets of county results would make their way to the state board of canvassers for final adjudication, with four (Lexington, Orangeburg, Union, and Williamsburg) ending up as dispensary victories. Of the remaining seven counties, five also wound up in the wet column. Although one of them, Florence, was a county in which nearly half of the yearly revenue came from the dispensary, the other four had been dry prior to 1913.

With only two exceptions, the 1913 dispensary contests were fought on the same ground as the 1909 referenda. Of the eighteen mill counties that had adopted prohibition in 1905, only one (Union County) sought an election to readopt its dispensary. Of the six continuously dispensary counties, only one (Florence County) held an election to rid itself of its liquor shops. Among the eighteen counties that adopted prohibition in 1909, by contrast, ten held new elections four years later, and eight of those ten readopted their liquor stores. Obviously, the 1909 dry counties were weaker supporters of dry laws than their neighbors upstate; these counties only held elections when prompted to do so by state law rather than voluntarily, as had the 1905 dry counties. It is not surprising, then, that the 1909 dry counties might be more likely to change their position on the liquor question than were the 1905 dry counties.

What is less clear is why half of the 1909 dry counties readopted their liquor shops (or nearly did so in the case of Sumter County), while the other half either gave prohibition large majorities or failed to gather the required number of petitions to hold an election. All of the 1909 counties were located in the eastern part of the state. All were largely agricultural counties with few or no textile mills. All but two had majority African American populations. Most important, they would each be characterized as apathetic prohibition counties; each had held prohibition contests only when prompted by the state, and yet when they did so, none had more than 28 percent of their voters support the continuation of their liquor shops. As these counties appear so similar, we might wonder what changed in some of them but not in others and what would bring about such differing outcomes only four years later?

The arguments made in the campaigns leading up to the referenda point us toward some potential answers. Aware of citizens' concerns about taxes and loss of dispensary revenue in their counties, prohibitionists acknowledged these issues as they campaigned. As SCASL superintendent Harley toured the state, he attempted to blunt these concerns. "I have utterly failed to make myself understood," he told one audience, "if I have given the impression that one should be careless about profits." That being the case, Harley continued, "the health, happiness, progress, and prosperity of the public is your best asset. In the cultivation of these you reap the natural result, the harvest of profit."[58]

While Harley showcased his newfound business acumen, other speakers chided men who, "convinced the illicit sale of whiskey cannot be suppressed, have voted for the dispensaries in order that their county may obtain a profit," having thereby "lowered the sense of virtue and honor exhibited by those counties."[59] Springfield preacher James H. Fanning struck an even more strident tone, condemning "the man who will vote to reestablish a den of vice, of sin, of debauchery, of degradation, provided he . . . understand the debauchery entailed upon the State of South Carolina by the old dispensary system and the horde of office disgracers elected under the regime of the vast octopus" as those who "will have merited the displeasure of high heaven and will receive their reward as promised in the Holy Bible."[60]

A less moralistic dry argument was found in fears and frustrations of blind tiger activity and its likelihood to create lawlessness. In Calhoun County, for example, "many farmers lined up against the sale of whiskey on the ground, among other things, that the public roads on Saturday nights were unsafe because of drunken rowdies . . . who had a habit of discharging their firearms promiscuously. . . . Others claim that matters are worse instead of better [under prohibition] and that there has been little or no hindrance to the sale of illicit liquor without any revenue therefrom."[61] Those concerned about blind tigers included "many business men and planters who do not scruple to take their toddies yet vote for prohibition in the belief that, with whiskey hard to get, better order will prevail in their towns and on their plantations."[62]

Prohibitionist arguments, whether biblical or business centered, were largely accepted by the majority of South Carolina's citizenry. Yet they had limited sway among those grappling with the limitations caused by "divisions of infected territory interspersed throughout prohibition territory that render it easy and convenient for a large proportion of those in prohibition territory to secure all the whiskey they desire, thereby neutralizing largely the beneficial effects of prohibition in territory where the majority of voters have endorsed and desire it."[63] Instead of the promised prohibition prosperity, those dry counties remaining nearby dispensary counties were left with little but "high taxes and blind tigers running riot."[64]

While such circumstances pushed some to advocate for statewide prohibition, it led many others to the opposite conclusion. As a Lexington County liquor campaigner reminded his audience, "Liquor is a bad thing, the dispensary is bad—but we have a lot of blind tigers and no profits . . . [we also have] visions of good roads, paved streets, more and better schools, [and] lower taxes."[65] Summing up the pro-dispensary argument, the editor of the *Sumter Watchman and Southron* enumerated the situation as it existed following the adoption of prohibition in that county:

> The closing of the county dispensary was followed by a train of evils that counter-balanced the good. Blind tigers have multiplied within the town and throughout the county and this form of lawlessness has been attended by a growing disrespect for and contempt of law, drunkenness has decreased but little if at all, and the burden of trying to enforce the law has been shifted from the shoulders of the liquor drinkers to those of the taxpayers. The blind tigers have profited, the express companies have reaped a harvest, and the mail order whiskey houses in other states have grown rich as a direct result of the closing of the dispensary. The direct and indirect evils of intemperance we still have with us, for there has not been a day since the dispensary was closed that an occasional or habitual drunkard could not obtain liquor for a debauch. . . . The experience of the last four years holds out not a glimmer of hope of improvement for the future. . . . This effort to control or suppress the use of liquor in one place when it is freely sold in another with the sanction of law will prove a farce and a failure.[66]

Following the readoption of the dispensary in Calhoun County, the *Calhoun Advance,* meanwhile, was even more blunt: "When the dispensary was voted out immediately council doubled the taxes of our citizens. Will the present council reduce our taxes now since the dispensary has returned?"[67]

Three themes, then, made themselves apparent in the campaign discussions of 1913. The first had to do with the ability of prohibition, if retained as a policy, to accomplish its stated goals. While nearly all speakers acknowledged the difficulties of keeping down blind tigers and the increasing willingness of honest citizens to look the other way while entering their social clubs, prohibition arguments were a little easier to maintain in counties far removed from dispensary counties. At least in these cases speakers could assert that it would be more difficult for middlemen to obtain liquor if no legal source existed nearby, which might dissuade some illegal activity. Proximity to another county's legal liquor would also have meant that more folks would probably have made this trip, increasing the likelihood of having drunkards on the roads making their way back home. Although few citizens were willing to admit defeat at the hands of the blind tigers in their own counties, the argument that "our people go to the 'wet' counties and buy liquor; we have the trouble while they get the profits therefrom" might have gained quite a bit more traction among voters in counties near already established dispensaries.[68]

The other two arguments made for dispensary readoption were economic and can be seen as two sides of the same coin. Both focused on profits lost to the county as a result of going dry. If faced with less revenue, counties could opt for one of two courses. The first would be to make do with less, meaning fewer roads would be built and less school improvements would be made throughout the county. The other, more direct way that loss of dispensary revenue would impact voters was through their tax rates. Counties faced with a loss of liquor money might have sought to accomplish the same goals and thus asked of their citizens a higher county tax rate or the levying of a special tax for road construction or the betterment of county schools. In an environment in which state tax levels were continually rising, voters subject to such levies might have reasoned that the readoption of the dispensary would if not reverse their financial fortunes, at least put a stop to their constant draining away.

Taken together, voters' judgment of the feasibility of prohibition as a policy depended primarily on their financial assessment and their understanding of how well enforcement might work. Counties that were far enough removed from existing legal liquor to at least give the illusion that liquor could be prevented from crossing county lines and those that saw little financial cost in maintaining dry laws stayed the course as prohibition counties. Those that took a greater financial hit or whose voters reasoned that easily available legal liquor was too close for comfort were more likely to opt for a return to their dispensaries (table 10.3).

Table 10.3. Three factors influencing the readoption of dispensaries, 1913

County	High revenue loss (fewer county improvements)	High tax increase	Close proximity to dispensary county	Readopted dispensary, 1913
Abbeville	x	x		
Bamberg	x		x	Yes
Barnwell	x	x	x	Yes
Berkeley				
Calhoun		x		Yes
Chester		x		
Chesterfield				
Clarendon				
Colleton				
Dorchester		x	x	Yes
Fairfield				
Hampton				
Kershaw	x			
Laurens		x		
Lee	x			
Lexington		x	x	Yes
Orangeburg	x	x	x	Yes
Sumter	x	x		Yes
Williamsburg	x			Yes

Sources: South Carolina General Assembly, State Comptroller General, *Annual Report;* South Carolina General Assembly, State Dispensary Auditor, *Annual Report.*

Note: x denotes that the county had that condition. A blank field denotes that the county did not have that condition.

By the end of 1913 fifteen of South Carolina's now forty-three counties had dispensaries,[69] and Sumter County had seemingly given a majority to the dispensary as well, before having the result overturned. Although prohibitionists might have counted as safely dry the remaining twenty-seven counties, altogether they amounted to only two-thirds of the state. In the remaining third, it seemed, the battle against liquor could not be safely won at the county level.

COUNTY VOTES AND COUNTY PROFITS

No doubt dispensary customers rejoiced at the prospect of having more easily available liquor, as did counties looking to boost their revenues through liquor sales. Looking at the impact on liquor profits as a whole, the increase in the number of dispensary counties predictably added to dispensary sales, up from $3,071,948 in 1913 to 3,663,826 in 1914.[70] These profits, however, were not spread evenly. Liquor boards in the counties that had previously held a monopoly on liquor sales now confronted declining profits because of greater competition from counties nearby. Each of the six counties with existing dispensaries lost sales when the new counties' dispensaries opened in late 1913 and throughout 1914 (table 10.4).

It is difficult to gauge how many customers elected to patronize newly opened dispensaries in their home counties rather than those across county lines. What sales figures can show is that in two instances sales in old dispensary counties decreased after the new dispensaries began operating. The first such case occurred in counties that had liquor shops in towns relatively close to formerly dry counties, for example, Salley's dispensary, located in Aiken County on the border of Orangeburg County. The second occurred in

Table 10.4. Dispensary sales by county (dollars), 1912–1914

County	Sales in 1912	Sales in 1913	Sales in 1914
Aiken	**330,042**	**282,038**	**232,957**
Beaufort	**142,337**	**152,350**	**132,775**
Barnwell	—	67,990	245,482
Bamberg	—	34,144	118,315
Charleston	**631,904**	**592,106**	**578,467**
Calhoun	—	28,428	66,784
Dorchester	—	29,172	86,242
Florence	**499,996**	**566,674**	**564,116**
Georgetown	**147,730**	**167,005**	**158,689**
Jasper	12,172	18,567	23,339
Lexington	—	—	107,640
Orangeburg	—	—	326,057
Richland	**897,845**	**982,889**	**811,133**
Union	—	150,579	170,525
Williamsburg	—	—	41,297
Total	2,662,026	3,071,948	3,663,826

Source: South Carolina General Assembly, State Dispensary Auditor, *Annual Report.*

Note: Figures for the six counties with existing dispensaries that lost sales when new dispensaries opened in other counties are shown in bold.

Table 10.5. Distance to dispensaries and dispensary sales, 1913–1914

Old dispensary county (town)	Gain/loss in sales, 1913–14	Neighboring formerly dry counties	Gain/loss in sales, 1913–14	Miles to old dispensary county
Aiken (Salley)	-$49,081	Barnwell	+$177,492	29
		Orangeburg	+$326,057	15
Charleston	-$13,639	Dorchester	+$57,070	25
Florence	-$2,557	Williamsburg	+$41,297	39
Georgetown	-$8,315	Williamsburg	+$41,297	42
Richland (Columbia)	-$171,756	Lexington	+$107,640	15
		Calhoun	+$38,355	38

Source: South Carolina General Assembly, State Dispensary Auditor, *Annual Report.*

Note: Beaufort was omitted from this analysis because its neighboring county with liquor (Jasper) was formed as a wet county in 1912.

the two largest dispensary towns, Charleston and Columbia, where visitors from neighboring counties would likely have been frequent, even if the distance from their home counties was a bit greater. Table 10.5 details the shift in dispensary revenue between South Carolina counties as well as the distance between existing dispensary towns and formerly dry counties. The closer old dispensary towns were to formerly dry counties, the greater the decline in their sales once new liquor shops were opened.

More important than sales figures was the profit made by county liquor shops and their contribution to the county's revenues. Here, too, the impact on the old dispensary counties was dramatic and generally negative. In the new dispensary counties, where legal sales were often touted as the panacea for a county's financial woes, such claims proved to be unfounded. Among the fifteen dispensary counties in 1914, only two saw profits that contributed more than a third to their incoming revenue and only three others saw as much as a quarter of their bottom line accounted for by liquor profits (table 10.6).

PROHIBITION DOES NOT PROHIBIT ANYWHERE

As South Carolina's dry campaigners struggled throughout 1913 to convince their neighbors that dispensary money was not worth the deal they had made

Table 10.6. Percentage of dispensary profits to county revenue, 1913–1914

County	1913	1914
Aiken	25.0	19.5
Bamberg	—	33.9
Barnwell	—	26.9
Beaufort	27.3	28.8
Calhoun	—	19.2
Charleston	18.2	13.4
Dorchester	—	18.5
Florence	51.5	43.9
Georgetown	30.6	27.7
Jasper	—	6.7
Lexington	—	8.1
Orangeburg	—	27.5
Richland	35.8	20.7
Union	—	14.9
Williamsburg	—	6.6

Sources: South Carolina General Assembly, State Comptroller General, *Annual Report;* South Carolina General Assembly, State Dispensary Auditor, *Annual Report.*

with the devil, they likely looked on with envy at their neighbors across the region who had seemingly already won this battle. Yet across the South those victorious prohibitionists watched with dismay as their states, desirous of the very same liquor profits, licensed and taxed social clubs and near beer dealers. The impetus for this seeming change of heart was aptly stated by the mayor of Fayetteville, North Carolina, who, after three years of failed attempts to enforce prohibition in a supposed bastion of dry sentiment, declared, "The present abortion is unenforceable, a fraud upon its face, impossible in theory and practice, creates hypocrites and fosters hypocrisy, breeds criminals and is a public reproach upon the intelligence of our citizenship."[71] If the mayor was surprised by the enormity of the task, he would likely have been among the few who were. The advent of prohibition had turned North Carolina into "a paradise for 'moonshiners' . . . while in the cities and towns 'speak-easies spring up like mushrooms, the hotels find ways of selling the 'stuff' on the quiet. The clubs adopt all the well-known devices for successfully evading the law."[72]

Such complaints were common across the South. "Every city in Mississippi has had more blind tigers than legitimate saloons in the days when the sale of whiskey was carried on," reckoned the editor of the *Natchez News*,[73] while the superintendent of the Tennessee Anti-Saloon League begged his local organizers to "take steps to have the anti-saloon forces of your section represented" so as to destroy the "liquor traffic that has so manipulated and controlled the politics of the large cities of the State that the officials . . . make absolutely no effort . . . to enforce the law."[74] In Montgomery a reporter sent to cover an Alabama Anti-Saloon League meeting wandered into a resort down the street and "after every other person had ordered beer, whiskey or highballs, respectfully requested that he be served with a certain known soft-drink, made in Atlanta. The barkeep was exceedingly surprised, and declared that the soft-drink was something he did not sell. . . . Beer and whiskey were all that could be had in the prohibition capital of a prohibition state."[75]

As the initial southern prohibition experiment unfolded in five southern states (in Georgia in 1907, Mississippi and North Carolina in 1908, and Alabama and Tennessee in 1909), such rampant violations led many southerners increasingly to take for granted several of the same "truths" about liquor that had been found in South Carolina's prohibition counties. The first rested on religious notions of the inevitability of sin and the limits of reform measures to promote temperance. As a Tuscumbia, Alabama, citizen noted: "We have it on good authority that many strictly sober men who were known as such previous . . . are now gradually becoming habitual drinkers. . . . They are giving away to the baser appetites of the flesh. The spirit is weak when it dwells in a body fired by strong drink."[76] In such circumstances, argued Alabama governor Emmet O'Neal, there was little that could be done to make prohibition successful. "We advocate temperance. We uphold the highest standard of Christian character. We heed the healing voice of Christian charity, but we know that we cannot legislate virtue into men's lives."[77] Given men's propensity to drink, it was patently obvious that "prohibition does not stop drinking; it does limit the sale of whiskey in the smaller communities where law breakers can be easier watched. . . . In the larger cities, it has been found next to impossible to enforce the law."[78]

The blind tigers that arose in prohibition cities bred "a spirit of lawlessness; when men find they can violate a law with impunity it is not very long before other laws are violated."[79] Birmingham's chief of police echoed these thoughts, claiming that in his experience "blind tigers and other forms of vice go hand in hand. . . . There is nothing more detrimental to our moral life than the sale of liquors by women and children and in places frequented by women and children. It is a matter of frequent occurrence to see respectable looking white women brought into court for operating blind tigers. In many instances, girls of 12 years of age have been found serving drinks and sitting for company in apparently respectable houses."[80]

Charges of corruption similar to those made against South Carolina dispensary officials were also found in prohibition states. In Anniston, Alabama, "impeachment proceedings were instituted at a lengthy session of the city council . . . against Alderman J. A. Burgess of the third ward who is charged with irregularity in dealing with blind tigers of the city, from which he is said to have collected $100.50 under promise of immunity."[81] In Gulfport, Mississippi, blind tigers' influence on the city's political life was so great by 1912 that a mayoral candidate had to issue a statement refuting the contention that "the blind tiger element of this city are supporting me in the present campaign for mayor,"[82] and the chief of police similarly assured the town's residents, "The statement that . . . I am or ever have been associated with or interested in, in any way, with blind tigers, other than to raid and bring them to justice, is false and malicious."[83]

Also similar to South Carolina was the reasoning that prohibition could be more effective if enough distance could be put between dry counties (or states) and sites of legal liquor. As in South Carolina, those dry counties farthest from dispensaries often retained their dry laws, a sign that perhaps they felt secure in their ability to prevent legal liquor from coming into the territory from great distances. In this respect statewide prohibition was thought to bestow even greater advantages over local option or dispensary regimes. If whole states could be made dry, the distance to legal liquor might be so great that the flood could reasonably be slowed to a trickle, if not eliminated entirely.

By 1911 such claims had been debunked by the "approximately 20,000,000 gallons of liquors annually shipped by express, principally from mail order houses direct to consumers in prohibition states."[84] Similar to the North Augusta dispensary, many of these suppliers were located as near as possible to dry states or counties, as liquor dealers sought to move just beyond the law's reach. Following the onset of prohibition in Tennessee, for example, "the wholesale dealers of Nashville are to establish branch houses in Kentucky from which liquors can be purchased by people in Tennessee. . . . They state that they will not resort to any subterfuge to sell liquors . . . and that the Tennessee consumer who purchases from their branch houses will be supplied from the regular stock kept in such houses."[85] Farther west, in Osceola, Arkansas, a dry town located just south of Missouri, northwest of Memphis, and bordering the Mississippi River, "a meeting of citizens and officials will be held," wrote the *Jonesboro Daily Tribune*, "to prepare a statement and proofs including reports and maps showing how the section of the river for a number of miles above and below Osceola is infested with blind tigers on shanty boats."[86] The city of Bristol, Tennessee, offered an even more tempting target, being split in two by the Tennessee-Virginia state line. With the onset of prohibition in Tennessee, saloonkeepers flocked to Bristol, Virginia, and the city saw its revenue from liquor licenses jump from a mere seven thousand dollars in 1908 to over thirty-one thousand dollars the following year.

Nor was the out-of-state traffic confined only to private liquor companies. As in Aiken County, state and county governments were quick to capitalize on the liquor needs in newly created dry areas. Along the Virginia–North Carolina border three Virginia counties placed dispensaries in the towns closest to the state line, in Ridgeway, Boydton, and Virgilina. In Arkansas, Polk County sought to coax Oklahomans across the border to its county seat of Mena by licensing dispensaries in that town, and across the state along the Mississippi River saloons sprang up in Chicot and Desha Counties to entice citizens of Greenville, Mississippi.

Surveying the various leaks in their supposedly dry states, state and local officials had two choices. They could double down on prohibition by making existing laws tougher and enforcing them more consistently, or they could back off, acknowledging that these laws did not work and giving other liquor control schemes another try. Almost without exception state and local governments chose the second option, following the same path Augustans traveled when confronted with the loss of revenue to the North Augusta dispensary.

That lost revenue played a role in these deliberations is made clear by the thoughts of a Charlotte businessman, who in despair reviewed the litany of places North Carolina liquor dollars had helped enrich: "Richmond has recently been receiving from North Carolina for liquor not less than $20,000 daily. . . . Norfolk also does a huge liquor shipment business with North Carolina. . . . Of course a great deal of additional money goes to Kentucky, Maryland,

Pennsylvania and other more distant states." "How long," the businessman wondered, "can North Carolina endure such fearful bleeding as this? Whatever material progress we achieve, it will manifestly be far less than we could have achieved otherwise. We need these annual millions of tribute for many essential purposes right now; the people need them; the State needs them. . . . Every one of our cities and towns would be overjoyed to get this revenue."[87] In Wadesboro, North Carolina, citizens protested an effort to form a law-and-order league to fight blind tigers, complaining that "it is hard that they should pay taxes for the purpose of keeping up the town government and then be called on to look after the enforcement of law by private citizens and at private expense."[88]

The North Carolina prohibition law that citizens were charged with enforcing was only an anti-saloon measure and said nothing about legal sales at drugstores or in social clubs or near beer joints; thus, preventing liquor sales seemed especially difficult. The state legislature made it even more challenging a year later, when, in pursuing lost revenue, it passed a law specifically permitting sales within social clubs, provided they paid an annual tax of two dollars a member. In the revenue act of the same session the legislature countenanced the existence of near beer dealers as long as they paid a license fee to the state and locality in which they operated. Even more critical for liquor enforcers was the state supreme court's interpretation of the state law, which held that a town could not close down social clubs or near beer dealers unless its charter specifically authorized such a power.[89]

Now free to pursue liquor profits, "Charlotte has gone and done it," wrote the *Greensboro Record*. "It has fixed the license on near beer saloons at $1,000. Must be trying to recoup for the loss of whiskey license. Imitation is the highest form of flattery. Two days ahead of Charlotte, the little town of Selma did the same thing."[90] Although the state legislature did outlaw near beer dealers in 1911, social clubs continued unabated across many towns in the state, and North Carolina's municipalities used increasingly higher license fees to recoup their losses from other types of liquor licensing. Charlotte again led the way, with the city board "licensing every club that has applied. . . . It is argued that if the well-to-do are to be allowed locker privileges, the same right exists in the man of lesser means whose club is located upstairs in a second-rate storeroom on a back street. . . . Therefore, the aldermen are receiving the money with open hands."[91] Nor was it only North Carolina's largest city that hosted such clubs, as word came into the *Observer* of "a number of men from Salisbury having incorporated the Pocahantas [*sic*] Club which was to be social and convivial in nature, having lockers for the members."[92] In Lexington "the aldermen adopted an ordinance placing an annual tax . . . on locker clubs or any other sort of clubs where whiskey was handled in any shape or form or manner."[93]

In Tennessee retailers initially skirted the statewide four-mile law by converting their saloons into social clubs or near beer joints or opening new saloons four miles from any schoolhouse. While the rural saloons were quickly shut down, the state supreme court gave some cover to urban social clubs, holding that "where evidence showed that a lodge was a bona fide one and that the furnishing of liquor was purely incidental, that the lodge was not engaged in the handling of liquor for sale." Alongside this dispensation the court also gave a warning, writing: "It is a matter of common knowledge that . . . clubs have sprung up . . . and obtained charters whose apparent purpose is to evade . . . these [liquor] statutes. It is hardly necessary to say that such a club can find no warrant for its existence. . . . It will be the duty of the court to scrutinize closely, in order to see that no such device is attended with success."[94]

Close scrutiny of social clubs was not easily forthcoming, especially in Tennessee's largest cities. The state prohibition law left enforcement in the hands of local authorities, which in the state's urban areas meant leaving the law at the mercy of those who did not support it. In the spring of 1910, not even a year after statewide prohibition had been enacted, Tennessee Anti-Saloon League superintendent E. E. Folk wrote that these places were "wide open as never before, for many years. . . . Crimes of all kinds are rampant. . . . The situation is becoming alarming, desperate. It is fast growing intolerable. Something must be done."[95]

Nashville mayor Hilary Howse made little effort to enforce prohibition for the better part of four years, reinstituting liquor licenses in 1912 in clear violation of the statewide ban and admitting in 1913 that "the State-wide prohibition law is violated in Nashville . . . with the knowledge and consent of the great majority of the people."[96] Despite this admission, Howse successfully stood for reelection, winning by a wide margin even though two of the city's leading newspapers, the ASL and WCTU, the heads of Nashville's colleges, and nearly all of the cities preachers had campaigned against him. His enemies attributed this victory to "the hundreds of saloons, dens and dives and their army of hangers-on, all the low and vicious elements of both races, with a corruption fund of stupendous proportions and an office-holding political machine of tremendous power."[97]

In Memphis, Mayor E. H. Crump advocated and practiced regulation rather than prohibition, believing that such oversight would "accomplish more good for the city . . . giving the city a good fire and police department, improving our streets, extending our sewer system, building subways, lighting up the town and giving the people a business administration."[98] Although the Memphis chief of police vowed to keep a close rein on liquor shops and limit their influence on the city's political and moral affairs, on Election Day in 1911 the *Commercial Appeal* found "main street and downtown saloons within a few doors of the polling places, where policemen were on duty, running wide open and doing a land office business. A negro porter came out of a side door of the Climax saloon at Second Street and Monroe Avenue with a tray of drinks and started to the voting booth. . . . 'Say nigger,' said a large white man, who had been taking an active part in the voting, 'For Lord's sake, put a napkin or something over that tray.'"[99] By 1912 Memphis, too, abandoned any prohibitionist pretense and reinstituted the sale of liquor licenses, with Crump claiming that he needed the revenue to build hospitals.

Faced with such seemingly outrageous violations of the statewide dry law, the Tennessee legislature did nothing to curb them during its 1911 session. Nor did the state supreme court intervene, content to rest on its narrow delineation of legitimate from illegitimate liquor dealers and trusting, despite all evidence to the contrary, that local officials would do the right thing. Thus, prohibition languished in Tennessee.

Surveying the state of Mississippi a year after the adoption of its statewide prohibition law in 1908, the *Jackson Clarion-Ledger* noted: "That whisky is still drunk here no one denies. There is no law against bringing it in by express, and members of social clubs are permitted to have their own private lockers."[100] Yet despite this obvious loophole in the law, the state legislature made no move to close it a year later, using its 1910 session only to outlaw drunkenness on railway passenger trains. It fell to Mississippi's supreme court to address the state's social clubs, and unlike Tennessee's high court, Mississippi justices took a harsher view of these establishments, writing, "We unhesitatingly adopt as sound the views of those courts which have held that such a device . . . in disposing of vinous and spirituous liquors was a violation of the law against unlicensed retailing."[101]

In closing that particular loophole, the court also denied towns across Mississippi further revenue, and this loss was a concern for both taxpayers and public officials, who confronted the difficult decision to either raise taxes or cut municipal services. "By this prohibition law," figured Gulfport, Mississippi, tax collector Bradley, "our city loses around $500 per annum, and there remains a yawning gap of $9,500 in the general fund which will have to be made up in some way by an additional tax levy."[102] Imagining this possibility, a Biloxi taxpayer begged to "protest most vigorously against the policy which has been pursued in this community relative to blind tigers. That they are here we all know, including the police officers themselves. As a tax-payer, I insist that we have two unnecessary policemen here who we are paying $1,440 per annum of our good hard-earned money uselessly. If the mayor . . . does not propose to suppress these blind tigers, why should we act as hypocrites and pretend that we do not know they are here? Why not permit them to run and save the city $1,440 of uselessly spent money every year?"[103]

Apparently, the state legislature agreed because in its 1912 session its members placed in their revenue bill a five hundred–dollar privilege tax "on each near beer joint, where there is sold, kept for sale, or offered for sale any drink that simulates in appearance, odor, taste and quality lager beer."[104] As the *Gulfport Daily Herald* pointed out, the legislature was savvy to incorporate the act into the revenue law: "It is said that the Governor could not have eliminated it because he would have had to veto the whole revenue bill."[105]

Mississippi cities were quick to take advantage of the new revenue stream. The *Meridian Dispatch* reported that "the city council of Vicksburg has been having a lively discussion about near beer, a term which is commonly used to include all kinds of concoctions that taste like beer, smell like beer—and sometimes may be beer. . . . It was contended that a tax of $350 should be placed on each dealer who sells it."[106] In Biloxi, according to the *Gulfport Daily Herald*, "this will net considerable revenue for the city at $250 per shop with at least a score of shops that will probably take out licenses.[107] By March 28, 1912, only two weeks after the law went into effect, "the state had derived $20,000 from the new near-beer licensing law."[108]

It was in Alabama that the most striking reversal of state liquor policy took place. Declaring prohibition unworkable, the state legislature repealed the law, replacing it with the Smith Act, which used the size of Alabama's cities as the basis for the number of saloons they might house and the license each might charge for such a privilege. Historian James Benson Sellers explains: "Birmingham, a city of over seventy-five thousand population, would be permitted one saloon to each three thousand population and each of these saloons would be required to pay a license of $3,000 annually. All towns and cities with populations ranging from one thousand to seventy-five thousand might have one saloon for each thousand population and the license fee for these saloons would be fixed at $1,500. Towns of less than 1,000 population could have one saloon paying a license fee of $900."[109]

In turning Alabama back into a local option state, the legislature also required that each county wishing to consider adopting saloons first hold an election in which the majority of voters would have to approve such a measure. With the revenue limits for each town clearly established, voters did not have to guess at how much their county or town's bottom line would be impacted. Not surprisingly, the counties that readopted their liquor stores were those with the most revenue to gain.

The first among them was Colbert County, which housed both Sheffield and Tuscumbia and on that basis stood to make roughly fifteen thousand dollars in revenue per year. Pointing to this possibility, the *Sheffield Standard* argued that "county and towns had, during the experiment, been deprived of much income from liquor licenses and taxes. The county alone was out nearly $20,000 also in costs of attempted enforcement and thousands of dollars more had been spent in court costs for trying violators of the prohibition law."[110] In response to this enumeration, the *Alabamian-Dispatch,* Colbert County's foremost prohibition paper, could only urge "voters to consider prayerfully before they took the backward step toward the return of the saloon. Let them remember, the editor begged, that it would be a sad day for mothers, wives and children when the saloon opened again."[111] Few were surprised when the wets carried the election.

Even fewer were surprised by the return of the saloon to Alabama's largest cities, where prohibition had long since been regarded as a failure and the potential revenues were the greatest. In Montgomery a voter wrote that under prohibition "we have experienced all the evils of the open saloon without any of the restrictions, deriving no revenue therefrom, and gaining no moral benefit whatever from the law."[112] In Birmingham it was local judge A. O. Lane who put the matter most succinctly, declaring that "every effort to suppress blind tigers in Birmingham had failed. He added that blind tigers were converting many young men into sneaks, undermining the social organism, and entailing a heavy expense upon the city, county and state."[113]

By the end of 1912 seven of Alabama's sixty-six counties had readopted liquor sales. Four of them stood to make the most in license fees as defined by the Smith Act. Two of the remaining three wet counties, Madison and Russell, were located on the border of Tennessee and Georgia, respectively, and opened dispensaries as well as saloons in the hopes of drawing drinkers from neighboring dry states. Russell County in particular, which stood just across the bridge from Columbus, Georgia, another major dry population area, hoped to emulate the North Augusta experience. The final Alabama liquor county, Pike, was located next to the state capital in Montgomery and, like Lexington County in South Carolina, sought to keep drinkers from going to the larger city right next door.

By the dawn of 1913 the momentum for prohibition across the South appeared to be at a standstill, if not in retreat. No major dry legislation had been passed in any southern state during the previous legislative session. No southern courts had rendered decisions to make alcohol more difficult to procure or to enhance enforcement machinery. Virtually every southern city practiced some form of liquor licensing, whether legally countenanced or not. Every southern states' border was lined with liquor shops, as dealers and municipalities sought to make money at the expense of their dry neighbors. For those men of means it was hardly necessary to be near a legal liquor haven to secure one's supply, as "the operation of the interstate commerce law and the State laws allow the wet cities and towns of a State to ship liquor into the dry territory of the same state."[114] The result, in the words of a Charlotte citizen, was that "as much whiskey was being drunk here now as in the days of the saloons. . . . When asked for an expression as to a solution of the problem—the consumption of whiskey being an admitted evil—he declared that nothing could be done."[115]

11

THE COMING OF A (TRULY) DRY SOUTH

By the end of the first decade of the twentieth century many southerners were questioning the efficacy of prohibition, not on the basis of its stated goals but, rather, on its means of achieving them. This distinction was clearly drawn by the editor of the *Augusta Chronicle* in a 1910 letter to one of the city's prominent ministers, the Rev. John Erwin. Erwin had recently accused the *Chronicle* and Augusta's citizenry of fostering acquiescence toward Georgia's prohibition law. In his reply, appropriately titled "We Differ Not So Much in the Diagnosis as in the Remedy," the *Chronicle*'s editor made his position clear.[1]

He began by noting that "our views as to the liquor traffic have always been much the same, no doubt, as those of Reverend Erwin and many others who conscientiously oppose it. We have always regarded it—at least as it is generally conducted—the greatest curse of the age." That this view was generally shared across the entire region the writer had no doubt, as he asked rhetorically: "Can there be any difference of opinion on the evils of intemperance— Or that without the promiscuous sale of intoxicating liquor we could have no great amount of drunkenness? Can any intelligent observant man look about him and fail to see and shudder at the wreckage that lies in the wake of intemperance? Could one human being with the heart in his breast refuse, if he had the opportunity, to put an end to all the misery, the heartaches, the poverty, the crime, caused by the drink habit?"[2]

What prevented meaningful action to redress the drink problem was not a disagreement about the evils of the liquor trade but, rather, the legislature's inability to devise a policy to combat it. Local option only worked if all counties and cities agreed to go dry; all were at risk if liquor was available in nearby counties or across state lines. Prohibition did scarcely better, as there was no means of preventing interstate shipments of liquor. These results convinced many that, try as they might to eradicate drink, "we haven't that power. Neither has the Reverend Erwin. Neither has the Mayor of Augusta, nor the Governor of Georgia. Neither has the press nor the pulpit nor the state."[3]

Rather than acknowledge this incapability, "a number of Georgia legislators—the majority of them playing politics with a great moral question, and all of them urged on by sentiment rather than cool judgment—sought to . . . dam up the stream . . . And the water—or rather the whiskey—broke over the dam. It has now all but swept the dam away." Confronted with the abject failure of their policy, "the Georgia legislature made its former act nothing more than a near prohibition law. In effect it said 'the state of Georgia recognizes that its prohibition law is going to be largely, if not generally, violated; therefore it demands of all those who intend to violate it a certain fee, to take the place of the revenue which it voluntarily surrendered when it abandoned its local option policy.'"[4]

As southern state legislators admitted that prohibition could not stop the sale of liquor, counties and cities, if they were advantageously located, reasoned as Augusta did, saying: "It is impossible for our limited police force to cope. . . . If we refuse to license these near-beer saloons ourselves, they will do business without paying their just proportion to the public expense. . . . Therefore we will do the best we can in a bad situation." The result was an ever-changing patchwork of county and municipal liquor laws as localities struggled to stay ahead of the blind tigers and their neighbors. Given this state of affairs, the editor concluded, "we take issue with him [Erwin] . . . on the proposition that Augusta is as bad as he has painted her, that she is the most debauched city in Georgia. She isn't. On the contrary, she is the best city in Georgia. Like most of her citizens, not as good as she ought to be and would like to be and is trying to be. Not good, perhaps, to the point of sanctification; but good as the world goes."[5]

This diatribe may sound strange to readers accustomed to histories that link the southern Baptist and Methodist understanding of saloons as sites of temptation for the young, whites' concerns about drinks' contribution to African American degradations of white women, and middle-class fears of liquor as fuel for lower-class violence. These factors, and the Anti-Saloon League's ability to harness them into a potent political machine capable of realizing its will in state legislatures, are given the lion's share of the credit for the success of the southern prohibition movement. Yet these cultural and organizational factors were in play prior to 1913, with state after state first trying and then backing away from outright prohibition. As they did so, state and local lawmakers did not come to see liquor as less problematic, nor were they openly defying the dictates of the Anti-Saloon League. Instead, they were pragmatically noting that prohibition did not work and that until it could be made to do so, other anti-liquor policies offered a better opportunity for the state to regulate liquor.

What allowed southerners to bring their anti-liquor crusade to a successful conclusion was the passage in 1913 of the federal Webb-Kenyon Act, which prohibited shipment of liquor into states that had already declared themselves dry. Armed with the possibility that prohibition could actually be effective, southern dry campaigners went back to their legislatures and asked them to give "real" prohibition a chance. As they did so, anti-liquor campaigners received support from nearly all of the South's big-city newspapers, which had previously come out against universal dry laws. Although not necessarily enamored of prohibition as a policy, southern wets agreed that the South's liquor problem needed to be fought by any means available and were willing to give prohibition a fair trial.

THE WEBB-KENYON ACT

Scholars have argued that prior to the passage of federal prohibition, the Webb-Kenyon Act was probably the most significant victory achieved by prohibition advocates. Not only did its passage invigorate the dry movement; it also "made effective state action against the liquor industry," according to Historian Richard Hamm. "It revitalized old laws and stimulated prohibitionists to turn to new tactics, including new liquor transportation regulations, prohibitions of liquor advertising statutes, and personal-use bans—so-called bone dry laws."[6] By giving federal approval to the regulation of interstate liquor traffic and its prohibition into dry territory, Webb-Kenyon secured the gains made in state legislatures up to that point, essentially helping to make the old laws, as well as newly created ones, work.

Although previous scholarship has pointed to the importance of Webb-Kenyon, the focus of these authors has been the role of the Anti-Saloon League in bringing about its passage, its impact on the dry movement, or the legal and political structure used to maintain it.[7] What has gone virtually unremarked upon is how the passage of Webb-Kenyon altered the perception of prohibition as an anti-liquor policy. Simply put, prior to the passage of Webb-Kenyon, all but the most diehard prohibitionists believed that the policy was completely unworkable in the real world. Prohibition could not prevent shipments of liquor across state (or even county) lines into dry territory. Unless a town, county, or state was surrounded on all sides by similarly strong dry sentiment, any experiment in prohibition that might be tried would end with competing government agencies doing what Aiken County had done in North Augusta—making money off each other's morality.

The Webb-Kenyon Act held out the possibility that "prohibition states are now for the first time afforded a fair opportunity to demonstrate whether or not prohibition does prohibit."[8] Although it did not guarantee that all states would pass dry laws, it did pledge the federal government's stamp of approval to keep dry areas' borders inviolate. As such, it elevated prohibition's viability when compared to other competing anti-alcohol policy choices. By the time of Webb-Kenyon's passage in 1913, local option, mile laws, and the dispensary had been tried and found wanting. Prohibition promised a way forward, and as southerners contemplated a future surrounded by dry neighbors, they were more willing to embrace this new option. By 1917 newspapers across the South (even those in cities that had previously supported liquor sales) were clamoring for stricter dry laws in an attempt to give prohibition a fair trial.

The act was the culmination of dry agitation across the South and Midwest that, in addition to expanding the amount of dry area, also brought to elected office congressmen whose constituents had made clear their desire for such laws. Alongside these preferences southern representatives in particular came to Washington vowing to protect the rights of their states and localities against federal power. Webb-Kenyon spoke to both concerns. Edwin Y. Webb, a congressman from North Carolina, "claimed that it 'never professed to make the federal government enforce the local prohibition laws.' Rather, it granted something 'we have always clamored for . . . the removal of the shackles which were heretofore on the states' action, so that the states could not act' to control 'the whole subject.'"[9]

The plainly written act (by congressional standards) stated that "the shipment or transportation . . . of any spirituous, vinous, malted, fermented or any other intoxicating liquor of any kind from one state, territory or jurisdiction of the United States . . . into any other state, territory or jurisdiction of the

United States . . . which said spirituous, vinous, malted fermented or any other intoxicating liquor is intended by any person therein to be received, possessed, sold or used in any manner . . . in violation of any law or such state, territory or district . . . is hereby prohibited."[10] Following the bill's passage in early February 1913, dry campaigners had to clear one more hurdle, as President William Howard Taft—whose lame-duck status meant he owed little fealty to the prohibition lobby—vetoed the bill. Taft's argument rested on the bill's presumed regulation of interstate commerce, which in his mind ran afoul of the main purpose of the Constitution, to relieve commerce from "the burdens which local states and jealousies had in the past imposed upon it."[11] The Anti-Saloon League had prepared for such executive action, lining up more than enough votes to override the veto, and Webb-Kenyon became law on March 1, 1913.

THE SOUTH'S SECOND PROHIBITION WAVE, 1913–1917

In employing Webb-Kenyon to reach their dry nirvana, prohibitionists would have to wage two more campaigns. First, they would have to convince state governments to create laws to specifically protect their dry territories. The earliest of these laws, such as those passed in Texas in 1913, focused on limiting intrastate shipments from wet to dry areas while still allowing personal use, sacramental use, and interstate shipments. Other state legislatures were pressured to prohibit interstate shipments to their respective states because their existing laws did "not prohibit private-use shipments, and will not unless the state forbids it, and the state cannot where it allows sale to individuals by anyone in the state."[12] Unless such state legislation was put in place, according to the *Richmond Times Dispatch,* "local officers of the various express companies . . . will pay no attention to the Webb law."[13] By the fall of 1913 dry advocates across the South followed the lead of "Dr. G. W. Young, president of the Georgia Anti-Saloon League . . . to request the approaching session of the State legislature to pass a law forbidding the transportation of intoxicants by common carriers made possible by the enactment of the Webb law regulating interstate shipments."[14]

In seeking such regulations, southern dry advocates had to convince their fellow citizens that "prohibition in 1915 will bear no resemblance to prohibition in 1907." "That was a gross caricature on the real thing," declared the *Selma Times.* "It was an unending grievance to all right-minded citizens who believe in the sanctity of the law in a Democratic State." The paper asked Alabama prohibitionists to "please give us something different this time . . . if you have it in your repertoire."[15] Chief among southerner's concerns was the unease they felt at trying to legally compel their fellows to refrain from liquor. "Men," opined Joseph C. Taylor, the head of the Virginia Association for Local Self-Governance, "can no more be made by law abstainers than they can be compelled by law to be religious. The solution of the temperance problem lies in a gradual education of the public as to the evils of intemperance and the abuse of alcoholic liquors, and not in the imposition of law from without."[16]

The Webb-Kenyon law allowed southern prohibitionists to meet this challenge by appealing to both local and individual autonomy. Webb-Kenyon, explained G. W. Eichelberger, head of the Anti-Saloon League of Mississippi, merely asked states to take a firm stance on the status of liquor in their communities, not as individuals. On the one hand, the law promised that "if a state declares for prohibition, it should be enabled to enforce the prohibition law. . . . On the other hand . . . shipment direct to individuals for their own use should be permitted. . . . While this privilege will undoubtedly be abused, we believe it is reasonable, but the amount allowed to be shipped at one time should be limited."[17] Such limitations would have the effect of markedly reducing the amount of drunkenness, poverty, and crime that resulted from drink in many southern communities.

State legislatures were quick to comply. One after the other they passed laws permitting only personal-use shipments and restricting even these to as small an amount as possible. A North Carolina law adopted two days after Webb-Kenyon typified such legislation. "The law made possession 'at any one time' of more than small amounts of liquor—one gallon of spirituous, three gallons of vinous, or five gallons of malt liquors—or the delivery of more than five gallons of hard liquor or twenty gallons of beer or wine within one month to one person or firm—prima facie evidence of violation of the state's law against liquor sales."[18]

With severe anti-shipping laws in force, dry campaigners next focused their attack on the sites of sale within each state (locker clubs and near beer saloons) and finding ways to more fully empower local officials to enforce these laws. Because they paid state taxes, it initially seemed that "the locker clubs and the near-beer saloons by common consent or otherwise, are considered and looked upon as being legitimate. It appears that they are not run in violation of state law, and if they are not certainly they cannot be a violation of the Webb bill."[19] Dry advocates responded that because southern state laws prohibited the manufacture and sale of liquor, "locker clubs and fraternal orders that use liquor, insofar as they order it for purposes of sale, must be considered by all reasonable people as violators of the prohibition law and also of the Webb law."[20]

As they pushed to close these loopholes in their respective prohibition laws, dry campaigners kept the pressure on legislators not to "even consider any policy that may mean a concession to the liquor interest."[21] "Far from reopening old issues that have been settled," drys argued, "we need to strengthen the law."[22] Laws eliminating local clubs and near beer saloons "can be enforced if any drink over $\frac{1}{2}$ of 1% of alcohol were legally defined as intoxicating, if municipal officials were made responsible to the state government, if the state were given power to intervene in local affairs, and if voluntary law enforcement leagues were established in every county. These things should be done."[23] Again, state legislatures complied, and as they did so, dry campaigners triumphantly promised the end to liquor trouble was nearly at hand: "The claims of the liquor press and the friends of the traffic that the Webb law was of no effect are being disproved daily. In Alabama especially have good results been obtained by the use of the Federal Law in conjunction with our Alabama Fuller law. . . . Decatur, formerly under the domination of blind tigers and corrupt officials, is as dry as the desert. . . . In Etowah and other counties there have been similar activities and from all over the country comes the intelligence that this new law is helping suppress illegal liquors. . . . The only thing now necessary to enforce the law is the determination on the part of the people and an honest judge."[24]

Even formerly wet newspapers that doubted the efficacy of prohibition urged respect for the new laws, as they argued for giving them a fair trial. "It is for all of us—for those who opposed as well as for those who approved and supported this legislation," declared the *Richmond Times-Dispatch*, "to obey the law, to uphold its officers and to give prohibition a fair, complete and conclusive trial. If the plan succeeds, there will be few to wish its repeal. If in actual practice it shows itself competent sensibly to decrease drunkenness, poverty and crime, as its protagonists have declared it would do, no pride of opinion will tempt thinking men to withhold its need of praise."[25]

As they accommodated themselves to the new laws, southerners recog-

nized their inherent inconsistency. Acknowledging that towns without saloons were better than those with them, many still wondered about the wisdom of permitting anyone to drink, if liquor was in fact the source of the
trouble. "If we want prohibition, why not go to it and have it and try it out?"
questioned the *Greensboro Record.* "If a man insists he is a prohibitionist why
allow his neighbor to have two quarts a month? Because two quarts of likker
will do the work of a gallon or a barrel so far as the present jag is concerned,
and the one present jag is the paramount always, and subsequent jags are
taken up in the usual order. The prohibition question will never be settled . . .
as long as any shipment is allowed."[26]

Part of the difficulty for dry campaigners in meeting this challenge was the
perceived limitations of the Webb-Kenyon Act, which in Virginia caused "a
quart-a-month clause [to be] inserted . . . because there was grave doubt of the
right of the State to forbid all interstate traffic in alcoholic liquors."[27] The case
that ultimately rendered a verdict on this aspect of the Webb-Kenyon Act orig-
inated with the passage of a 1915 West Virginia law forbidding all transportation of liquor within the state, the introduction of any alcohol into the state,
and the reception and storage of any transported liquor. On January 8, 1917,
the Supreme Court sustained West Virginia's law. Chief Justice Edward D.
White, writing for the majority, argued that "there was no constitutional right
to receive personal use shipments." According to historian Richard Hamm:
"White also concluded that Congress had the power to pass the Webb-Kenyon
Act and that it was not a delegation to the states of Congress's authority to regulate interstate commerce. Thus, the operation of the Webb-Kenyon Act and
the West Virginia law did prohibit the shipment of liquor into the state."[28]

In Virginia "news of the Supreme Court's actions reached State Attorney-General Pollard," who vowed "the decision will encourage the General
Assembly of Virginia at its next session to strengthen the present prohibition law."[29] The result of this decision was a new round of legislation, as states
across the South rushed to write their own Bone-Dry laws. By the end of 1917
most southern states had effectively outlawed all transportation and sales of
liquor within their borders (table 11.1). In this effort legislators received support not only from dry advocates but also from those who had previously denounced such efforts. As the *Memphis Commercial Appeal,* long a bitter opponent of prohibition, saw it, "Total prohibition must be achieved before the
effect of the elimination of alcohol upon society could be determined."[30]

Table 11.1. Southern state liquor laws, 1914–1919

State	Types of laws passed	Date enacted	Date effective
Alabama	Statewide prohibition of sale and manufacture; enforcement provisions.	01/1915	07/1915
	Bone-Dry law.	01/1919	01/1919
Arkansas	Prohibition of sale and manufacture.	03/1915	01/1916
	Bone-Dry law; enforcement provisions.	03/1917	06/1917
Florida	Sale in packages of less than a half-pint, no liquor drunk on premises.	01/1915	10/1915
	Statewide prohibition of sale and manufacture.	11/1918	01/1919
Georgia	Prohibition of sale and manufacture; enforcement provisions.	11/1915	05/1916
	Bone-Dry law.	03/1917	01/1918
Kentucky	Prohibit shipping to dry territory.	02/1914	02/1914
	Statewide prohibition.	02/1919	02/1919
Mississippi	Prohibition of sale and manufacture.	12/1912	12/1912
	Anti-shipping, enforcement provisions.	01/1914	01/1914
	Reduction of amount permitted to be shipped.	01/1916	01/1916
	Bone-Dry law.	02/1918	02/1918
North Carolina	Prohibition of sale and manufacture.	01/1911	01/1911
	Search and seizure law.	01/1913	01/1913
	Bone-Dry law.	02/1917	02/1917
South Carolina	Prohibition of sale and manufacture enforcement provisions.	09/1915	01/1916
	Reduction of amount permitted to be shipped.	02/1918	02/1918
Tennessee	Prohibition of sale and manufacture; ouster law to remove any local official not enforcing dry laws.	01/1915	01/1915
	Bone-Dry law.	01/1917	01/1917
Virginia	Prohibition of sale and manufacture; enforcement provisions.	09/1914	11/1916

Source: Cherrington, *Anti-Saloon League Yearbook,* 161–210.

GEORGIA'S DRY CAMPAIGN, 1913–1917

At the time of Webb-Kenyon's passage in March 1913, the South was divided into nominally prohibition states and states that practiced some version of local option. Although there was little practical difference in liquor sales between the two groups, the distinction was meaningful for dry campaigners as they plotted their next move. In nominally prohibition states arguments about prohibition could more easily rest on making real what had already been enshrined in law, presumably with the backing of popular opinion. In local option states campaigners faced the more difficult challenge of convincing voters to first adopt dry laws before then going the extra step of giving these laws greater force.

When the Georgia Anti-Saloon League began a campaign "to pass a law forbidding the transportation of intoxicants by common carriers made possible by the enactment of the Webb-Kenyon law," it framed its request as a desire of the people for a "real" prohibition law. Such a measure, if passed, would, according to the *Columbus Ledger,* improve on "our present prohibition act that is far from perfect all must admit. The long lines of both blacks and whites at the express offices in the various cities in Georgia almost daily clearly demonstrate this fact.... If we are to have to prohibition in Georgia, it should be prohibition as we have little patience with compromise or make-believe."[31]

In asking for a "real prohibition law, one that will prohibit not only the manufacture and sale of it in the state, but the shipment of it into the state," the *Columbus Daily Enquirer* chastised the "many men who are prohibitionists for the 'other fellow' only. These men desire some loophole through which they may receive at least a little liquor as they want it."[32] Such a dispensation willfully ignored the harmful effects of looking the other way while locker clubs and near beer saloons did a thriving business. Referring to the Augusta city tax of five hundred dollars on near beer joints, an Augusta citizen asked: "Does any reasonable man think that anyone is going to pay $500 to sell simply near-beer? He could not afford to pay $5, if only soft drinks are to be sold." Instead of such an obvious farce, the citizen wrote, "I believe in a square deal, and whenever we get a genuine prohibition law I will support it with all my might."[33]

Although the Webb-Kenyon Act made such a law possible as early as 1913, it was not until two years later that Governor Nathaniel Harris, moved as he said he was by the "large numbers of petitions from grand juries, from church organizations, from civic bodies, from called meetings, public officers and thousands of individual citizens from nearly all the business callings and professions in the state" to enact a real prohibition law, called a special session of the Georgia legislature to accomplish just that. Harris made an exceptionally clear case for prohibition to lawmakers: "The people demand that more stringent laws be enacted so that the benefits of the legislation can be more fully enjoyed.... The celebrated Webb-Kenyon Act passed by the national Congress ... prohibiting the shipment of intoxicating beverages into dry states ... has never yet been adopted in Georgia. I earnestly advise the legislature to put this act into operation.... The state authorities will have the cooperation of the national government ... in the prevention of many of the violations of the prohibition law and this cooperation can make effective ... preventing the shipment for unlawful purposes into the state prohibited articles."[34]

While many legislators acknowledged the governor's contention that Webb-Kenyon had made prohibition more enforceable, others were still reticent as they contemplated the "question of providing in some way to the state treasurer $340,000 which the enactment of [anti-liquor] legislation will take away."[35] Dry campaigners were ready with replies, some urging legislators not to worry, as "statistics will show that it costs more to punish and defend crime than is derived in the revenue from the licenses granted to those feeders and breeders of crime."[36] Others reminded those worried about lost revenue that while "prohibition under local option, where one city is dry and a close neighbor is wet, may hurt transient business considerably ... where they are all dry, neither resident nor transient business suffers. The dollars don't go out of circulation just because the saloon cash register is silenced."[37]

For those still not convinced, Augusta reverend Howard T. Cross undertook a "careful inquiry," which revealed that "the average daily sales for the average bar in Augusta are $30, or total receipts for the year about $10,000 each." With the total number of saloons in Augusta at roughly one hundred, Reverend Cross calculated that "out of the pockets of our people has come the enormous sum of $1,000,000 annually for the questionable privilege of quenching thirst in barrooms, to say nothing of locker clubs and out of town mail orders. ... Utilized in a constructive way, this is what could be done each year [with that same amount of money]. Erect homes for 100 families ... supply groceries for 100 families ... supply clothing for 100 families ... supply lights for 100 families ... savings account for 100 families."[38] Reverend Cross concluded his calculation by implying that the social life of Augusta (and presumably any other Georgia city) could be made materially better even if the loss of liquor meant the loss of revenue.

Convinced that prohibition could indeed prohibit and that the material welfare of the state would be enhanced if it did, Georgia's legislature passed first a law outlawing locker clubs and near beer sales and then, a year later, banning interstate liquor shipments entirely. Surveying the result, the *Augusta Chronicle,* long known as an opponent of prohibition, took a wait-and-see attitude, noting that "there are those who declare that if the sale and use of intoxicants could be completely stopped the state would be much benefitted and there would never be a return to it. There are others who aver such laws can never be enforced and that it is useless to try.... The people will never be satisfied until the new law has been given a fair trial.... But we shall see what we shall see.[39]

SOUTH CAROLINA'S DRY CAMPAIGN, 1913–1915

In South Carolina winning the war against liquor would require more than the passage of a statewide Webb enforcement act, although doing so was the initial goal of Reverend Harley and the SCASL. Assessing the political environment following the largely pro-dispensary referenda of 1913, when asked about the feasibility of a statewide prohibition referendum, Harley wrote, "We do not see the need now of throwing the whole State into turmoil and strife with a liquor election."[40] Instead, an increasingly gun-shy Harley favored working through the state legislature, vowing to have the liquor question settled once and for all, but "first is a bill which will destroy the blind tiger situation and make the Webb law effective. The plan of the Anti-Saloon League is to fight for this measure before anything else is done. We do not believe it wise to introduce a statewide prohibition bill until provision is made for its enforcement."[41]

Frustrated by this slow pace, drys began questioning the commitment of the SCASL and of Harley in particular. "I would like to ask whether the Anti-Saloon League has gone out of business in South Carolina," remarked one pastor. "It was quite active last year, its inactivity now is passing strange."[42] Harley responded that "the Anti-Saloon League has only one active man in the field, the superintendent," adding: "We have never endorsed any man for political office unless it comes to a showdown between a purely liquor candidate and a prohibitionist. There are a number of men in the race for governor who stand with prohibitionists in their fight. If the league, as these brethren seem to desire, should come into this fight, we believe it would . . . divide the forces and we would get ourselves into no end of trouble if we should endorse any man as a candidate or have anything to do with the Governor's race. We could not afford to antagonize the good men in the race who conscientiously stand for local option . . . for we believe that these men would sign any prohibition bill passed by the legislature."[43]   While Harley was gearing up for his campaign to strengthen already existing laws, another group was also preparing to enter the fray. Made up of leading prohibitionists from throughout the state and led by J. K. Breedin, editor of the *Manning Herald,* its members vowed to "undertake a systematic campaign for a special election next September, at which, so the prohibitionist's believe, the people will vote out the liquor traffic altogether." The committee's avowed purpose was "(1) organizing the said counties: (2) to circulate petitions; (3) to raise money to defray costs; (4) to collect and present these petitions; (5) to arrange a vigorous campaign in case an election is called; (6) do anything else that is necessary for the accomplishment of this purpose. . . . We invoke the assistance and cooperation of the Anti-Saloon League the women's temperance associations and newspapers, and all other agencies which stand for civic righteousness."[44]

The better part of the fall of 1914 saw two prohibition committees, each attempting to gather supporters yet working for different legislative outcomes. Breedin's citizens' committee continued to advocate for a statewide referendum, which Harley and the SCASL, writing in November 1914, vowed never to support:

> Under our constitution, every man of every color who pays taxes on $300 worth of property or who can read and write the constitution can . . . vote on the liquor question. The prohibitionists who are urging a referendum ought to study the experience of Florida and Texas as an object lesson. It is not only possible, but probable, that the liquor trust will establish agencies in South Carolina . . . and with their thousands of dollars they would see to it that Negroes and others are registered and ready to vote when the election is held. . . . When the legislature meets, our bills for both the law enforcement measure and for [legislative] statewide prohibition will be

ready. Our purpose is to save the State, if possible, the turmoil and strife
and expenses attendant upon a liquor election. If, however, the matter is
thoroughly hashed out in a caucus meeting, a majority of the prohibitionists
in the House and Senate think it wise to refer the matter to the people, then
we will acquiesce, but not before.[45]

Three weeks later the SCASL acquiesced. By January 1915 it was clear
the momentum was with the citizens' committee, and at a meeting with the
SCASL "the proposition of Mr. Breedin and his committee was decided upon
and that will be the only one before the state legislature on the State-wide issue."[46] A committee of ten was appointed to meet with the assembly to craft
prohibition legislation. Tellingly, the five members appointed by Reverend
Harley were all from Spartanburg, while the members appointed by the citizens' committee included Columbia men and former state officials.[47]

A NEW PROHIBITION CAMPAIGN

While the committee of ten worked to draft the legislation, Breedin set about
crafting an organization and message that would move state legislators where
the ASL had not. Breaking with Harley's predominantly religious tone, Breedin asserted that "the real prohibitionist is no self-vaunting specimen of su-
perior virtue, but a clear thinking man who sees in alcohol a waste of money,
lost energy, impaired health, blighted careers, blasted hopes, unhappiness,
a shortened life."[48] From this hard-nosed practical vantage point, he argued
that "the reasons for prohibition urged a few years ago are just as potent today; but there are other reasons which are appealing to the popular imagina-
tion such as the diversion of money from the purchase of staples to the purchase of liquor. The towns having no dispensaries have enjoyed a measure of
trade in proportion to the purchasing ability of the community; whereas the
towns with dispensaries have divided with the dispensaries. . . . Our revenue
must be based on the inexhaustible wealth of the country and the labor of its
inhabitants."[49]

Drawing out his economic argument, Breedin imagined the market as the
primary vehicle for the enhancement of public life, in contrast to the state,
which had used the dispensary to fund social uplift. "The idea of a stable commercial economy being based on the sale of liquors is contrary to a proper con-

ception of business as well as being incorrect from an economic standpoint," he argued. "The highest development of business proceeds from economical utilization of all the resources of the state, the greatest being sober productive citizens."[50] To support his argument, Breedin pointed to "the tax levy in Kansas [which] has been reduced from 5.5 mills to 1.2 mills under prohibition. Why is that? Because money not wasted on liquor became part of the permanent wealth of the state and thus a lower levy on great wealth will produce a greater amount raised for the maintenance of the state."[51]

Turning to conditions in the Palmetto State, Breedin was fond of contrasting dispensary sales with those of other businesses as a way of driving home the economic potential lost to liquor. "A merchant in lower Carolina remarked some days ago that the dispensary in the little town in which he lives makes more money than all the other businesses; fifteen in all, combined. Many former supporters of the dispensary are championing prohibition for this reason. I do not regard this as a higher motive for supporting prohibition but it is a sound one."[52] All through late 1914 and into 1915 citizens' committee rallies resulted in petitions to the legislature demanding the right to vote on statewide prohibition.

THE 1915 PROHIBITION REFERENDUM

As had been the case six years earlier, prohibitionists working in the legislature turned to Senator H. B. Carlisle (Spartanburg), in conjunction with the newly formed committee of ten, to draft a statewide prohibition bill.[53] Unlike six years earlier, this bill asked the legislature only to authorize a referendum on the liquor question to be binding statewide, arguing that "the holding of a referendum is a pure Democratic movement . . . [that] will make all surrounding conditions better and enable the people to prosper."[54] It was hoped by dry forces that this approach might be more palatable to voters accustomed to having a say in matters concerning alcohol.

Although the prohibitionists' aim had not changed, the legislative environment they found in 1915 was more favorable to their request than had been the case six years earlier. During the previous half-decade counties across the state had been given multiple opportunities to explore the possibility of county dispensaries, and the results of these referenda created a clear sense of where each constituency stood. Unlike in 1909, when the legislators felt pressure to vote for local option so that their counties might use dispensaries to lure wayward Georgians or North Carolinians, in 1915 it was only lawmakers from currently wet counties who would be tempted to support the existing system.

Aware that they had a majority of almost two to one, dry spokesmen used hearings on the bill in part to highlight the role dispensaries played in undermining the collective good in already dry counties. "We do not want for the people of neighboring counties to sell whiskey to our people. Our greatest trouble is in whiskey being shipped in and we want you to make that impossible," wrote one citizen, while another testified that because a neighboring county readopted its dispensaries, "in the city court the charges of drunkenness and disorderly conduct had increased 300 percent."[55]

Drys also sought to appeal to legislators from counties with very thin dispensary majorities in the 1913 referenda. Of the fifteen dispensary counties seven had seen wets win by one hundred votes or less, and dry campaigners made certain that voices from these counties were prominently heard. Typical of these petitions was that of businessmen in Blackville: "We the undersigned businessmen of Blackville wish to testify that according to our observation and knowledge the consumption of alcoholic liquors . . . interferes so seriously with a man's worth in any position and involves such a heavy drain on the resources of the country that we respectfully petition the legislature of our State to prohibit the bringing in of whiskey or the sale of it."[56]

When the dispensary campaigners had their say a week later, most of the conversation was focused on Charleston, with many of the same arguments being made as had been made before, albeit with fewer supporters. Charleston's mayor was especially strident in his remarks: "We tell you that it cannot be enforced in Charleston County. . . . None of the past panaceas of liquor laws has been of real service to us. Each of Charleston's mayors since 1893 has told this same thing. Put the responsibility on us . . . and we will ameliorate those conditions that are intolerable. My conviction is that there is but one solution in Charleston and that is under a well-regulated high license system. . . . Let us drink and you can drink or not as you please."[57]

Unfortunately for dispensary advocates, these arguments about unenforceability and a plea to let each county decide the matter for themselves was far less palatable than had been the case six years earlier, as most legislators agreed with the Bamberg County senator who wondered, "What guarantee have we got that they will enforce it [a high license law], as they have voted for the dispensary and have not been able to enforce that?"[58]

Given the considerable hostility to the local option position, all commentators expected the prohibition bills to pass, even though many were surprised by the eventual margin of the dry victories: ninety-nine to seventeen in the House and thirty-three to nine in the senate. The prohibition majorities would have actually been greater had not two representatives from Greenville voted against them because they did not include soft drinks on the list of items to be prohibited, and two senators did likewise in the hopes that coffee might also make the list.[59] Excluding these legislators, the final tally of votes in both houses shows legislators echoing the results of recent county referenda to a remarkable degree (table 11.2).

The referendum question itself was a piece of dry craftsmanship. Not wanting to get too far ahead of public opinion and propose too drastic a shift in policy, the drys drafted a statute allowing for "two ballots. . . . One, for the manufacture and sale of alcoholic liquors and beverages in South Carolina; the other, against the manufacture and sale of alcoholic liquors and beverages in South Carolina." It was made clear to voters that the referendum result "has nothing to do with the gallon a month law regulating the importation of liquors."[60] By continuing to permit the importation of liquor for personal use, South Carolina drys avoided running afoul of the possible limits of the Webb-Kenyon Act and also turned the ensuing election into a referendum

Table 11.2. Legislative support for prohibition referendum by county vote, 1913

	Dispensary county	Split vote	Prohibition county
Representatives and senators united against prohibition	5	—	—
Representatives and senators disagree about prohibition	1	1	—
Representatives and senators united in support of prohibition	2	4	27

Source: South Carolina, *Journal of the Senate.*

Note: Senators from Florence and Union Counties were not present for the vote. A split vote meant that the county had readopted dispensaries in 1913 but had only done so after a close vote that required adjudication by the courts.

on the dispensaries. In doing so, dry advocates hoped to appeal to residents of dry counties who had found that their own local prohibition laws "cannot, to any reasonable degree, be effective or satisfactory ... against any crime or evil because the division of infected territory interspersed throughout a large area of prohibition territory render it easy ... for a large proportion of those in prohibition territory to secure all the whiskey they desire...." Further, dry campaigners argued that prohibition counties should not trust those with dispensaries to eliminate them via local option because "the fewer the counties in a state having dispensaries the more difficult it is to abolish then through local election because the revenue from them is so great that it demoralizes the moral sentiment."[61]

Instead of supporting the dispensary system, which had been tried and found wanting, drys asked South Carolinians to give prohibition a fair trial. Drys did not promise that prohibition would eliminate all whiskey sales and manufacturing. Instead, they vowed that, in the words of a Timmonsville resident, "state-wide prohibition laws and with courageous, energetic and honest officials to execute them the innumerable evils resulting from ... the intemperate use of intoxicants would be so greatly reduced that all fair-minded men would admit that prohibitory laws were as effective in suppressing the evils of intemperance as any other laws for the suppression of the crimes ... for which they were intended."[62]

By bringing back in voters from already prohibition counties, many of which had populations far greater than their dispensary counterparts, it was

Table 11.3. Dispensary profits of total taxes by county, 1909 and 1914 (percentage)

	1909	1914		1909	1914
Aiken	43	29	Florence	41	56
Bamberg	37	28	Georgetown	40	36
Barnwell	41	26	Lexington	24	15
Beaufort	45	47	Orangeburg	40	35
Calhoun	30	22	Richland	44	39
Charleston	45	19	Union	—	23
Dorchester	33	17	Williamsburg	26	10

Sources: South Carolina General Assembly, State Comptroller General, *Annual Report;* South Carolina General Assembly, State Dispensary Auditor, *Annual Report.*

assumed the drys would be able to command a significant majority. In addition to the demographic reality, liquor shop supporters were also confronting the limitations of dispensary profits, which had decreased with the reopening of several county dispensaries following the 1913 referenda (table 11.3).

THE END OF THE AIKEN COUNTY DISPENSARIES

For prohibition supporters in Aiken County the timing of the statewide referendum could not have been better. Throughout the campaign season Aiken was rocked by a scandal on the county board of control that rivaled anything in the long history of the dispensary. Trouble had been brewing for several years, as it had grown to be common knowledge across the county that "the dispensary has figured largely in county and city politics, in many cases the deciding factor, and has contributed to the upbuilding and tearing down of political fortunes. There has been a sentiment in Aiken county . . . that only the exceptional man could be elected to office without the support of the dispensary, and then only by accident."[63]

In the 1914 countywide elections several candidates ran successfully against the incumbents and in doing so ushered in what was thought to be the end of the whiskey ring. By May 1915 the new board had been approved by the governor and had settled in to begin its work "electing officials for the several dispensaries throughout the county, cutting salaries and making plans for innovations aimed at lifting the dispensary out of county politics." To their surprise, wrote the *Journal and Review,* "officials of the institution who have been in control for several years past . . . openly defied Governor Manning . . . and expressed the intention of holding on to their jobs, although their successors have been duly elected."[64] For about a week Aiken County's dispensaries were shut down by the governor as the two competing county boards struggled for control of the institution, the new board claiming its rightfully elected position, the old board claiming its right to hold over for another month until its term officially ended. The matter was settled by Governor Manning, who ruled in favor of the newly elected board.

Just when Aikenites imagined the dispensaries would resume normal operations, they received another jolt. "This afternoon when the new chairman of the dispensary board, H. P. Dyches, served notice on the dispenser of No. 1 Dispensary at Aiken, T. J. Southall, that his successor . . . had this morning been commissioned . . . Mr. Southall refused to comply with the demand that he turn over his keys" to his store or stocks.[65] After six weeks of wrangling, during which the dispensary remained closed, Southall first reluctantly agreed to surrender his keys, then, after notifying the board of his intention to do so, "refused again . . . to give up. The board met and decided to give Mr. Southall another chance to transfer the keys and the stock formerly in his control. . . . A messenger was sent to him in Augusta . . . with the statement that unless he surrendered that afternoon it would be necessary to break down the doors." When no further reply came from Southall, the dispensary board forcibly opened the dispensary doors and took stock of the store's contents. "When the stock was checked . . . and the books gone over, Mr. Southall was found to be short in his cash $2,159."[66] A week later an Aiken grand jury appointed a three-man committee to investigate the matter further. In the course of its review the committee reported that "this is not the first time that Mr. Southall has been short and . . . had been permitted to violate the law" by members of the previous dispensary board.[67]

Aikenites had just finished digesting news of the Southall affair when further trouble broke out on the county board. This time the source was the board itself and the conflict between H. P. Dyches and M. B. Smith, on the one hand, and W. T. Hite, on the other. Hite accused Dyches and Smith of colluding against him (and by extension the people of Aiken County) by over-purchasing dispensary liquor and overpaying dispensary staff. Hite especially took issue with Smith, who had been asked by the governor to serve when another dispensary board member stepped down. In May 1915 Hite issued an injunction against Smith, asserting that "Smith is a usurper . . . with no right to vote. As a taxpayer he [Hite] alleges he is injured or will be if no relief is granted by loss to the county through moneys being paid out illegally to dispensers and others illegally elected by the vote of Smith."[68] Once again, the county dispensaries were closed by the governor while the matter was sorted through, with a judge eventually ruling in favor of Smith's position on the board. By July an incensed Hite quit as county board member, citing continuing irregularities promulgated by Dyches and Smith, including "the purchase of a mule with dispensary funds" and "the payment for boarding [the mule] to Dyches and Son."[69]

The dispensaries were again closed as the governor searched for yet another board member. By this point most Aikenites had seen enough. By the time of the prohibition referendum in September, following a year in which the county dispensaries had been closed far more times than they had been operating, the editor of the *Aiken Journal and Review* predicted: "Prohibition will win, but what percent of voters will cast their ballots? As far as Aiken County is concerned, little interest is being shown. . . . The people in favor of the dispensary have made no interest to get out the votes. . . . The people seem tired of the dispensary and no doubt it will go."[70] When the votes were counted, Aikenites supported prohibition by a better than four-to-one margin. Statewide, the story was the same: prohibition outpolled the dispensary by a count of 41,735 to 16,809. North Augusta's little shop in the hollow was to be shut down, South Carolina voters "sending word to Augusta that you cannot hope in the future to purchase liquors from the foot of the bridge."[71]

CONCLUSION

On September 23, 1916, the *Columbus Enquirer* urged its readers: "Let us give it a trial. It is our duty to do so. . . . It would be unfair to those who have worked so earnestly in behalf of this prohibition law to make any effort to repeal or modify it in any way unless, after a fair and square trial of it, it should prove to be not what its advocates have claimed it would be." With these words one editor spoke what many across the South hoped for, an end to the constant political wrangling over the liquor question and in its place a real test of the new law's possibilities. The *Enquirer* expressed sympathy for the prohibitionists' fondest hopes, painting such a picture that even the staunchest supporter of the liquor trade could hardly have scoffed should they come to pass:

> Those who have all these years been advocating prohibitory laws have done so in the interest of humanity. They have contended that prohibiting the manufacture and sale of intoxicating liquors within the state would be vastly beneficial to mankind in general. They have contended that many a child who has heretofore, on account of the sale of these liquors, gone hungry and scantily clad would be better provided for if there were no liquor sold in the state, because the money that was spent for drink would go to purchase food and clothing for the home. . . . If it shall prove beneficial, as those who have advocated it contend, then no one who has even the semblance of sympathy and the milk of human kindness in his make-up will for a moment advocate a return to former conditions.

Alongside these dry dreams the *Enquirer* also issued a challenge to those who pursued them without regard for conditions on the ground: "If the law should, by any circumstance, after a fair test has been made, prove to be a failure, if the good that has been claimed would come from its proper enforcement fails to come, and it is proven conclusively that it is not a good thing, it stands to reason that those who have urged the enactment and the enforcement of such a law, will admit their error and will be among the leaders of those who would advocate the repeal of the law."[1] The *Columbus Enquirer* was not the only Georgia or South Carolina newspaper to endorse the notion of a "fair and square" trial for prohibition. By 1916 southerners in general had coalesced around this notion. What a fair and square trial meant, of course, varied in the eye of the beholder. It could mean "urging that all men be aggressive against violators of the law, and not merely passive sympathizers," or that "those who lament the law must obey it nonetheless."[2]

Increasingly, especially after the Supreme Court's decision supporting the Webb-Kenyon Act in January 1917, it meant advocating prohibition, "ironclad, written in the statute books."[3] Many of these advocates were long-standing supporters of the dry cause, such as J. M. Mitchell, the leader of Columbia's Prohibition Enforcement League, who wrote: "If whiskey is poison, should we not put down the foe? Why not have absolute prohibition. . . . Let's have it. An enemy like this should be resisted and destroyed. Our motto should be no compromise."[4] For many of these commentators the usefulness of prohibition was obvious, as "the way to quit drinking is to quit drinking."[5] In their minds there was little question that the law, if properly enforced, would work.

Others supported prohibition for exactly the opposite reason—"not because we believe in it or believe it the right method but because there is an agitation that will never go down until it is tried out honestly and sincerely."[6] Nothing would convince drys of their folly short of a true test, after which the truth would be easily seen. "If South Carolina keeps its citizens from drinking 'strong waters,'" wrote the *Charleston Evening Post*, "it will accomplish a great benefit while it achieves a great deal. . . . If it shows poor results it will be from intrinsic defects."[7] Like it or not, at least until further information on the efficacy of dry laws was available, "public sentiment has at last come to a full approval of such a program—and that settles it."[8]

The prohibition question would remain settled in the South quite a bit longer than most realized at the time. In 1917, just as most southern states were passing bone-dry prohibition, dry advocates, arguing that no state could be truly dry unless all states were dry, successfully lobbied Congress to pass the

Eighteenth Amendment.[9] In January 1919, when state legislatures across the South might have gathered to reflect on the progress of their dry laws, federal prohibition was enshrined in the Constitution, effectively muting any voices that still questioned the efficacy of such a policy. It is of course mere conjecture to suggest what path southern prohibition would have taken had the federal law not intervened. To ask the question does throw light on the region's complex relationship with alcohol. As we have seen, at all levels of government southerners grappled with various strategies to combat liquor, trying to adapt not only to the problems but also to the opportunities liquor brought about.

State legislatures vacillated on prohibition, finding it seemingly impossible to enforce when other states around them were freely selling liquor to their populations. Unable to crack down on those outside their jurisdictions, several southern states abandoned their initial attempts to establish statewide dry laws. It was only after passage of the Webb-Kenyon Act in 1913 that southern state legislatures felt empowered enough to assert that dry laws could work as good policy and at that time enacted bone-dry statutes.

South Carolina's counties were given three opportunities to weigh in on dispensaries in their midst. Of the state's forty-two counties only sixteen went dry at the first opportunity in 1905 and remained dry throughout the local option era. The remainder included twenty counties that changed their liquor status (nine more than once) and six consistently dispensary counties. Analyses of these referenda make clear that the proximity of millworkers to dispensary towns was the chief factor in making a county consistently prohibitionist. Among those counties with few mill hands, the choice to adopt the dispensary or prohibition rested primarily with the profits such liquor shops could bring.

At the local level Aiken County initially showed slight interest in the liquor question. Its dispensaries brought in only modest sums and caused little social disorder, with most of Horse Creek Valley's millworkers opting to drink in Augusta's saloons. Georgia's adoption of prohibition made the dispensary an issue in Aiken County as its citizens sought profits while North Augustans' campaigned against the liquor shop because of their fear of the chaos it would bring to their town. By 1915 liquor profits had largely dried up, dispensary board corruption was brought to light, and Aiken County voted in large numbers in favor of prohibition.

These fluctuations, taking place over short periods of time among the same groups of people, remind us that prohibition was not an inevitable outcome of the southern anti-liquor crusade. It was merely one of many possible policies southerners could and did try to combat what they saw as the evil of liquor. Prohibition happened only when it seemed to promise the best answer to the liquor problem, one that could be enforced with little damage to the economy. Yes, southerners embraced anti-liquor laws and did so for reasons that often set them apart from their fellow citizens in other parts of the country. Yet this embrace was halting and at times uncertain, and in their moments of deepest doubts about the wisdom of prohibition, southerners sounded very much like pragmatic Yankees—or like our current crop of politicians trying to weigh the health risks of legalizing "dangerous" substances against the allure of higher tax revenues.

NORTH AUGUSTA AFTER THE DISPENSARY

In 1916, as the new year began, newspapers across South Carolina announced the closing of the state's most infamous liquor shop. The *Sumter Watchman and Southron* announced: "The North Augusta dispensary, about which so much has been written, is no more. The remaining stock has been shipped to the Aiken dispensary and the place is for rent."[10] Although the dispensary's closing seemed to promise sober prosperous days, in hindsight it became the first in a series of events that transformed the thriving town of North Augusta into something more akin to a small southern backwater.

A year to the day of the dispensary's demise, James U. Jackson's Hampton Terrace Hotel burned completely, leaving behind nothing but the brick remains of the famous smokestack that had once served as a beacon for incoming visitors. Across the river fires consumed the Bon Air Hotel on February 3, 1921, severely curtailing Augusta's role as a tourist destination. The final blow was dealt in 1925, when the latest in a series of floods destroyed much of North Augusta's commercial area. By the time James U. Jackson died, in October of that year, his dream of a grand town had been reduced to a small bedroom community of the city across the river.

The damage caused by persistent flooding persuaded North Augusta's businessmen to abandon the riverfront area and seek safer spaces farther uphill on Georgia Avenue. By 1937 the dispensary building was the only one remaining in the once bustling intersection. After a second life as a hotel (Ye Olde Dispensary Inn) the building remained vacant, standing alone amid an increasing tangle of vegetation. It was finally demolished in 1995 after a significant fire.[11]

As of this writing, the land where the dispensary once stood remains empty, although North Augusta officials, buoyed by the building of Clark's Hill dam upriver and a resulting change in floodplain designation, have again undertaken development along the town's riverfront. The first decade of the twenty-first century saw the development of Hammonds Ferry, a mixed-use residential, commercial, and green space project. In early 2013 the North Augusta City Council proposed "Project Jackson." Named after James U. Jackson, the latest revitalization effort envisions as its centerpiece a minor league baseball stadium on the site where the dispensary building once stood. If Project Jackson is completed, the ballpark will likely lure Augusta's minor league baseball team (as well as its fans and their money) across the river, much as the dispensary did one hundred years earlier.

Even as they look forward to future riverfront development, North Augustans continue to recall the dispensary as part of the town's historic halcyon days. Prominently located in the North Augusta Arts and Heritage Center is a model of North Augusta in 1910 that "represents some of the more historic structures that existed throughout the city."[12] There—alongside miniature replicas of the Bridge and Interurban Trolley Line, which made the town's development possible; the palatial houses of James U. Jackson and others who first called North Augusta home; and the Hampton Terrace Hotel, which made the town a tourist destination with few peers—is a model of South Carolina's most infamous dispensary, the little shop in the hollow.

NOTES

INTRODUCTION

1. "Dispensary Rumored for North Augusta," *Aiken Journal and Review,* August 9, 1907.

2. "North Augusta," *Augusta Chronicle,* November 1, 1908.

3. William Mealing, letter to the editor, *Augusta Chronicle,* January 21, 1908.

4. "Give Us Dividends," *Aiken Journal and Review,* August 2, 1907.

5. See, e.g., Coker, *Liquor in the Land of the Lost Cause;* Davis, *Attacking the Matchless Evil;* Isaac, *Prohibition and Politics;* Link, *Paradox of Southern Progressivism;* Ownby, *Subduing Satan;* Sellers, *Prohibition in Alabama;* Whitener, *Prohibition in North Carolina;* Willis, *Prohibition in Middle Florida.*

6. Platt, *Child-Savers;* Tindall, *Emergence of the New South;* Grantham, *Southern Progressivism,* 178–99; Trost, *Gateway to Justice.*

7. Willis, *Southern Prohibition,* 137.

8. *North Carolina White Ribbon,* October 29, 1908.

9. Ownby, *Subduing Satan,* 170.

10. Coker, *Liquor in the Land of the Lost Cause,* 123–74.

11. Stewart, *Moonshiners and Prohibitionists,* 5.

12. Carlton, *Mill and Town,* 132–33.

13. U.S. Bureau of the Census, *Thirteenth Census, 1910;* U.S. Bureau of the Census, *Religious Bodies, 1906.*

14. For details on the particular laws in the various southern states, see Bailey, *Prohibition in Mississippi;* Blakely, *Sale of Liquor in the South;* Davis, "Attacking 'The Matchless Evil'"; Eubanks, *Ben Tillman's Baby;* Heath and Kinard, "Prohibition in South Carolina, 1880–1940"; Hendricks, "South Carolina Dispensary System"; Hohner, "Prohibition and Virginia Politics"; Hunt, "A History of the Prohibition Movement in Arkansas"; Isaac, *Prohibition and Politics;* Leab, "Temperance Movement in Tennessee"; Patton, *History of the Prohibition Movement in Mississippi;* Pearson and Hendricks, *Liquor and Anti-Liquor in Virginia;* Roblyer, "The Road to State-Wide prohibition in Tennessee"; Sellers, *Prohibition Movement in Alabama;* Simkins, *Tillman Movement;* Wallace, "South Carolina State Dispensary"; Whitener, *Prohibition in North Carolina.*

1. THE POLITICS OF THE SOUTH CAROLINA DISPENSARY

1. For more on the South Carolina dispensary, see Eubanks, *Ben Tillman's Baby;* Heath and Kinard, "Prohibition in South Carolina"; Hendricks, "South Carolina Dispensary System"; Johnson, *Government Liquor Monopoly;* Tatum, *South Carolina Dispensary;* Wallace "South Carolina State Dispensary"; Wines and Koren, *Liquor Problem in Its Legislative Aspects.*

2. The best scholarly sources on Tillman are Kantrowitz, *Ben Tillman and the Reconstruction of White Supremacy;* Simkins, *Tillman Movement;* Simkins, *Pitchfork Ben Tillman.*

3. State of South Carolina, *Journal of the Senate,* 1892, 24.

4. Ibid.

5. Ibid.

6. Ibid., 25.

7. Ibid., 27.

8. It was assumed that the vast majority of customers would be men because only women of very low morals would frequent a liquor store.

9. Sallie F. Chapin, "Dispensary Law Is a Great Thing for Temperance," *Chicago Lever,* July 13, 1893; *State,* December 25, 1892.

10. Simkins, *Pitchfork Ben Tillman,* 240.

11. Tatum, *Salient Features,* 5–6.

12. Ibid.

13. Hemphill, "South Carolina Dispensary," 414.

14. Wines and Koren, *Liquor Problem,* 146.

15. Ibid.

16. Ball, *State That Forgot,* 243.

17. Tillman, quoted in *South Carolina House Journal,* 1893, 34–41.

18. State of South Carolina, *Acts of South Carolina,* 1892, 62.

19. State of South Carolina, *Acts of South Carolina,* 1896, 368.

20. *State,* July 1, 1893.

21. Ibid., June 30, 1893.

22. *New York Times,* June 5, 1894.

23. Ibid., June 30, 1893.

24. Charles A. Storman, Orangeburg County Board of Control, to Governor Benjamin R. Tillman, January 26, 1894, box 44, Benjamin R. Tillman Papers, South Carolina Department of Archives and History.

25. J. Welch, dispenser, Union S.C., to Governor Benjamin R. Tillman, January 21, 1894, box 44, Benjamin R. Tillman Papers, South Carolina Department of Archives and History.

26. J. Douthit, Anderson County Board of Control, to Governor Benjamin R. Tillman, February 8, 1894, box 44, Benjamin R. Tillman Papers, South Carolina Department of Archives and History.

27. *State,* January 28, 1894.

28. *Charleston News and Courier,* January 16, 1894.

29. Little has been written on the Darlington Riot beyond the firsthand accounts from the time. The lone scholarly source devoted entirely to this subject is Holley, "Darlington Riot of 1894." For Tillman's role in and view of the insurgency, see Simkins, *Pitchfork Ben Tillman.*

30. J. Buckner Floyd, Darlington County dispenser, to Governor Benjamin R. Tillman, March 28, 1894, box 45, folder 14, Benjamin R. Tillman Papers, South Carolina Department of Archives and History.

31. *New York Times,* March 31, 1894.

32. Huguermir, brigadier general, Charleston militia, to Governor Benjamin R. Tillman, quoted in *State,* April 1, 1894.

33. *State,* March 30, 1894.

34. Governor Benjamin R. Tillman to South Carolina Municipal Authorities, October 1, 1894, box 9, State Board of Control Folder, South Carolina Dispensary Records, South Carolina Department of Archives and History.

35. W. W. Hursey, Mayor of Florence, to Governor Benjamin R. Tillman, October 10, 1894, box 45, Benjamin R. Tillman Papers, South Carolina Department of Archives and History.

36. G. F. Tolly, Mayor of Anderson, to Governor Benjamin R. Tillman, January 6, 1894, box 44, Benjamin R. Tillman Papers, South Carolina Department of Archives and History.

37. J. W. Roach, Dispenser 4th Ward, Columbia, to Governor Benjamin R. Tillman, December 4, 1894, box 45, Benjamin R. Tillman Papers, South Carolina Department of Archives and History.

38. W. W. Rhodes, Dispenser, Summerville, to Governor Benjamin R. Tillman, December 5, 1894, box 45, Benjamin R. Tillman Papers, South Carolina Department of Archives and History.

39. County Dispenser, name unreadable, Blacksburg, to Governor Benjamin R. Tillman, November 3, 1894, box 45, Benjamin R. Tillman Papers, South Carolina Department of Archives and History.

40. F. M. Mixon, Mayor of Charleston, to Governor Benjamin R. Tillman, January 15, 1894, box 9, F. M. Mixon file, State Board of Control Folder, State Dispensary Records, South Carolina Department of Archives and History.

41. E. L. Jones, Mayor of Newberry, to Governor Benjamin R. Tillman, January 10, 1894, box 9, State Board of Control Folder, State Dispensary Records, South Carolina Department of Archives and History.

42. Simkins, *Tillman Movement,* 198.

43. Wines and Koren, *Liquor Problem,* 164–65.

44. H. Elmore Martin, Chief of Police, Charleston to Governor Benjamin R. Tillman, February 1, 1894, box 44, Benjamin R. Tillman Papers, South Carolina Department of Archives and History.

45. Eubanks, *Ben Tillman's Baby,* 148.

46. McCollough v. Brown, 41 (S.C. 1893), 220.

47. Ibid., 221.

48. Ibid.

49. Committee of Fifty, *Liquor Problem,* 157.

50. South Carolina General Assembly, *South Carolina House Journal,* 1894, 35–36.

51. *Charleston News and Courier* October 9, 1894.

52. South Carolina General Assembly, *Acts and Resolutions of South Carolina, 1895,* 71.

53. *State,* May 7, 1895.

54. Ibid., June 6, 1895.

55. South Carolina General Assembly, *Acts and Resolutions of South Carolina, 1897,* 40.

56. *State,* January 20, 1897.

57. Ibid., August 20, 1897.

58. Ibid., September 3, 1898.

59. Ibid., September 6, 1898.

60. Upon discovering Ellerbe's deceit, Gonzales wrote a series of scathing articles exposing the governor. Further details of Tillman's role in forcing Ellerbe's hand can be found in Simkins, *Pitchfork Ben Tillman,* 377; and Wallace, *History of South Carolina,* 392.

61. Governor Miles B. McSweeney to Senator Benjamin R. Tillman, August 15, 1899, box 9, Benjamin R. Tillman Papers.

62. Senator Benjamin R. Tillman to John O. Wilson, August 11, 1899, box 9, Benjamin R. Tillman Papers, South Carolina Department of Archives and History.

63. *Charleston News and Courier,* July 28, 1900.

64. Ibid., September 4, 1900.

65. Hendricks, "South Carolina Dispensary System," 330–31.

66. *Charleston News and Courier,* July 28, 1900.

67. Ibid.

68. *State,* July 19, 1900.

69. Ibid.

70. *Charleston News and Courier,* July 19, 1900.

71. Ibid., July 25, 1900.

72. *South Carolina Baptist,* quoted in the *State,* August 16, 1900.

73. Simkins, *Pitchfork Ben Tillman,* 379.

2. THE ECONOMIC CONTEXT OF THE DISPENSARY

1. *Anderson Intelligencer,* January 19, 1901.

2. For more on South Carolina's taxation policy, see Hudson, *Entangled in White Supremacy.*

3. Ibid., 227.

4. *Anderson Intelligencer,* January 16, 1903.

5. South Carolina General Assembly, *South Carolina House Journal,* 1906, 11.

6. Ibid.

7. Green, *This Business of Relief,* 120–21.

8. Ibid., 125.

9. For more on the good roads movement across the South, see Ingram, *Dixie Highway;* Preston, *Dirt Roads to Dixie.*

10. Hyatt, "Statistics of Good Roads in South Carolina," 21–25.

11. *Manning Times,* February 4, 1903.

12. Watson, "Economic Value of Good Roads," 9–16.

13. *Edgefield Advertiser,* May 8, 1901.

14. Hand, "Relation of Good Roads to Schools," 17–20.

15. Ibid.

16. *Charleston News and Courier,* January 10, 1906.

17. *Winnsboro News and Herald,* December 13, 1901.

18. *Newberry Herald and News,* January 14, 1902.

19. Ibid., October 16, 1903.

20. *Winnsboro News and Herald,* December 13, 1901.

21. *Abbeville Press and Banner,* June 11, 1902.

22. *Newberry Herald and News,* July 28, 1903.

23. *Anderson Intelligencer,* August 12, 1903.

24. *Newberry Herald and News,* July 28, 1903.

25. South Carolina General Assembly, *House Journal* 1890, 129, 133.

26. Ibid., 134.

27. Ibid.

28. For more on taxation and southern schools, see Carter, "State Support for Public Schools"; Johns et al., *Economics and Financing of Education;* Margo, *Race and Schooling in the South;* Mort, *State Support for Public Education.*

29. Hudson, *Entangled in White Supremacy,* 265.

30. State of South Carolina, State Superintendent of Education, *Annual Report,* 1909, 11.

31. State of South Carolina, State Superintendent of Education, *Annual Report,* 1900.

32. Bartels, "History of South Carolina Schools," 13.

33. Ibid.

34. Ibid., 14.

35. See Hudson, *Entangled by White Supremacy,* 266–67.

36. South Carolina General Assembly, State Superintendent of Education, *Annual Report,* 1909, 61.

37. Ibid.

38. South Carolina General Assembly, *Journal of the Senate,* 1895.

39. *Charleston News and Courier,* January 9, 1908.

40. This table excludes the four counties that were not formed at the time of the dispensary (Allendale, Dillon, Jasper, and McCormick). I also exclude four counties that were formed after the dispensary began operations (Bamberg, Calhoun, Dorchester, and Lee). Each of these counties began with dispensaries already located in a number of their towns, put there by liquor county boards in the counties from which they had been formed. The dispensary law prevented these towns from removing dispensaries. Greenwood and Marlboro Counties are also excluded, as they never had dispensaries. The two counties with nine hundred square miles and only one dispensary town (Charleston, Georgetown) have unusual reasons that made dispensary expansion unlikely. The city of Charleston included roughly two-thirds of that county's population and featured ten dispensaries within its borders, making further expansion unnecessary. Georgetown was the only incorporated town in Georgetown County, and because the state dispensary law required that dispensaries be placed only in incorporated towns, no further expansion was possible.

41. South Carolina General Assembly, State Dispensary Auditor, *Annual Report,* 1893–1905; U.S. Bureau of the Census, *Twelfth Census, 1900.*

42. D. H. Thompkins, private secretary to Tillman to H. G. Judge, March 9, 1894, box 45, Benjamin R. Tillman Papers, South Carolina Department of Archives and History; James E. Payne to State Board, n.d., box 4, State Board of Control Folder, South Carolina Dispensary Records, South Carolina Department of Archives and History.

43. South Carolina General Assembly, State Dispensary Auditor, *Annual Report,* 1893–1905; South Carolina General Assembly, Railroad Commission of South Carolina, *Annual Report,* 1905.

44. Ibid.

45. *Charleston Evening Post,* January 11, 1898.

46. South Carolina General Assembly, Superintendent of Education, *Report to General Assembly,* 1901–5.

47. Ibid.

48. *Charleston News and Courier,* January 10, 1906.

49. *Charlotte Observer,* September 3, 1905.

50. South Carolina General Assembly, State Comptroller General, *Annual Report,* 1905; South Carolina General Assembly, State Dispensary Auditor, *Annual Report,* 1905.

51. Ibid.

52. Ibid.

53. Ibid.

54. *Charleston News and Courier,* July 26, 1905.

55. *Keowee Courier,* August 2, 1905.

56. *Newberry Herald and News,* August 18, 1905.

3. THE SOCIAL COSTS OF THE DISPENSARY

1. See, e.g., Blocker, *Retreat from Reform;* Bordin, *Women and Temperance;* Carlton, *Mill and Town;* Clark, *Deliver Us from Evil;* Coker, *Liquor in the Land of the Lost Cause;* Epstein, *Politics of Domesticity;* Greenwood, *Bittersweet Legacy;* Hamm, *Shaping the Eighteenth Amendment;* Kerr, *Organized for Prohibition;* Link, *Paradox of Southern Progressivism;* Ownby, *Subduing Satan;* Pegram, "Temperance, Politics and Regional Political Culture"; Sims, *Power of Femininity in the New South;* Stewart, *Moonshiners and Prohibitionists;* Szymanski, *Pathways to Prohibition;* Timberlake, *Prohibition and the Progressive Movement;* West, *From Yeoman to Redneck;* Willis, *Southern Prohibition.*

2. Carlton, *Mill and Town,* 132; see also West, *From Yeoman to Redneck.*

3. Wilson, "Preachin', Prayin' and Singin' on the Public Square." On the history of southern evangelical churches, see Eighmy, *Churches in Cultural Captivity;* Loveland, *Southern Evangelicals and the Social Order;* Spain, *At Ease in Zion.*

4. Ownby, *Subduing Satan,* 15.

5. Moment, *Temperance in Light of the Letter and the Spirit of the Bible,* 5. For more on the evangelical view of and campaign against liquor, see Coker, *Liquor in the Land of the Lost Cause.*

6. *North Carolina Biblical Recorder,* January 16, 1907.

7. *State,* August 6, 1900.

8. Ibid., November 30, 1904.

9. Ibid., August 17, 1903.

10. Ibid., January 21, 1900.

11. Ibid., October 9, 1905.

12. Ibid., October 19, 1902.

13. Ibid., August 16, 1900.

14. Ibid.

15. Ibid., December 3, 1906.

16. Ibid., October 12, 1905.

17. Ibid., October 9, 1905.

18. Ibid., September 10, 1900.

19. Ibid., August 28, 1900.

20. For more on the liquor industry prior to the onset of prohibition, see Baron, *Brewed in America;* Cochran, *Pabst Brewing Company;* Downard, *Cincinnati Brewing Industry;* Duis, *Saloon;* Kerr, *Organized for Prohibition* (esp. chap. 1); Lender and Martin, *Drinking in America;* Mittleman, *Brewing Battles;* Rorabaugh, *Alcoholic Republic.*

21. Kerr, *Organized for Prohibition,* 17–18.

22. See Duis, *Saloon,* 33; and Mittelman, *Brewing Battles,* 102–49.

23. Ledger G, General Dispensary, December 1, 1903–November 1904, 122–23, 186, 196, 226, 230, 242–52, 268–69, 276–77, 294, 370, 448, Records of Dispensary.

24. *Augusta Chronicle,* July 25, 1897.

25. Ibid., October 7, 1897.

26. John W. Aviret to Governor Benjamin R. Tillman, April 25, 1893, box 44, Benjamin R. Tillman Papers, South Carolina Department of Archives and History.

27. George Meyer to Governor Benjamin R. Tillman, June 15, 1893, box 44, Benjamin R. Tillman Papers, South Carolina Department of Archives and History; my emphasis.

28. Eubanks, *Ben Tillman's Baby,* 136.

29. County Dispenser's reports, 1900–1905, SCDAH.

30. *State,* June 24, 1905.

31. *Charleston News and Courier,* April 27, 1905.

32. *State,* July 19, 1905.

33. *Newberry News and Observer,* August 16, 1905.

34. *Beaufort Post,* August 20, 1905.

35. *Darlington News Era,* October 10, 1905.

36. *State,* June 24, 1905.

37. *Spartanburg Herald,* August 8, 1904.

38. *Charleston Sunday News,* April 27, 1902.

39. *State,* August 11, 1893.

40. *Winnsboro News and Herald,* November 22, 1905.

41. *Anderson Intelligencer,* July 18, 1905.

42. *Winnsboro News and Herald,* November 22, 1905.

43. Atlanta Brewing and Ice Company to M. H. Mobley, May 29, 1906, box 5, Board of Directors folder, State Dispensary Records, South Carolina Department of Archives and History.

44. J. P. Thackston to E. W. Herman, no date given; quoted in Eubanks, *Ben Tillman's Baby,* 162.

45. *State,* June 30, 1902.

46. Ibid., November 5, 1903.

47. Hendricks, *Dispensary System,* 348, 335.

48. *People's Advocate,* May 29, 1893. There is little historical basis to support the conclusion of a black crime wave. See Ayers, *Vengeance and Justice,* for further discussion.

49. *State,* January 25, 1904.

50. Ibid., December 25, 1904.

51. County Dispensers Reports, 1900, 1905, State Dispensary Records, South Carolina Department of Archives and History.

52. West, *From Yeoman to Redneck,* 149.

53. Ibid., 150.

54. J. R. Deane to Governor Coleman L. Blease, November 18, 1911; quoted in West, *From Yeoman to Redneck,* 151.

4. FROM STATEWIDE DISPENSARY TO LOCAL OPTION

1. Johnson, *Government Liquor Monopoly,* 14.

2. Ibid., 15.

3. Ibid.

4. *State,* February 9, 1904.

5. South Carolina General Assembly, *Journal of the Senate,* January 20, 1904, 76.

6. *State,* February 15, 1904.

7. Ibid., February 13, 1905.

8. Hendricks, *South Carolina Dispensary,* 339–40.

9. Eubanks, *Ben Tillman's Baby,* 185.

10. South Carolina General Assembly, *House Reports and Resolutions,* 1906.

11. Christensen, "State Dispensaries of South Carolina," 78.

12. State of South Carolina, *House Reports and Resolutions,* 1906.

13. Christensen, "State Dispensaries of South Carolina," 80.

14. State of South Carolina, *House Reports and Resolutions,* 1906.

15. Ibid.

16. Ibid.

17. Christensen, "State Dispensaries of South Carolina," 79–80.

18. State of South Carolina, *House Reports and Resolutions,* 1906, 217.

19. Ibid.

20. State of South Carolina, *House Reports and Resolutions,* 1907, 586.

21. *Spartanburg Herald,* August 22, 1905.

22. *Charleston News and Observer,* July 26, 1905.

23. Ibid.

24. Ibid.

25. Ibid.

26. Hudson, *Entangled in White Supremacy,* 226.

27. Edgar, *South Carolina,* 455.

28. *Beaufort Gazette,* July 15, 1909.

29. *Newberry Herald and News* June 13, 1905.

30. Ibid., August 18, 1905.

31. *Beaufort Gazette,* July 1, 1909.

32. South Carolina General Assembly, State Dispensary Auditor, *Annual Report,* 1905; South Carolina General Assembly, State Comptroller General, *Annual Report,* 1905.

33. Tindall, *South Carolina Negroes,* 176.

34. U.S. Bureau of the Census, *Negro Population, 1905,* 232.

35. One of the other remaining dispensary counties was Charleston.

36. *Charleston News and Courier,* July 26, 1905.

37. Ibid., December 5, 1906.

38. *State,* July 30, 1906.

39. Ibid., June 16, 1905.

40. Ibid., May 9, 1906.

41. Ibid., July 31, 1906.

42. *Baptist Courier,* August 27, 1906.

43. *State,* July 26, 1906.

44. Ibid.

45. Ibid.

46. Ibid.

47. Ibid., July 31, 1906.

48. Ibid., August 1, 1906; my emphasis.

49. Ibid., July 31, 1906.

50. *Edgefield Advertiser,* August 22, 1906.

51. *Aiken Journal and Review,* July 5, 1906.

52. *State,* August 6, 1906.

53. Ibid., September 14, 1906.

54. *Charleston News and Courier,* January 18, 1907.

55. Ibid., February 11, 1907.

56. South Carolina General Assembly, *Journal of the Senate,* 1907, 689.

57. *Charleston News and Observer,* January 28, 1907.

58. South Carolina General Assembly, *Journal of the Senate,* 1907, 690–91.

5. AUGUSTA, AIKEN COUNTY, AND NORTH AUGUSTA

1. The history of Aiken County's founding is best told in Vandevelde, *Aiken County.*

2. *Augusta Chronicle,* December 5, 1902. For more on the Hamburg and Ellenton massacres, see Isabel Vandevelde, *Aiken County.*

3. For more on the history of Horse Creek Valley, see Carlton, *Mill and Town;* Conroy, "Horses Don't Eat Moon Pies"; Downey, "Riparian Rights and Manufacturing in Antebellum South Carolina"; Simon, *Fabric of Defeat;* Woodward, "Cotton Mill Village in the 1880's."

4. For more on southern agriculture during this period, see Fite, *Cotton Fields No More.*

5. *Aiken Journal and Review,* April 19, 1905.

6. Fite, *Cotton Fields No More,* 40.

7. *Augusta Chronicle,* July 23, 1905.

8. Among southern cities Augusta as a research focus has received far less attention than most. The city's chief historian has no doubt been Edward J. Cashin, who authored numerous books detailing the history of his native city. Although Cashin's focus was more typically on Colonial Era and pre–Civil War Augusta, two of his works offer important analyses of the city during the Progressive Era: Cashin, *Story of Augusta;* Cashin and Eskew, *Paternalism in the Southern City.* Aside from Cashin's work, the other most helpful source for Augusta's Progressive Era politics is German, *Queen City of the Savannah.*

9. Much of the scholarly literature on southern railroads has been consumed with the role of northern financial interests. Their presumed ill-effects on the development of the New South was frequently mentioned by commentators at the time and received its first full airing in Woodward, *Origins of the New South.* The standard history of southern railroad development is Stover, *Railroads of the New South.* For a more refined discussion of the political debates surrounding railroad development see Doster, *Railroads in Alabama Politics.*

10. Jones and Dutcher, *Memorial History of Augusta,* 418–19.

11. City of Augusta, Georgia, *Augusta City Directory* (Augusta: Maloney Printing Company, 1897–1903); City of Augusta, Georgia, *R. L. Polk and Co. Augusta City Directory* (Augusta: R. L. Polk, 1904–17).

12. H. H. Hickman, Reports of the President, 1901, Gregg-Graniteville Collection, University of South Carolina–Aiken.

13. Kohn, *Cotton Mills of South Carolina,* 457.

14. Tracy I. Hickman, Reports of the President, 1907, Gregg-Graniteville Collection, University of South Carolina–Aiken.

15. Sands, *St. Paul's Mission in Horse Creek Valley,* 10.

16. *Aiken Journal and Review,* March 4, 1905.

17. Each of Augusta's original North-South streets were named after Revolutionary War generals; over time, however, these names gradually fell out of use in favor of a simple numerical system. By the early twentieth century both sets of names were used interchangeably. In this text I will introduce both names initially and then will use the numerical system.

18. *Augusta Chronicle,* February 12, 1891.

19. Ibid.

20. McDaniel, *North Augusta,* 51.

21. For more on Aiken's Winter Colony, see Lawrence, *Horses, Heroes and High Society;* Smith, *Life and Sport in Aiken.*

22. For more on sick northerners seeking respite through southern tourism, see Silber, *Romance of Reunion.*

23. Geddings, "Aiken."

24. Ibid.

25. Ibid.

26. Ibid.

27. *State,* November 5, 1900.

28. Ibid., April 18, 1904.

29. Ibid.

30. *New York Times,* February 28, 1892.

31. *State,* November 5, 1900.

32. *Augusta Chronicle,* March 6, 1906.

33. *Atlanta Constitution,* March 7, 1903.

34. *Augusta Chronicle,* March 6, 1906.

35. *State,* April 18, 1904.

36. *Aiken Journal and Review,* April 26, 1905.

37. *Augusta Chronicle,* December 2, 1889.

38. Ibid., December 1, 1903.

39. Ibid., August 15, 1902.

40. Ibid., August 20, 1902.

41. Ibid., August 29, 1902.

42. *Aiken Journal and Review,* August 29, 1902.

43. Ibid., May 26, 1902.

44. *Augusta Chronicle,* August 20, 1903.

45. *Aiken Journal and Review,* April 16, 1904.

46. *Augusta Chronicle,* October 7, 1902.

47. Ibid., October 2, 1902.

48. Ibid., November 15, 1906.

49. Ibid., November 25, 1906.

50. Ibid., October 4, 1906.

51. *Aiken Journal and Review,* November 13, 1906.

52. *Augusta Chronicle, November* 15, 1906.

53. Ibid., October 6, 1906.

54. Ibid.

55. Ibid., October 4, 1906.

56. *Aiken Journal and Review,* September 28, 1906.

57. Ibid., November 20, 1906.

58. Ibid., November 29, 1903.

59. Ibid., October 11, 1906.

60. Ibid., September 28, 1906.

61. Ibid.

62. *Augusta Chronicle,* April 15, 1902.

6. LIQUOR IN AUGUSTA AND AIKEN COUNTY, 1900–1906

1. *State,* September 24, 1896.

2. Ibid.

3. Ibid., August 4, 1903.

4. Ibid., June 15, 1902.

5. *Augusta Chronicle,* May 3, 1904.

6. Ibid., September 24, 1904.

7. *Charleston News and Courier,* June 12, 1905.

8. *Augusta Chronicle,* June 16, 1905.

9. *Aiken Journal and Review,* August 3, 1905.

10. *State,* October 16, 1905.

11. *Aiken Journal and Review,* October 16, 1905.

12. *State,* January 4, 1905.

13. Ibid., October 27, 1905.

14. Carlton, *Mill and Town;* West, *From Yeoman to Redneck.*

15. Carlton, *Mill and Town,* 163.

16. *State,* December 24, 1904.

17. *Aiken Recorder,* October 9, 1904.

18. *State,* September 5, 1906.

19. South Carolina General Assembly, *Acts and Resolutions adopted by the State of South Carolina,* 1894, 735–36.

20. *Charleston News and Courier,* July 26, 1905.

21. Ibid.

22. Unlike most other southern states, Georgia has not had a full-length scholarly history of its temperance movement. Despite this lack, several excellent studies have shed light on the various facets of the state's anti-alcohol movement. For a discussion of the Georgia anti-liquor movement prior to the Progressive Era, consult the eight hundred–plus magnum opus by Henry Anselm Scomp, *King Alcohol in the Realm of King Cotton.* The Woman's Christian Temperance Union of Georgia was the primary temperance organization in the state for virtually the entire Progressive Era. The best histories of the Georgia WCTU are Ansley, *History of the Georgia Woman's Christian Temperance Union;* Hardesty, "'Best Temperance Organization in the Land'"; Rabby, "Woman's Christian Temperance Union in Georgia." For a discussion on the seminal role played by southern white fears of race war and the Atlanta Race Riot that heightened these fears, see Bauerlein, *Negrophobia;* Dittmer, *Black Georgia in the Progressive Era;* Mixon, "Atlanta Riot of 1906"; Moore, "Negro and Prohibition in Atlanta"; Thompson, "Race, Temperance and Prohibition in the Postbellum South." For a discussion of the role Georgia's evangelicals played in the anti-liquor movement, see Coker, *Liquor in the Land of the Lost Cause.*

23. Scomp, *King Alcohol in the Realm of King Cotton,* 648.

24. Ibid., 679–80.

25. Ibid., 680.

26. *Athens Daily Banner,* January 14, 1892.

27. Ibid., July 7, 1891.

28. *Atlanta Constitution,* July 14, 1891.

29. Ibid., August 11, 1891.

30. Coulter, "Athens Dispensary," 20–21.

31. *Athens Daily Banner,* October 6, 1891.

32. Ibid., May 26, 1893.

33. *Oglethorpe Echo,* April 28, 1893.

34. Georgia General Assembly, Georgia State Comptroller General, *Annual Report,* 1898, 1900, 1902, 1904, 1906.

35. Coulter, "Athens Dispensary."

36. *Augusta Chronicle,* November 15, 1904.

37. Ibid., November 12, 1904.

38. Ibid., July 25, 1904.

39. Ibid.

40. Ibid.

41. Ibid.

42. Ibid.

43. Ibid., September 26, 1904.

44. Ibid., October 21, 1904.

45. Ibid., November 16, 1904.

46. Ibid., September 22, 1904.

47. Ibid., November 12, 1904.

48. Ibid., September 10, 1904.

49. Ibid., September 26, 1904.

50. Ibid., November 12, 1904.

51. City of Augusta, Ga., *City Council Report,* 1902–7.

52. Licenses listed in *Augusta Chronicle,* September 14, 1904, September 21, 1905, and September 23 1906.

53. *Augusta Chronicle,* September 12, 1904.

7. THE DISPENSARY COMES TO NORTH AUGUSTA

1. The best scholarly account of the 1906 Georgia gubernatorial race is found in Grantham, *Hoke Smith and the Politics of the New South.* For further discussion of the links between the 1906 gubernatorial contest and the race riot in Atlanta that occurred later that same year see Bauerlein, *Negrophobia;* Woodward, *Tom Watson Agrarian Rebel.* For more on the riot, see Burns, *Rage in the Gate City;* Godshalk, *Veiled Visions.*

2. Rabby, "Woman's Christian Temperance Union in Georgia," 114.

3. Ibid.

4. Georgia Woman's Christian Temperance Union, *Annual Report,* 1906, 71.

5. White, "Prohibition," 140.

6. Georgia Woman's Christian Temperance Union, *Annual Report,* 1906, 71.

7. *Savannah Morning News,* July 3, 1907.

8. *Augusta Chronicle,* July 19, 1907.

9. Ibid., July 7, 1907.

10. *Atlanta Constitution,* July 25, 1907.

11. Ibid.

12. Georgia General Assembly, *Acts of the State of Georgia,* 1907, 81.

13. *Atlanta Constitution,* July 31, 1907.

14. *Augusta Chronicle,* August 2, 1907.

15. Ibid.

16. *Aiken Journal and Review,* December 12, 1907.

17. Ibid.

18. *Marlboro Democrat,* December 27, 1907.

19. *Aiken Journal and Review,* December 16, 1907.

20. Ibid.

21. Ibid.

22. *Augusta Chronicle,* December 7, 1907.

23. Ibid.

24. *Aiken Journal and Review,* December 16, 1907.

25. Ibid.

26. *Augusta Chronicle,* December 7, 1907.

27. *Aiken Journal and Review,* December 16, 1907.

28. Ibid., December 10, 1907; my emphasis.

29. Ibid., December 24, 1907; City of Augusta, Georgia, *Augusta City Directory,* 1907.

30. Augusta Lodge, BPO Elks No. 205: *Officers;* Acacia Lodge No. 315, *History of Acacia Lodge No. 315,* 1–7; North Augusta South Carolina First Baptist Church, *History of the First Baptist Church,* 3–10; North Augusta (S.C.) Grace United Methodist Church, *History of Grace United Methodist Church;* Augusta (Ga.) First Presbyterian Church, *Directory of Membership,* 1908.

31. *Aiken Journal and Review,* December 24, 1907; City of Augusta, Georgia, *Augusta City Directory,* 1907.

32. *Aiken Journal and Review,* November 29, 1907.

33. Ibid., December 16, 1907.

34. *Augusta Chronicle,* December 7, 1907.

35. Ibid.

36. Ibid.

37. *Aiken Journal and Review,* December 16, 1907.

38. Ibid.

39. *Greenwood Index,* January 13, 1908.

40. *Anderson Mail,* January 13, 1908.

41. *Orangeburg Sun,* August 25, 1909.

42. *Sumter Watchman and Southron,* January 15, 1908.

43. *Augusta Chronicle,* January 23, 1908.

44. Ibid., January 24, 1908.

45. Ibid.

46. Ibid., January 28, 1908.

47. *Charleston Evening Post,* January 29, 1908.

48. *Augusta Chronicle,* February 6, 1908.

49. Ibid., January 3, 1908.

50. Ibid., March 18, 1908.

51. Ibid.

52. Ibid., April 13, April 9, April 10, 1908; *Charleston News and Courier,* April 14, 1908.

53. *Augusta Chronicle,* March 30, 1908.

54. Ibid., March 10, 1908.

55. Ibid., April 15, 1908.

56. Ibid., March 26, 1908.

57. *Columbia Record,* April 22, 1908.

8. THE TOWN AND COUNTY THE DISPENSARY BUILT

1. *State,* January 4, 1908.

2. *Augusta Chronicle,* October 2, 1908.

3. Ibid., September 23, 1908.

4. *Orangeburg Times and Democrat,* February 21, 1908.

5. Ibid., January 17, 1908.

6. *Augusta Chronicle,* February 18, 1908.

7. Ibid., October 2, 1908.

8. Ibid., November 1, 1908.

9. Ibid., June 30, 1908.

10. Ibid., January 10, 1909.

11. Ibid.

12. Ibid., December 6, 1909.

13. Ibid., December 20, 1908.

14. Ibid., October 7, 1908.

15. Ibid., January 10, 1909.

16. Ibid., October 13, 1912.

17. Ibid., December 10, 1908.

18. The South Carolina Anti-Saloon League was not one of its more successful state organizations, nor has it left many documents to allow scholars a glimpse into its activities. Most of the information on the SCASL can be found in the Anti-Saloon League's annual yearbooks. The standard histories of the national Anti-Saloon League are Kerr, *Organized for Prohibition;* Odegard, *Pressure Politics.* The league's own retelling of its history can be found in Cherrington, *History of the Anti-Saloon League.*

19. *Charleston News and Courier,* March 7, 1908.

20. Duncan, "Reverend John Lawton Harley," 187.

21. Through 1909 four of the five southern states that adopted statewide dry laws did so without resorting to referenda (Ala., Ga., Miss., and Tenn.). The only state where dry campaigners sought a referendum was North Carolina.

22. *State,* January 22, 1909.

23. Ibid., January 21, 1909.

24. *Charleston News and Observer,* January 22, 1909.

25. *State,* January 21, 1909.

26. Ibid., January 25, 1909.

27. *Charleston News and Courier,* December 6, 1908.

28. *State,* February 26, 1909.

29. Ibid.

30. Ibid., January 25, 1909.

31. Ibid.

32. Ibid., February 23, February 26, 1909.

33. Ibid., March 2, 1909.

34. *Newberry Herald and News,* December 1, 1908.

35. *Manning Times,* July 10, 1909.

36. *Charleston News and Courier,* July 21, 1909.

37. Ibid., January 9, 1909.

38. *Newberry Herald and News,* December 1, 1909.

39. Ibid., July 27, 1909.

40. *Charleston News and Observer,* January 9, 1909.

41. Ibid., January 23, 1909.

42. *Edgefield Advertiser,* August 12, 1909.

43. Since the 1905 referenda three counties (Chester, Chesterfield, and Laurens) had received legislative approval to hold special referenda on their liquor shops. Each had voted for prohibition. South Carolina General Assembly, State Electoral Commission, *Report to General Assembly,* 1907, 1908.

44. *Charleston News and Courier,* December 1, 1909.

45. Ibid., June 27, 1908.

46. *Augusta Chronicle,* September 17, 1908.

47. Ibid., January 30, 1910.

48. Ibid., January 4, 1910.

49. Cecil Seigler, "Aiken County," in South Carolina General Assembly, Superintendent of Education, *Report to South Carolina General Assembly,* 1909.

50. *State,* August 25, 1909.

51. *Horse Creek Valley News,* July 11, 1910.

52. For more on the inferiority of African American schools, see Anderson, *Education of Blacks in the South.*

53. *Augusta Chronicle,* May 10, 1908.

54. Ibid., September 17, 1908.

55. Ibid.

56. Ibid., February 18, 1909.

57. *Charleston News and Observer,* April 13, 1909.

58. Ibid.

59. *Augusta Chronicle,* March 7, 1909.

60. Ibid., March 1, 1909.

61. Ibid., September 6, 1907.

62. Ibid., January 14, 1912.

63. Ibid.

64. Ibid.

65. Ibid., January 17, 1912.

66. Ibid., January 23, 1912.

67. Ibid., July 15, 1912.

68. *State,* December 1, 1912.

69. *Charleston News and Courier,* January 11, 1908.

70. Ibid., January 15, 1908.

71. *State,* July 8, 1909.

72. *State,* August 17, 1913.

9. AUGUSTA'S SALOONS REVIVED, 1908–1913

1. Park, *Report of the Thirtieth Annual Session of the Georgia Bar Association,* 170–71.

2. Ibid., 172.

3. Ibid., 174.

4. *Columbus Daily Enquirer,* July 3, 1908.

5. *Augusta Chronicle,* January 18, 1908.

6. *Columbus Daily Enquirer,* March 10, 1908.

7. U.S. Department of Commerce and Labor, *Financial Statistics of Cities,* 1909.

8. *Augusta Chronicle,* October 26, 1908.

9. Ibid., March 9, 1908.

10. Ibid., October 26, 1908.

11. Ibid.

12. Ibid., December 1, 1911.

13. *Macon Telegraph,* January 20, 1909.

14. *Augusta Chronicle,* December 31, 1908.

15. *Columbus Daily Enquirer,* July 3, 1908.

16. *Macon Telegraph,* July 11, 1911.

17. Ibid., June 10, 1908.

18. *Atlanta Constitution,* August 31, 1908.

19. *Chattanooga News,* September 1, 1908.

20. *Macon Telegraph,* September 1, 1908.

21. *Columbus Daily Enquirer,* July 3, 1908.

22. *Macon Telegraph,* September 1, 1908.

23. *Columbus Daily Enquirer,* July 3, 1908.

24. *Montgomery Advertiser,* June 18, 1910.

25. *Augusta Chronicle,* August 4, 1907.

26. *Marietta Journal,* August 15, 1907.

27. *Augusta Chronicle,* August 18, 1907.

28. Ibid., August 17, 1907.

29. Ibid.

30. Ibid., August 19, 1907.

31. *Columbus Daily Enquirer,* August 22, 1907.

32. *Aiken Journal and Review,* August 27, 1907.

33. The *Macon Telegraph* in the last six months of 1907 kept close track of the various amounts of locker taxes in cities across Georgia.

34. Ibid., August 12, 1907.

35. Ibid., December 31, 1907.

36. *Augusta Chronicle,* July 3, 1908.

37. Ibid., January 1, 1908.

38. Ibid., March 12, 1908.

39. Ibid., August 23, 1908.

40. Ibid., December 21, 1908.

41. Ibid., August 22, 1908.

42. Ibid., July 15, 1909.

43. Ibid., September 23, 1912.

44. Ibid., February 1, 1909.

45. Ibid., January 7, 1909.

46. Ibid., January 18, 1909.

47. Ibid., July 12, 1909.

48. Ibid., December 20, 1908.

49. Ibid., June 14, 1908.

50. Ibid., July 6, 1909.

51. *Roanoke Times,* June 7, 1910.

52. *Augusta Chronicle,* July 6, 1909.

53. Ibid., January 10, 1909.

54. *Macon Telegraph,* April 19, 1908.

55. *Roanoke Times,* June 7, 1910.

56. *Augusta Chronicle,* January 10, 1909.

57. Augusta Chamber of Commerce, *Annual Report,* 1908.

58. Ibid.

59. *Aiken Journal and Review,* August 27, 1907.

60. *Macon Telegraph,* November 12, 1912; *Augusta Chronicle,* June 23, 1913.

61. Ibid., February 2, 1914.

62. Ibid., December 18, 1914.

63. Ibid., March 4, 1908.

64. Ibid., October 9, 1908.

65. Ibid., December 29, 1910.

66. Ibid., November 28, 1911.

67. Augusta (Ga.) City Council, *Yearbook of the City Council of Augusta, Georgia,* 1910–11.

68. *Augusta Chronicle,* April 26, 1911.

69. Ibid., July 19, 1910.

70. Ibid., June 15, 1910.

71. Ibid., June 27, 1910.

72. Ibid., May 23, 1910.

10. THE SOUTH STEPS BACK FROM PROHIBITION, 1909–1913

1. *State* August 19, 1909.
2. Ibid.
3. Ibid.
4. *Charleston News and Courier,* August 30, 1910.
5. *Manning Times,* July 13, 1910.
6. *Newberry Herald and News,* July 22, 1910.
7. *Yorkville Enquirer,* September 8, 1910.
8. *Sumter Watchman and Southron,* September 8, 1910.
9. *State,* September 2, 1910.
10. Ibid., September 8, 1910.
11. Ibid., August 9, 1910.
12. South Carolina General Assembly, *Journal of the Senate,* 1911, 84–85.
13. For more on Blease as governor, see Burnside, "Governorship of Coleman Livingston Blease."
14. *State,* November 24, 1913.
15. Ibid., May 1, 1913.
16. Ibid., January 21, 1913.
17. Hudson, *Entangled in White Supremacy,* 268–69.
18. *State,* March 6, 1913.
19. Ibid., March 21, 1913.
20. Ibid., February 19, 1913.
21. Ibid., July 20, 1913.
22. *Edgefield Advertiser,* February 5, 1913.
23. *Newberry Observer,* February 5, 1913.
24. *State,* September 23, 1913.
25. Moore, *South Carolina Highway Department,* 29.
26. Ibid.
27. Holmes, "Sand-Clay Roads," *Southern Good Roads,* April 1911.
28. Spoon, "Construction of Sand-Clay and Burnt-Clay Roads."
29. Watson, "Earth, Sand-Clay and Gravel Roads," *Southern Good Roads,* April 1911.
30. *Manning Times,* January 15, 1913.
31. *Laurens Advertiser,* August 6, 1913.
32. Ibid., May 21, 1913.
33. *State,* May 7, 1913.
34. *Charleston News and Courier,* May 28, 1913.
35. *Beaufort Gazette,* April 8, 1913.
36. *State,* December 29, 1913.
37. Ibid., August 29, 1913.
38. *Charleston News and Courier,* March 3, 1913.
39. *State,* June 7, 1913.
40. *Charleston News and Courier,* May 10, 1913.

41. *State,* June 2, February 14, 1913.

42. Ibid., November 17, 1913.

43. Ibid., September 18, 1913.

44. *Sumter Watchman and Southron,* September 20, 1913.

45. *Spartanburg Journal,* April 23, 1913.

46. *State,* October 6, 1913.

47. *Newberry Herald and News,* March 24, 1911.

48. *State,* March 26, 1911.

49. *Outlook,* July 27, 1912, 101:650–51.

50. *State,* July 12, 1912.

51. *New York Times,* July 21, 1912.

52. *Greenville Journal,* February 5, 1913.

53. *Edgefield Advertiser,* April 23, 1913.

54. *State,* September 15, 1913.

55. Ibid., August 30, 1913.

56. Ibid.

57. Ibid.

58. *Augusta Chronicle* April 28, 1913.

59. *State,* August 25, 1913.

60. Ibid., March 30, 1913.

61. *Charleston News and Courier,* March 13, 1913.

62. *State,* August 29, 1913.

63. Ibid., September 7, 1913.

64. *Charleston News and Courier,* June 12, 1913.

65. *State,* July 18, 1913.

66. *Sumter Watchman and Southron,* May 3, 1913.

67. *Calhoun Advance,* August 23, 1913.

68. *State,* September 1, 1913.

69. Jasper County was founded from parts of Beaufort and Hampton Counties in 1912 and retained its dispensaries that had been operating in Beaufort County.

70. South Carolina General Assembly, State Dispensary Auditor, *Annual Report,* 1914, 15.

71. *Charlotte Observer,* February 15, 1912.

72. *Augusta Chronicle,* June 5, 1908.

73. *Natchez News,* September 29, 1911.

74. W. R. Hamilton, Tennessee Anti-Saloon League Superintendent to local ASL affiliates, November 21, 1911, Tennessee State Library and Archives.

75. *Montgomery Advertiser,* January 22, 1911.

76. Ibid., February 22, 1911.

77. *Gulfport Daily Herald,* January 17, 1911.

78. *Natchez News,* September 29, 1911.

79. Ibid.

80. Sellers, *Prohibition in Alabama,* 170–71 n. 126.

81. *Montgomery Advertiser,* January 14, 1911.

82. *Gulfport Daily Herald,* July 6, 1912.

83. Ibid., June 20, 1910.

84. Ibid., July 1, 1911.

85. *Biloxi Daily Herald,* July 2, 1909.

86. *Jonesboro Daily Tribune,* April 16, 1911.

87. *Charlotte Observer,* December 23, 1912.

88. Ibid., February 21, 1910.

89. Whitener, *Prohibition in North Carolina,* 171.

90. *Greensboro Record,* May 28, 1909.

91. *Charlotte Observer,* October 11, 1911.

92. Ibid., February 24, 1910.

93. Ibid.

94. Moriarty v. State of Tennessee, 1909, 124.

95. Isaac, *Prohibition and Politics,* 173.

96. Ibid., 174.

97. Ibid., 176.

98. *Memphis Commercial Appeal,* February 11, 1910.

99. Ibid.

100. *Jackson Clarion-Ledger,* January 13, 1909.

101. Nogales Club v. State of Mississippi, 1910, 69.

102. *Biloxi Daily Herald,* August 12, 1908.

103. *Gulfport Daily Herald,* July 15, 1910.

104. Mississippi General Assembly, *Laws of the State of Mississippi,* 1912, 75.

105. *Gulfport Daily Herald,* March 28, 1912.

106. *Meridian Dispatch,* June 14, 1912.

107. *Gulfport Daily Herald,* April 9, 1912.

108. Ibid., March 28, 1912.

109. Sellers, *Prohibition in Alabama,* 164–65.

110. *Sheffield Standard,* June 13, 1911.

111. Sellers, *Prohibition in Alabama,* 168.

112. *Montgomery Advertiser,* June 18, 1910.

113. Sellers, *Prohibition in Alabama,* 170.

114. *Richmond Times Dispatch,* January 17, 1910.

115. *Charlotte Observer,* July 22, 1912.

11. THE COMING OF A (TRULY) DRY SOUTH

1. *Augusta Chronicle,* July 8, 1910.

2. Ibid.

3. Ibid.

4. Ibid.

5. Ibid.

6. Hamm, *Shaping the Eighteenth Amendment;* Timberlake, *Prohibition and the Progressive Movement;* Kousser, *Shaping of Southern Politics.*

7. Szymanski, *Pathways to Prohibition;* Hamm, *Shaping the Eighteenth Amendment;* Timberlake, *Prohibition and the Progressive Movement;* Kousser, *Shaping of Southern Politics.*

8. *Charleston News and Courier,* July 9, 1913.

9. Hamm, *Shaping the Eighteenth Amendment,* 216.

10. *New York Times,* March 2, 1913.

11. Hamm, *Shaping the Eighteenth Amendment,* 218.

12. *Richmond Times Dispatch,* March 10, 1913.

13. Ibid., March 9, 1913.

14. *Augusta Chronicle,* June 24, 1913.

15. *Selma Times,* January 15, 1915.

16. *Richmond Times-Dispatch,* May 15, 1914.

17. *Gulfport Daily Herald,* February 8, 1913.

18. Hamm, *Shaping the Eighteenth Amendment,* 223.

19. Ibid.

20. *Columbus Ledger,* March 23, 1913.

21. Isaac, *Prohibition and Politics* 179.

22. Whitener, *Prohibition in North Carolina,* 135.

23. Isaac, *Prohibition and Politics,* 179.

24. *Alabama Citizen,* October 11, 1913.

25. *Richmond Times-Dispatch,* November 1, 1916.

26. *Greensboro Record,* February 10, 1917.

27. *Richmond Times-Dispatch,* January 29, 1917.

28. Hamm, *Shaping the Eighteenth Amendment,* 225.

29. *Richmond Times-Dispatch,* January 9, 1917.

30. Isaac, *Prohibition and Politics,* 252.

31. *Columbus Ledger,* January 17, 1916.

32. *Columbus Daily Enquirer,* November 17, 1916.

33. *Augusta Chronicle,* December 18, 1914.

34. *Macon Telegraph,* November 4, 1915.

35. Ibid., July 6, 1915.

36. *Augusta Chronicle,* June 23, 1913.

37. *Macon Telegraph,* October 7, 1916.

38. *Augusta Chronicle,* December 15, 1914.

39. Ibid., November 14, 1915.

40. *State,* October 14, 1914.

41. Ibid., December 15, 1914.

42. Ibid., July 22, 1914.

43. Ibid., July 22, 1914.

44. Ibid., October 23, 1914.

45. Ibid., December 15, 1914.

46. Ibid., January 4, 1915.

47. *Newberry Herald and News,* December 25, 1914.

48. *State* July 28, 1915.

49. Ibid., December 30, 1914.

50. *Charleston News and Courier,* June 24, 1915.

51. *State,* September 12, 1915.

52. Ibid., November 25, 1914.

53. Ibid., January 4, 1915.

54. Ibid., January 20, 1915.

55. Ibid.

56. Ibid.

57. Ibid., January 27, 1915.

58. Ibid.

59. Ibid., January 14–February 14, 1915.

60. Ibid., July 11, 1915.

61. Ibid., September 7, 1913.

62. Ibid.

63. Ibid., April 22, 1915.

64. *Aiken Journal and Review,* April 21, 1915.

65. *State,* April 24, 1915.

66. Ibid., June 8, 1915.

67. Ibid., June 20, 1915.

68. Ibid., May 25, 1915.

69. *Augusta Chronicle,* July 13, 1915.

70. *Aiken Journal and Review,* September 10, 1915.

71. *Augusta Chronicle,* September 7, 1915.

CONCLUSION

1. *Columbus Enquirer,* September 23, 1916.

2. *State,* June 13, 1916; *Charleston Evening Post,* January 1, 1916.

3. *State,* February 11, 1917.

4. Ibid., February 7, 1917.

5. *Albany Herald,* November 24, 1916.

6. *Macon Telegraph,* November 12, 1915.

7. *Charleston Evening Post,* January 1, 1916.

8. *Augusta Chronicle,* May 2, 1916.

9. The best scholarly discussion of the political maneuvering that brought forth the Eighteenth Amendment is found in Hamm, *Shaping the Eighteenth Amendment.*

10. *Sumter Watchman and Southron,* January 1, 1916.

11. Trinkley, *Cultural Resources Survey of North Augusta,* 47, 67, 78, 79.

12. City of North Augusta, "Guide to the North Augusta in 1910 Model," 2.

BIBLIOGRAPHY

MANUSCRIPT COLLECTIONS

South Carolina

South Carolina Department of Archives and History, Columbia
    Benjamin R. Tillman Papers
    South Carolina State Dispensary Papers
        State Board of Control, General Correspondence, 1893–1907
        Reports of the County Dispensers, 1893–1907
        Annual Reports of the South Carolina State Dispensary, 1895–1907
Graniteville Manufacturing Co. Papers, Gregg-Graniteville Library, Gregg-Graniteville Archives, University of South Carolina–Aiken

Tennessee

Tennessee State Library and Archives
    Correspondence from W. R. Hamilton, Nashville, November 21, 1911, GP 36, Governor Ben W. Hooper Papers. "The Saloon and Anarchy." Online exhibit. tn.gov/tsla/exhibits/prohibition/images/temperance/36541.jpg.

GOVERNMENT SOURCES

Federal

U.S. Bureau of the Census. *Financial Statistics of Cities Having a Population over 30,000, 1909.* Washington, D.C.: Government Printing Office, 1913.
——. *Negro Population, 1905.* Washington, D.C.: Government Printing Office, 1908.
——. *Religious Bodies, 1906.* Washington, D.C.: Government Printing Office, 1910.
——. *Thirteenth Census, 1910.* Washington, D.C.: Government Printing Office, 1913.
——. *Twelfth Census, 1900.* Washington, D.C.: Government Printing Office, 1902.

State

Georgia General Assembly. *Acts and Resolutions of the General Assembly of the State of Georgia, 1906, 1907, 1910, 1916.* Atlanta: State Printer.

——. Georgia State Comptroller General. *Annual Report of the Comptroller General to the General Assembly of the State of Georgia, 1906–1913.* Atlanta: State Printer.

Mississippi Legislature. *Laws of the State of Mississippi,* 1912. Memphis: E. R. Clarke and Brothers, 1913.

South Carolina General Assembly. *Acts and Resolutions of the General Assembly of the State of South Carolina, 1892–1907.* Columbia: State Printer.

——. South Carolina State Comptroller General. *Annual Report of the Comptroller General of the State of South Carolina to the General Assembly.* Columbia: State Printer.

——. *Journal of the House of Representatives, 1892–1915.* Columbia: State Printer.

——. *Journal of the Senate.* Columbia: State Printer.

——. South Carolina Secretary of Education. *Annual Report of the South Carolina Secretary of Education to the General Assembly of the State of South Carolina, 1895–1907.* Columbia: State Printer.

——. South Carolina State Dispensary Auditor. *Annual Report of the South Carolina State Dispensary Auditor to the General Assembly of the State of South Carolina, 1893–1915.* Columbia: State Printer.

Local

City of Augusta, Georgia. *Mayor's Message and Official Reports of the Departments of the City of Augusta, 1902–1916.* Augusta: Chronicle Job Office.

City of Augusta, Georgia. *Augusta City Directory.* Augusta: Maloney Printing Co., 1897–1903.

City of Augusta, Georgia. *R. L. Polk and Co. Augusta City Directory.* Augusta: R. L. Polk and Co., 1904–17.

City of North Augusta, South Carolina. "Guide to the North Augusta in 1910 Model." North Augusta: Arts and Heritage Center of North Augusta, 2010.

Court Cases

McCollough v. Brown, 41 S.C. (1893)
Moriarty v. State of Tennessee, 122 Tenn. (1909)
Nogales Club v. State of Mississippi, 97 Miss. (1910)

NEWSPAPERS

Abbeville (S.C.) Press and Banner, 1895–1915

Aiken (S.C.) Journal and Review, 1895–1915

Aiken (S.C.) Recorder, 1906–10

Alabama Citizen (Tuscumbia), 1913

Albany (Ga.) Herald, 1916

Anderson (S.C.) Intelligencer, 1895–1914

Anderson (S.C.) Mail, 1907

Athens (Ga.) Daily Banner, 1891–1907

Atlanta (Ga.) Constitution, 1906–16

Augusta (Ga.) Chronicle, 1891–1916

Beaufort (S.C.) Gazette, 1905–13

Beaufort (S.C.) Post, 1905

Biloxi (Miss.) Daily Herald, 1908–12

Calhoun (S.C.) Advance, 1913

Charleston (S.C.) Evening Post, 1892–1915

Charleston (S.C.) News and Courier, 1892–1915

Charlotte (N.C.) Observer, 1900–1914

Chattanooga (Tenn.) News, 1908

Chicago (Ill.) Lever, 1893

Columbia (S.C.) People's Advocate, 1893

Columbia (S.C.) Record, 1907

Columbia (S.C.) State, 1892–1915

Columbus (Ga.) Daily Enquirer, 1913–16

Columbus (Ga.) Ledger, 1913–16

Darlington (S.C.) News Era, 1904–5

Edgefield (S.C.) Advertiser, 1905–15

Greensboro (N.C.) Record, 1915–17

Greenville (S.C.) Baptist Courier, 1905–6

Greenville (S.C.) Journal, 1913

Greenwood (S.C.) Index, 1907

Gulfport (Miss.) Daily Herald, 1911–15

Horse Creek Valley (S.C.) News, 1910

Jackson (Miss.) Clarion-Ledger, 1909

Jonesboro (Ark.) Daily Tribune, 1911

Keowee (S.C.) Courier, 1899–1915

Laurens (S.C.) Advertiser, 1913

Macon (Ga.) Telegraph, 1907–16

Manning (S.C.) Times, 1909

Marietta (Ga.) Journal, 1907–10

Marlboro (S.C.) Democrat, 1907

Memphis (Tenn.) Commercial Appeal, 1910

Meridian (Miss.) Dispatch, 1912

Montgomery (Ala.) Advertiser, 1910–16

Natchez (Miss.) News, 1911

Newberry (S.C.) Herald and News, 1905–15

Newberry (S.C.) News and Observer, 1903–15

New York Times, 1894–1915

Oglethorpe (Ga.) Echo, 1893

Orangeburg (S.C.) Sun, 1907

Orangeburg (S.C.) Times and Democrat, 1909–15

Richmond (Va.) Times-Dispatch, 1912–17

Roanoke (Va.) Times, 1910

Savannah (Ga.) Morning News, 1906–16

Selma (Ala.) Times, 1915

Sheffield (Ala.) Standard, 1911

Spartanburg (S.C.) Herald, 1904–5

Sumter (S.C.) Watchman and Southron, 1906–15

Winnsboro (S.C.) News and Herald, 1901–15

Yorkville (S.C.) Enquirer, 1910

CHURCH AND FRATERNAL ORGANIZATION SOURCES

Acacia Lodge No. 315 AFM. *History of Acacia Lodge No. 315 AFM, North Augusta, South Carolina.* North Augusta: Historical Committee, Acacia Lodge, 1956.

Augusta Lodge, BPO Elks No. 205. *List of Members and Officers.* Augusta: BPO Elks, 1904.

Biblical Recorder. Journal. Baptist State Convention of North Carolina. Raleigh, N.C.: Biblical Recorder, 1907.

First Presbyterian Church, Augusta, Ga. *Directory of Membership of First Presbyterian Church.* Augusta: First Presbyterian Church, 1908.

Georgia Woman's Christian Temperance Union. *Report of the Twenty-Fourth Annual Convention of the Woman's Christian Temperance Union of Georgia.* Columbus: Gilbert Printing Co., 1906.

Griffeth, June Duffie. *The History of Grace United Methodist Church, North Augusta, South Carolina: A Time for Reflecting.* North Augusta: Grace United Methodist Church, 1989.

Maddox, L. V., et al. *A History of the First Baptist Church, North Augusta, S.C., 1902–1962.* North Augusta: First Baptist Church, 1962.

Moment, Alfred H. *Temperance in Light of the Letter and the Spirit of the Bible: A Sermon Preached before the North Carolina State Convention of the Woman's Christian Temperance Union.* Raleigh: October 1, 1905.

Sands, Anna. *St. Paul's Mission in Horse Creek Valley.* Graniteville, S.C.: St. Paul's Episcopal Church, 1914.

White Ribbon. Journal. North Carolina Woman's Christian Temperance Union. High Point, N.C.: WCTU, 1895–1905.

GOOD ROADS PAMPHLETS

Hand, W. C. "The Relation of Good Roads to Schools." *Bulletin of the University of South Carolina,* no. 20, January 1910, 17–20.

Holmes, M. Goode. "Sand-Clay Roads." *Southern Good Roads,* April 1911.

Hyatt, F. H. "Statistics of Good Roads in South Carolina." *Bulletin of the University of South Carolina,* no. 20, January 1910, 21–25.

Spoon, William L. "The Construction of Sand-Clay and Burnt-Clay Roads." *Southern Good Roads* (April 1910).

Watson, E. J. "Earth, Sand-Clay and Gravel Roads." *Southern Good Roads,* April 1911.

———. "The Economic Value of Good Roads." *Bulletin of the University of South Carolina,* no. 20, January 1910, 9–16.

SECONDARY SOURCES

Abbot, Lyman. "A Governor Accused." *Outlook* 101, no. 13, July 27, 1912, 650–51.

Anderson, James D. *The Education of Blacks in the South, 1860–1935.* Chapel Hill: University of North Carolina Press, 1988.

Ansley, Lula Barnes. *History of the Georgia Woman's Christian Temperance Union: From Its Organization, 1883–1907.* Columbus, Ga.: Gilbert Printing, 1914.

Ayers, Edward L. *Vengeance and Justice: Crime and Punishment in the Nineteenth Century American South.* New York: Oxford University Press, 1985.

Bailey, Thomas Jefferson. *Prohibition in Mississippi.* Jackson, Miss.: Hederman Bros., 1917.

Ball, William Watts. *The State That Forgot: South Carolina's Surrender to Democracy.* Columbia: Bobbs-Merrill, 1932.

Baron, Stanley. *Brewed in America: A History of Beer and Ale in the United States.* Boston: Little, Brown, 1962.

Bartels, Virginia B. "The History of South Carolina Schools." *South Carolina Center for Educator Recruitment, Retention and Advancement.* Columbia: State of South Carolina Department of Education, 1984.

Bauerlein, Mark. *Negrophobia: A Race Riot in Atlanta, 1906.* San Francisco: Encounter Books, 2001.

Blakely, Leonard. *The Sale of Liquor in the South.* Columbia University Studies of History, Economics and Public Law 127. New York: Columbia University Press, 1912.

Blocker Jack S. *Retreat from Reform: The Prohibition Movement in the United States, 1890–1913.* Westport: Greenwood Press, 1976.

Bordin, Ruth. *Women and Temperance: The Quest for Liberty and Power, 1873–1900.* New Brunswick: Rutgers University Press, 1990.

Burns, Rebecca. *Rage in the Gate City: The Story of the 1906 Atlanta Race Riot.* Athens: University of Georgia Press, 2009.

Burnside, Ronald D. "The Governorship of Coleman Livingston Blease of South Carolina, 1911–1915." Ph.D. diss., Indiana University, 1963.

Carlton, David L. *Mill and Town in South Carolina 1880–1920.* Baton Rouge: Louisiana State University Press, 1982.

Carter, Wingard. "State Support for Public Schools in South Carolina since 1895." Master's thesis, University of South Carolina, 1936.

Cashin, Edward J. *The Story of Augusta.* Augusta: Richmond County Historical Society, 1991.

Cashin, Edward J., and Glenn T. Eskew, eds., *Paternalism in the Southern City: Race Religion and Gender in Augusta, Georgia.* Athens: University of Georgia Press, 2001.

Cherrington, Ernest Hurst. *The Anti-Saloon League Yearbook.* Westerville, Ohio: American Issue, 1920.

———. *A History of the Anti-Saloon League.* Westerville, Ohio: American Issue, 1913.

Christensen, Niels, Jr. "The State Dispensaries of South Carolina." *Annals of the American Academy of Political and Social Science,* vol. 32: *Regulation of the Liquor Trade* (November 1980): 75–85.

Clark, Norman. *Deliver Us from Evil: A New Interpretation of the American Prohibition.* New York: Norton, 1976.

Cochran, Thomas C. *The Pabst Brewing Company: The History of an American Business.* New York: New York University Press, 1948.

Coker, Joe L. *Liquor in the Land of the Lost Cause: Southern White Evangelicals and the Prohibition Movement.* Lexington: University Press of Kentucky, 2007.

Committee of Fifty. *The Liquor Problem: A Summary of the Investigations Conducted by the Committee of Fifty, 1893–1903.* New York: Houghton Mifflin, 1905.

Conroy, Pat. "Horses Don't Eat Moon Pies." In *Faces of South Carolina: Essays on South Carolina in Transition,* edited by Franklin Ashley. Columbia: University of South Carolina Press, 1974.

Coulter, E. Merton. "The Athens Dispensary." *Georgia Historical Quarterly* 50, no. 1 (March 1966): 14–36.

Davis, William Graham. "Attacking 'the Matchless Evil': Temperance and Prohibition in Mississippi, 1817–1908." Ph.D. diss., Mississippi State University, 1975.

Dittmer, John. *Black Georgia in the Progressive Era, 1900–1920.* Urbana: University of Illinois Press, 1977.

Doster, James F. *Railroads in Alabama Politics 1875–1914.* Tuscaloosa: University of Alabama Press, 1957.

Downard, William L. *The Cincinnati Brewing Industry: A Social and Economic History.* Athens: Ohio University Press, 1973.

Downey, Thomas M. "Riparian Rights and Manufacturing in Antebellum South Carolina: William Gregg and the Origins of the Industrial Mind." *Journal of Southern History* 65 (February 1999): 77–108.

Duis, Perry. *The Saloon: Public Drinking in Chicago and Boston 1880–1920.* Urbana: University of Illinois Press, 1999.

Duncan, Watson B. "Reverend John Lawton Harley." *Twentieth Century Sketches of the South Carolina Conference, M.E. Church, South.* Columbia: State Co., 1914.

Edgar, Walter. *South Carolina: A History.* Columbia: University of South Carolina Press, 1998.

Eighmy, John Lee. *Churches in Cultural Captivity: A History of the Social Attitudes of Southern Baptists.* Knoxville: University of Tennessee Press, 1988.

Epstein, Barbara Leslie. *The Politics of Domesticity: Women, Evangelism and Temperance in Nineteenth Century America.* Middletown: Wesleyan University Press, 1981.

Eubanks, John Evans. *Ben Tillman's Baby: The Dispensary System of South Carolina, 1892–1915.* Augusta, Ga.: by the author, 1950.

Fite, Gilbert. *Cotton Fields No More: Southern Agriculture, 1865–1980.* Lexington: University Press of Kentucky, 1984.

Geddings, W. H. "Aiken: A Winter Resort." In *A Reference Handbook of the Medical Sciences, 1881–1885,* edited by Albert H. Buck. New York: William Wood and Co., 1886.

German, Richard Henry Lee. "The Queen City of the Savannah: Augusta, Georgia, during the Urban Progressive Era, 1890–1917." Ph.D. diss., University of Florida, 1971.

Godshalk, David Fort. *Veiled Visions: The 1906 Atlanta Race Riot and the Reshaping of American Race Relations.* Chapel Hill: University of North Carolina Press, 2005.

Grantham, Dewey. *Hoke Smith and the Politics of the New South.* Baton Rouge: Louisiana State University Press, 1967.

———. *Southern Progressivism: The Reconciliation of Progress and Tradition.* Knoxville: University of Tennessee Press, 1983.

Green, Elna C. *This Business of Relief: Confronting Poverty in a Southern City, 1740–1940.* Athens: University of Georgia Press, 2003.

Greenwood, Janet Thomas. *Bittersweet Legacy: The Black and White "Better Classes" in Charlotte, 1850–1910.* Chapel Hill: University of North Carolina Press, 1994.

Hamm, Richard F. *Shaping the Eighteenth Amendment: Temperance Reform, Legal Culture, and the Polity, 1880–1920.* Chapel Hill: University of North Carolina Press, 1995.

Hardesty, Nancy A. "'The Best Temperance Organization in the Land': Southern Methodists and the Woman's Christian Temperance Union in Georgia." *Methodist History* 28 (April 1990): 187–94.

Heath, Frederick M., and Harriet H. Kinard. "Prohibition in South Carolina, 1880–1940: An Overview." *Proceedings of the South Carolina Historical Association,* 118–32. Charleston: South Carolina Historical Association, 1980.

Hemphill, R. I. "The South Carolina Dispensary." *Arena* 12 (May 1895): 14–17.

Hendricks, Ellen Alexander. "The South Carolina Dispensary System, Part II." *North Carolina Historical Review* 22 (April 1945): 320–49.

Hohner, Robert A. "Prohibition and Virginia Politics, 1901–1916." Ph.D. diss., Duke University, 1965.

Holley, Gerald Dillard. "The Darlington Riot of 1894." Master's thesis, University of South Carolina, 1970.

Hudson, Janet G. *Entangled in White Supremacy: Reform in World War I Era South Carolina.* Lexington: University Press of Kentucky, 2009.

Hunt, George Murrell. "A History of the Prohibition Movement in Arkansas." Master's thesis, University of Arkansas, 1933.

Ingram, Tammy. *Dixie Highway: Road Building and the Making of the American South, 1900–1930.* Chapel Hill: University of North Carolina Press, 2014.

Isaac, Paul E. *Prohibition and Politics: Turbulent Decades in Tennessee, 1885–1920.* Knoxville, University of Tennessee Press, 1965.

Johns, Roe L., Edgar L. Morphet, and Kern Alexander. *The Economics and Financing of Education,* 4th ed. Englewood Cliffs, N.J.: Prentice-Hall, 1983.

Johnson, William E. *Government Liquor Monopoly as Demonstrated by the South Carolina Liquor Dispensary.* Washington, D.C.: Board of Temperance of the Methodist Church, 1920.

Jones, Charles C., and Salem Dutcher, *Memorial History of Augusta, Georgia.* Syracuse: D. Mason and Co., 1890.

Kantrowitz, Stephen. *Ben Tillman and the Reconstruction of White Supremacy.* Chapel Hill: University of North Carolina Press, 2000.

Kerr, K. Austin. *Organized for Prohibition: A New History of the Anti-Saloon League.* New Haven: Yale University Press, 1985.

Kohn, August. *The Cotton Mills of South Carolina.* Columbia: South Carolina Department of Agriculture, Commerce and Immigration, 1907.

Kousser, J. Morgan. *The Shaping of Southern Politics: Suffrage Restriction and the Establishment of the One-Party South, 1880–1910.* New Haven: Yale University Press, 1974.

Lawrence, Kay. *Horses, Heroes and High Society: Aiken from 1540.* Columbia: King Press, 1971.

Leab, Grace. "The Temperance Movement in Tennessee, 1860–1907." Master's thesis, University of Tennessee, 1916.

Lender, Mark Edward, and James Kirby Martin. *Drinking in America: A History.* New York: Free Press, 1987.

Link, William A. *The Paradox of Southern Progressivism 1880–1930.* Chapel Hill: University of North Carolina Press, 1992.

Loveland, Anne C. *Southern Evangelicals and the Social Order, 1800–1860.* Baton Rouge: Louisiana State University Press, 1980.

Margo, Robert A. *Race and Schooling in the South, 1880–1950: An Economic History.* Chicago: University of Chicago Press, 1994;

McDaniel, Jeanne M. *North Augusta: James U. Jackson's Dream*. Charleston: Arcadia Publishing, 2005.

Mittleman, Amy. *Brewing Battles: A History of American Beer*. New York: Algora Publishing, 2008.

Mixon, Gregory L. "The Atlanta Riot of 1906." Ph.D. diss., University of Cincinnati, 1989.

Moore, John Hammond. "The Negro and Prohibition in Atlanta, 1885–1887." *South Atlantic Quarterly* 69 (Winter 19070): 38–57.

———. *The South Carolina Highway Department, 1917–1987*. Columbia: University of South Carolina Press, 1987.

Mort, Paul R. *State Support for Public Education*. Washington, D.C.: American Council on Education, 1933.

Odegard, Peter H. *Pressure Politics: The Story of the Anti-Saloon League*. New York: Columbia University Press, 1928.

Ownby, Ted. *Subduing Satan: Religion, Recreation and Manhood in the Rural South, 1865–1920*. Fred W. Morrison Series in Southern Studies. Chapel Hill: University of North Carolina Press, 1990.

Park, Orville, ed. *Report of the Thirtieth Annual Session of the Georgia Bar Association*, Macon, Ga.: J. W. Burke and Co., 1913.

Patton, W. H. *History of the Prohibition Movement in Mississippi*. Oxford: Mississippi Historical Society, 1909.

Pearson, C. C., and J. Edwin Hendricks. *Liquor and Anti-liquor in Virginia, 1619–1919*. Durham: Duke University Press, 1967.

Pegram, Thomas R. "Temperance, Politics and Regional Political Culture: The Anti-Saloon League in Maryland and the South, 1907–1915." *Journal of Southern History* 63 (February 1997): 57–90.

Platt, Anthony. *The Child-Savers: The Invention of Delinquency in Chicago*. Chicago: University of Chicago Press, 1969.

Preston, Howard Lawrence. *Dirt Roads to Dixie: Accessibility and Modernization in the South, 1885–1935*. Knoxville: University of Tennessee Press, 1991.

Rabby, Glenda A. "The Woman's Christian Temperance Union in Georgia, 1883–1918." Master's thesis, Florida State University, 1978.

Roblyer, Leslie F. "The Road to State-Wide Prohibition in Tennessee, 1899–1909." Master's thesis, University of Tennessee, 1927.

Rorabaugh, W. J. *The Alcoholic Republic: An American Tradition*. New York: Oxford University Press, 1981.

Scomp, Henry Anselm. *King Alcohol in the Realm of King Cotton, or A History of the Liquor Traffic and of the Temperance Movement in Georgia from 1733–1877*. Chicago: Press of the Blakely Print Co., 1888.

Sechrist, Robert. *The Prohibition Movement in the United States*. Ann Arbor, Mich.: Inter-University Consortium for Political and Social Research, 1983

Sellers, James Benson. *The Prohibition Movement in Alabama, 1702–1943*. James Sprunt

Series in History and Political Science 26. Chapel Hill: University of North Carolina Press, 1943.

Silber, Nina. *The Romance of Reunion: Northerners and the South 1865-1900.* Chapel Hill: University of North Carolina Press, 1993.

Simkins, Francis Butler. *Pitchfork Ben Tillman: South Carolinian.* Columbia SC: University of South Carolina Press, 2002.

———. *The Tillman Movement in South Carolina.* Durham: Duke University Press, 1926.

Simon, Bryant. *A Fabric of Defeat: The Politics of South Carolina Millhands, 1910-1948.* Chapel Hill: University of North Carolina Press, 1998.

Sims, Anastasia. *The Power of Femininity in the New South: Women's Organizations and Politics in North Carolina, 1880-1930.* Columbia: University of South Carolina Press, 1997.

Smith, Harry Worcester. *Life and Sport in Aiken and Those Who Made It."* New York: Derrydale Press, 1935.

Spain, Rufus. *At Ease in Zion: Social History of Southern Baptists, 1865-1900.* Tuscaloosa: University of Alabama Press, 2003.

Stewart, Bruce. *Moonshiners and Prohibitionists: The Battle over Alcohol in Southern Appalachia.* New Directions in Southern History. Lexington: University Press of Kentucky, 2011.

Stover, John F. *Railroads of the New South, 1865-1900.* Chapel Hill: University of North Carolina Press, 1955.

Szymanski, Anne-Marie. *Pathways to Prohibition: Radicals, Moderates and Social Movement Outcomes.* Durham: Duke University Press, 2003.

Tatum, W. O. *The South Carolina Dispensary: Synopsis of Its History and Analysis of Its Salient Features.* Columbia: Daily Record Print Co, Office of the Dispensary, 1907. Pamphlet located in State Board of Directors, Correspondence, box 1, South Carolina Dispensary Records, South Carolina Department of Archives and History, Columbia.

Thompson, Harold Paul. "Race, Temperance and Prohibition in the Postbellum South: Black Atlanta, 1865-1890." Ph.D. diss., Emory University, 2005.

Timberlake, James. *Prohibition and the Progressive Movement, 1900-1920.* Cambridge: Harvard University Press, 1963.

Tindall, George Brown. *The Emergence of the New South, 1913-1945.* Baton Rouge: Louisiana State University Press, 1967.

———. *South Carolina Negroes 1877-1900.* Southern Classics Series. Columbia: University of South Carolina Press, 2002.

Trinkley, Michael, et al. *Cultural Resources Survey of North Augusta Riverfront Project.* Columbia: Chicora Foundation, 2004.

Trost, Jennifer. *Gateway to Justice: The Juvenile Court and Progressive Child Welfare in a Southern City.* Athens: University of Georgia Press, 2005.

Vandevelde, Isabel. *Aiken County: The Only South Carolina County Founded during Reconstruction.* Spartanburg: Reprint Co. Publishers, 1999.

Wallace, David Duncan. *The History of South Carolina*. New York: American Historical Society, 1934.

Wallace, Rita Foster. "The South Carolina State Dispensary, 1893–1907." Master's thesis, University of South Carolina, 1996.

West, Stephen A. *From Yeoman to Redneck in the South Carolina Upcountry, 1850–1915*. Charlottesville: University of Virginia Press, 2008.

White, John E. "Prohibition: The New Task and Opportunity of the South." *South Atlantic Quarterly* 7 (April 1908): 130–42.

Whitener, Daniel Jay. *Prohibition in North Carolina, 1715–1945*. James Sprunt Series in History and Political Science 27. Chapel Hill: University of North Carolina Press, 1946.

Willis, Lee L. *Southern Prohibition: Race, Reform, and Public Life in Middle Florida, 1821–1920*. Athens: University of Georgia Press, 2011.

Wilson, Charles Reagan. "Preachin', Prayin', and Singin' on the Public Square." In *Religion and Public Life in the South: In the Evangelical Mode*, edited by in Charles Reagan Wilson. New York: Alta Mira, 2005.

Wines Frederic H., and John Koren. *The Liquor Problem in Its Legislative Aspects*. 2nd ed. Boston: Houghton Mifflin, 1898.

Woodward, C. Vann. *The Origins of the New South, 1877–1913*. Baton Rouge: Louisiana State University Press, 1971.

———. *Tom Watson Agrarian Rebel*. Savannah: Beehive Press, 1938.

Woodward, W. E. "A Cotton Mill Village in the 1880's." *The Way Our People Lived: An Intimate American History*, 319–58. New York: Dutton, 1944.

INDEX